Responsible Sale and Service of Alcohol

for the tourism, hospitality and retail industries

T0302379

James Murphy

(G) Goodfellow Publishers Ltd

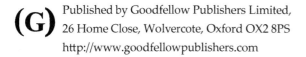 Published by Goodfellow Publishers Limited,
26 Home Close, Wolvercote, Oxford OX2 8PS
http://www.goodfellowpublishers.com

British Library Cataloguing in Publication Data: a catalogue record for this title is available from the British Library.

Library of Congress Catalog Card Number: on file.

ISBN: 978-1-910158-18-0

 Design and typesetting by P.K. McBride, www.macbride.org.uk

Cover design by Cylinder

Printed by Marston Book Services, www.marston.co.uk

Contents

Preface

Responsible Sales and Service of Alcohol has been developed for students and those working in the tourism, hospitality, culinary arts and retail industries who are involved in the sale and supply of alcohol, including those in supervisory and management positions. This book examines a wide range of topics associated with the sale and service of alcohol in the tourism, hospitality and retail industries. Its aim is to provide readers with a greater awareness of the effects of alcohol, and of their moral and legal obligations to act responsibly when supplying alcohol beverages or when dealing with alcohol misuse in their workplace.

Alcohol in the modern world

Alcohol is a vital trading commodity in the world economy today; from the production to the marketing, distribution and sale, its economic influence is vast (NBWA, 2014). In many countries, the production and sale of alcohol is a very important part of the overall local economy, as the taxes and Government levies on it can be substantial (ICAP, 2004). Alcohol is widely available and it is consumed for many different purposes which include entertaining, special events, socialising and business events. Alcoholic beverages consumed responsibly can enhance healthy social interaction and increase relaxation levels. Unfortunately irresponsible or abusive consumption patterns can lead to dangerous outcomes, including anti-social behaviour, malicious damage, violence and health related problems. Alcohol has become such an integral part of the culture of so many societies that we sometimes forget to treat it with the respect and care attributed to other addictive and mood altering substances like drugs. It is therefore critical for all industries involved in the sale, service and marketing of alcoholic beverages to minimise these risks, and to operationalise a duty of care for their customers and employees, especially those under the age of 18 or who are intoxicated. The President of the International Bartenders Association maintains that prevention is the best defence (Lee, as cited in IBA, 2008). It is in the context of these challenges that establishments, industry bodies, drinks companies, governments, local communities and training providers in recent years have adopted community schemes and training programs, in a partnership approach, to raise standards in promoting the responsible sale, service, marketing and consumption of alcohol.

Employees and managers working across the tourism, hospitality and retail sectors can play a crucial role in supporting this work by encouraging their customers, colleagues, family and friends to enjoy alcoholic beverages in a responsible manner. Everyone can make a difference towards creating the environment that makes a workplace safe, secure and more sociable.

Overview of the book

The chapters are each structured with specific learning aims and objectives, tables, illustrations and models of the significant issues in the topic areas. Chapter 1 introduces the major industries which benefit from the sale and supply of alcohol. It also outlines the impact of misuse and abuse across the community, and sets out the rationale for businesses to implement responsible service, sale and marketing practices for alcohol. Chapter 2 provides the background to the origin of alcohol and its role in modern society, and highlights the rates of consumption linked to this product. Chapters 3 and 4 explore the nature of alcohol, explaining its scientific composition, how it is produced, plus the general and some more specific effects of alcohol on the human body and its vital organs. These chapters also set out guidelines for safe drinking, and establish the strengths of alcoholic beverages and their impact on cognitive, sexual and sporting performances, including hangovers and the risk taking behaviours associated with alcohol consumption. Chapter 5 introduces the relationship between alcohol, health and well-being. It also sets out in detail the harmful and beneficial outcomes associated with alcohol consumption and the adverse reactions of consuming alcohol with prescribed medications or illegal drugs. Chapter 6 establishes the major requirements for management and employers regarding their legal and moral responsibilities when dealing with alcohol in the workplace. It also sets out specific policies to help them in assisting employees suffering from alcohol addiction problems to receive the necessary treatment and support. Chapter 7 looks at how to reduce the alcohol related crime and disorder caused by a small minority of individuals, which can harm the safety and security of employees, customers and society. The ways in which national governments, major industries and individual establishments have collaborated to reduce the negative health impacts of harmful drinking patterns through rigorous training programs, and agreed national standards for the marketing, sales and service of all alcoholic products are covered in Chapters 8 and 9. These chapters also identify best practice procedures and strategies which can be adopted to help individual establishments and large commercial operations to meet their obligations to serve alcohol in a responsible manner. Finally, Chapter 10 discusses the combined efforts of policy makers in creating regulatory and legislative structures which contribute towards increasing the understanding of the benefits of moderate alcohol consumption at the individual and societal levels.

I hope that you enjoy reading, consulting and adopting the policies, strategies and best practices highlighted in this book. *Responsible Sale and Service of Alcohol* is dedicated to raising the awareness, knowledge and skills involved in selling, serving and marketing alcohol in a responsible manner for the tourism, hospitality and retail industries worldwide

James Murphy, MSc (Hosp Mgt), MA (H.Ed), Mgt Dip.

Lecturer, Programme Chairman, School of Culinary Arts and Food Technology, College of Arts and Tourism, Dublin Institute of Technology

About the author

James Murphy is the winner of numerous national and international industry awards, including World Champion for Elite Bartenders in 1993. A former Education Chairman of the International Bartenders Association (IBA), he has managed in the bar and beverage industry for over 30 years. James is co-ordinator of licensed trade development programmes, chairman and author of the BSc (Honours) degree course in Bar Management and Entrepreneurship. He holds multiple Masters Degrees in Hospitality Management and Higher Education, is an expert witness, serves as an external examiner across international tourism and hospitality programmes and currently lectures full time in the bar and beverage management area at the Dublin Institute of Technology, School of Culinary Arts and Food Technology.

Also by James Murphy

Principles and Practices of Bar and Beverage Management (2013).

Principles and Practices of Bar and Beverage Management: *The Drinks Handbook* (2013).

Bartenders Association of Ireland – A History (1997).

Acknowledgements

If I was to mention everyone who helped in the compilation of this book then another would be required to include them all. So please accept a warm thanks to all those special people, with my apologies to anyone I may have inadvertently omitted. I would however like to express my thanks in particular to:

- My parents James and Elizabeth Murphy, my wife Jacinta and sons Ciaran and Ronan thank you all for your patience and support throughout the process of writing this book.

- The incredibly hard working team at Goodfellows Publishers Ltd for their support in the development of this book, especially Sally North and Tim Goodfellow.

- Governments, public service bodies, industry associations and community groups around the world whose collective work helps to develop policies and strategic programmes aimed at reducing alcohol related disorders and harmful consequences associated with abusive drinking patterns.

- Tourism, hospitality, retail and drinks companies and individual drinking establishments for their research and innovation in creating and implementing training programmes which help to create the awareness, knowledge and skills required to sell, serve and market alcohol in an enjoyable and responsible manner.

- The authors and researchers listed in the bibliography and web resources, whose work in the field of alcohol research is helping to build the knowledge base required by employers and managers to set high standards for the sale and service of alcohol.

- Last but certainly not least the picture credits. The author and publishers would like to thank the following for permission to reproduce copyright illustrative material: Figs. 1.2, fau.edu; Figs. 2.1, 2.2, History of the alcohol and tobacco division; Figs. 2.3, 5.3, 6.1, 8.1, 8.2, 8.3 Wiki Creative Commons; Fig. 3.1 BNIC ©; Fig. 3.2 stillcooker.com; Fig. 4.1 James Matthews, National Institute of Health,; Fig. 5.1 M. Häggström; Figs. 5.2 Student Wellness; Fig. 6.2 MMC; Fig. 8.5 Blomfield; Fig 10.1 Diageo; Fig. 10.2: Pernod-Ricard UK.

- Figs. 3.3, 5.4, 5.5, 5.6, 8.4, 9.1, were photographed by the author.

Every effort has been made to trace and acknowledge ownership of copyright and we will be glad to make suitable arrangements with any copyright holders whom it has not been possible to contact.

By the same author

The Principles and Practices of Bar and Beverage Management, a comprehensive text and resource book providing a complete guide to every aspect of bar management; a well defined pedagogic structure; links to relevant web and audio-visual resources; coverage of all the key topics plus the technical skills and practices in the bar and beverage sector; over 200 explanatory illustrations and tables; and numerous examples and case studies from within the industry.

ISBN 978-1-908999-36-8 Hardback;
        978-1-908999-37-5 Paperback 256pp;
        978-1-908999-44-3 eBook

The Principles and Practices of Bar and Beverage Management - The Drinks Handbook, a comprehensive training guide and authoritative resource, packed with facts, explanatory illustrations and practical guidance. This book provides a complete guide to beers, wines, spirit, liqueurs, ciders, hot beverages and soft drinks - where they're from, how they're made, how to serve and how to achieve maximum profits – and a detailed coverage of the World's leading brands of beers, spirits and liqueurs, an in-depth look at wines of the World and an indispensible listing of over 90 cocktail recipes.

ISBN 978-1-908999-58-0 Hardback 360pp;
        978-1-908999-59-7 eBook

See www.goodfellowpublishers.com for further details

1 The Rationale for Responsible Alcohol Sale and Supply

Aims and learning outcomes

This chapter introduces the major industries which benefit from the sale and supply of alcohol. It also outlines its impact through misuse and abuse across the community, and sets out the reasons why businesses need to implement responsible service and sale practices for alcohol. After reading this chapter, you should be able to:

■ Describe the overall structure of the hospitality, tourism and retail industries and the economic contribution which alcohol makes directly and indirectly to them.

■ Outline the rationale for businesses that sell or supply alcohol to adopt responsible service and sale practices.

■ Identify the impact of alcohol abuse and under-age drinking by individuals on the community, the workplace and in education.

1.0 The hospitality, tourism and retail industries

The hospitality industry

Alcohol is supplied and consumed in a large number of licensed premises within the general hospitality sector, which consists of:

■ **accommodation providers**: hotels, self-catering, bed and breakfast, camping and caravan sites, holiday centres, timeshare;

■ **catering providers**: restaurants, fast food outlets, takeaways, snack bars, tearooms, inns, bars;

■ **visitor and leisure attractions**: theatres and cinemas, nightclubs, museums, art galleries, theme parks, zoos, wildlife parks, sports centres, stately homes, gardens, heritage sites (religious, industrial, transport), historical sites, industrial visitor centres (for example, distilleries);

■ **transport providers**: cruise liners, train stations, airports.

Brotherton (2008) identifies the main sectors of the international hospitality industry as hotels, restaurants and contract foodservices (i.e. self-catering accommodation, or welfare and educational catering). Hospitality operators and establishments are also distinguished by the legislative and administrative parameters in which they operate.

The economic contribution of hospitality

Hospitality is a key driver for job creation across the world, and especially in Europe where 10 million people are directly employed and a further 6.4 million indirectly connected with the hospitality sector. One out of every 13 jobs is connected with hospitality. In countries like Cyprus and Malta, hospitality employs as many as 30% and 20% of the total populace, respectively. Each euro spent on hospitality results in additional 1.16 euros being invested in the wider economy. The hospitality industry also employs over 10% of the population in Spain, Portugal, Luxembourg, Ireland, Greece, Croatia and Austria (UNWTO, 2014).

Hospitality operators and their respective establishments are engaged in the provision of hospitality services, which in most circumstances includes alcoholic beverages, and they face similar strategic and operational issues in the responsible service of these drinks to their customers.

The tourism industry

Alcohol is widely consumed in licensed establishments across the tourism sector, which is one of the world's largest industries and also one of the most fragmented. It consists of tour operators, public sector organisations, regulatory bodies, distributors, tourism agencies, plus the sectors where alcohol consumption and service is most concentrated – the conference, exhibition and accommodation areas. This latter covers the licensed areas in hotels, villas, apartments, B&B and camping parks, where alcohol can be purchased for consumption in the public bar, restaurant or privately in the guests' rooms or chalets.

The structure of tourism

There is not a 'one size fits all' tourism structure. How each destination or country organises their tourism industry is determined by local factors, including resourcing, industry leadership, the size and importance of tourism to the local economy, and the attitude of the local government.

The tourism sector

Ribai, as cited in (UNWTO, 2014), maintains that 'the tourism sector has shown a remarkable capacity to adjust to the changing market conditions, fuelling growth and job creation around the world, despite the lingering economic and geopolitical challenges. Indeed tourism has been among the few sectors generating positive news for many economies.' The World Tourism Organisation agrees, stating that international tourist arrivals (overnight visitors) grew by 5% in 2013, reaching a record 1,087 million (UNWTO, 2014). Despite a global economy in low gear, international tourism results were well above expectations, with an additional 52 million international tourists travelling the world in 2013. For 2014, UNWTO forecast 4% to 4.5% growth, again above the long term projections. These figures were based on the 145 countries and territories which the World Tourism Organization actively monitors. A breakdown of these increased tourism figures across the continents indicated that:

■ Europe welcomed an additional 29 million visitors raising its total for 2013 to 563 million visitors

■ Asia and the Pacific grew by 14 million to reach 248 million visitors

■ The Americas increased by 6 million reaching 169 million visitors

■ Africa attracted an additional 3 million reaching a new record of 56 million visitors.

(UNWTO, 2014).

Tourism's economic contribution

The World Travel and Tourism Council – WTTC (2014) reported that 2013 was another successful year for the travel and tourism sector, off the back of an improving economy. The direct contribution of travel and tourism to the world economy grew by 3.1% in 2013, contributing US$2.2 trillion to the world gross domestic product (GDP) and 101 million jobs.

This economic growth for the third consecutive year outperforms other global sectors such as manufacturing, retail and distribution, public services and financial and business services. Travel and tourism represents US$7.0 trillion (2013 prices), 266 million jobs, US$754 billion in investment and US$1.3 trillion in exports.

1.4 million new jobs were generated directly in the sector in 2013, and in total, 4.7 million new jobs were created as a result of tourism activity. Travel and tourism's contribution equates to 9.5% of total GDP, which is essentially 1 in 11 of the world's total jobs (WTTC, 2014)

Tourism trends

The travel and tourism industry is estimated to add over 70 million jobs through the next decade, supporting a total of 328 million jobs – or 10% of the world's workforce. Two-thirds of those jobs will be created in Asia, where finding, training, developing and retaining talent is already a challenge (UNWTO, 2014). Hosting this humongous number of tourists is a lucrative business, which is why the hospitality industry is also growing exponentially. Not limited to hotels, restaurants and meeting venues, the hospitality boom offers multiple options to the customer, creating tough competition for the players.

But that's not where it stops. The WTTC estimate that by 2030, international tourist arrivals will reach 1.8 billion. That's a lot of people on the move, all requiring accommodation, food and beverages (which will include alcoholic drinks, served, it is hoped, in an informed and responsible manner).

The retail industry

The retail industry encompasses the sale of goods and services from individuals or businesses to the end-user. Retailers are part of an integrated system, and the last link in the supply chain. A retailer purchases goods or products in large quantities from manufacturers directly or through a wholesaler, and then sells smaller quantities to the consumer for a profit. Retailing can be done in either fixed locations like stores or markets, door-to-door or by delivery. In recent years an increasing amount of retailing is done using online websites, electronic payment, and delivery service providers. Retail establishments which sell alcohol can range from individual off-licenses to mixed trading premises where alcohol is sold in addition to other goods (for example supermarkets, convenience stores, petrol filling stations) (RRAI, 2010).

The structure of the retail industry

The retail business is still dominated by small family-run stores, but this market is increasingly being taken over by large retail chains (i.e. supermarkets and high street stores). Gradually the high street stores are being re-grouped into shopping malls. These are more defined and planned spaces for retail stores and their respective brands.

Ferrara (2014) states that the retail industry is usually classified by the type of products they sell, for example food, which typically requires cold storage facilities; soft goods or consumables, which includes clothing, other fabrics, footwear, cosmetics, medicines and stationery, and other goods that are consumed after one use or have a limited period in which you may use them.

Individuals working for retail businesses which encompass the sale of alcohol have statutory and non-statutory obligations to act responsibly when serving customers. These responsibilities include taking every precaution to ensure that under-age customers or drunken persons are not served alcohol. In most cuntries there are significant penalties which may be imposed on any retailer who is found to have sold alcohol in contravention of the relevant legislation.

The economic contribution of alcohol in the retail industry

In terms of total employment provided, about 22 million people work in the major distribution trades in the EU, 18% of these jobs are within the alcohol retail sector. In the USA, the beer industry alone includes 551,000 retail establishments and employs approximately 1.78 million Americans, paying them $54 billion in wages and benefits (NBWA, 2014).

Alcohol sales in the retail industry also benefit packaging manufacturers, shipping companies, agriculture, and other businesses whose livelihood depends on a healthy alcohol retail industry. There are also other industries affected by the performance of beverage alcohol companies: transport and haulage companies, government employees involved in the regulation and oversight of the beverage retail alcohol industry, consulting firms, firms that construct and decorate the various places where alcohol is sold, agricultural fertilizer suppliers, etc. Many of these are small, independent, or family-owned businesses (ICAP, 2006).

1.1   What is responsible sale and service of alcohol?

Responsible sale and service of alcohol is important for all levels of the hospitality, tourism and retail service industries, to minimise the harm associated with the use and abuse of alcohol by any person. Legally, liquor cannot be sold or supplied to a person who is intoxicated or disorderly, or is under the minimum age (18 in much of the world, 21 in the USA and some Asian countries, 16 or none in a few countries). *Responsible service of alcohol* is a term which represents the conditions set down by local governments and the industry to govern and manage the sale of alcohol on licensed premises and its effects on customers whilst under the care of the licensee and their staff. This includes the prevention of access by minors to alcohol and licensed venues and the safety of customers when exiting establishments. The regulation of the sale and supply of alcohol is necessary to apply control which ultimately leads to better business practices. Management and all staff who sell or supply alcohol must promote and support a safer environment for alcohol to be consumed, in a professional and responsible manner. By engaging in the responsible service of alcohol, a better environment is created for both customers and staff. Murphy (2013) maintains that businesses should therefore improve their RSA practices for the following reasons:

■ the establishments will gain a good reputation

■ there will be greater customer satisfaction

■ there will be less damage done to premises

■ potential legal problems will be reduced

■ there will be less police attendance

■ staff morale will be higher leading to greater productivity and fewer turnovers of staff

■ the environments for the consumption of alcohol beverages will be safer

■ there will be in complaints against licensed venues

■ there will be reduced levels of anti-social behaviour and social problems such as drink driving, excessive consumption and underage drinking.

1.2   Rationale for responsible alcohol sales and service

Responsible sales and service helps to improve the atmosphere of the premises, which ultimately leads to greater profits. Alcohol has long been a part of many cultures, and it continues to be an accepted part of the majority of modern lifestyles. Licensed premises must be aware of the need for responsible sale and service of alcohol to ensure the safety of the customers and staff. Excessive consumption of alcohol can impact on the community with violence, anti-social behaviour, malicious damage and domestic violence.

Further problems may also occur with alcohol related gambling, health and social problems. Research figures over the years had shown a significant relationship between alcohol consumption and crime. It also showed the effects on various social-economic groups in many communities. These studies have demonstrated the differences in consumption and alcohol-related harm between different ethnicities within countries, and have underlined the importance of further research on culture-related vulnerabilities (Neumark et al, 2004). Governments around the world have addressed the public concerns regarding alcohol abuse and misuse, through changes in policy and legislation, and numerous laws and measures have been passed to reduce or prevent intoxication, underage drinking and alcohol related problems. Babor et al

(2010) maintains that the level of effectiveness and vulnerability to harmful use of alcohol and alcohol-related harm around the world is based on each region's or country's ability to set alcohol policies. These developments have placed a direct obligation on licensed premises to prevent liquor abuse and misuse both inside and outside their establishments. In most countries, when the courts are considering issuing liquor licences for establishments, they must be satisfied that responsible serving practices will be implemented.

Duty of care

Duty of care is the responsibility that licensees, management and their staff have for the safety and wellbeing of customers, and for their employees. It is a concept that requires the establishment of systems which contribute towards creating a secure environment for their customers. Litigation cases over a number of years have highlighted that licensed premises can be vulnerable to civil liability actions, and if duty of care strategies are not in place, this obligation places more responsibility on management and staff. The hospitality, tourism and retail environments in which alcohol is consumed are varied and individually they present uniquely different challenges. The systems adopted must therefore be appropriate to that environment. Some of the techniques which can help an establishment plan its duty of care obligations include establishing a house policy; developing strategies to prevent underage drinking; promoting, if possible, safe transport options – local taxi services, courtesy bus; organising responsible alcohol promotions; and developing techniques to prevent guest intoxication.

In recent years trade associations nationally and internationally have developed guidelines for their members as to responsible practices in the sale and supply of alcohol. Each association has a generic policy towards their field, which is made available to their members, and can be utilised in their workplace. Businesses need to also develop their own set of house rules and policies which outline their position on providing alcohol to customers. They also need to ensure that their staff members are aware of and comply with the established practices and the legislation in place to protect not only themselves, but also their duty of care responsibilities to their customers.

(Name of the Premises)

If you are drunk, disorderly or violent on these premises, you will be requested to leave. If you fail to leave you will be committing an offence.

Figure 1.1: Responsible service of alcohol signage advising customers of their obligations.

1.3 Alcohol's impact on the community and the economy

Alcohol consumption has been said to play a fundamental role in the community life, and its consumption features strongly in most social and recreational activities of both a formal and informal nature. While the vast majority of the community, who consume alcohol, do so responsibly and sensibly, there are some to whom the consumption of alcohol can and does present problems. The wider community now expects those who serve and distribute alcohol do so responsibly and holds them responsible for the manner in which they serve alcohol. Local governments play an important role in addressing community concerns through legislative measures and, working with the drinks industry, through initiatives which help to reduce the social and economic costs of alcohol abuse.

Although there are positive social and health benefits from responsible alcohol use, there is a downside. Alcohol abuse is often associated with serious harm to individuals and the community. Alcohol abuse is unfortunately one of the leading causes of preventable death worldwide (Chartier et al, 2013). This abuse is largely driven by cultural factors, which include the issues that face rural and regional areas compared to those in urban areas. Some population groups, such as young people and indigenous communities, face particular issues.

Case example: Alcohol death by misadventure

Youth died after vodka drinking game

In 2009, a 19 year old undergraduate male died of alcohol poisoning following a drinking game that led to a lethal vodka binge. The deceased had consumed six to eleven cans of beer before he downed a large quantity of apple flavoured vodka in one slug straight from the bottle for a dare, at a party in his student flat. He had been celebrating a sporting win with friends. The young student had a blood alcohol level of 399 milligrams per 100 millilitres on admission to hospital, which is in the fatal range; he lay in a coma for 10 days until his death two days after his 19th birthday. At the inquest into his death his dad, in an emotional tribute, said that he was a 'lovely lad who loved life, loved sport and loved college life'. The Court Coroner described the loss of the young sportsman as 'unbearable' and said that while the dangers of alcohol were well recognised they were seldom so tragically illustrated. The jury returned a verdict of death by misadventure (Roseingrave, 2010).

Violence and crime involving alcohol

Another consideration must be the consequences associated with alcohol and the potential for a violence, which can occur in or around licensed venues and can include anti-social behaviour, malicious damage, assault crimes, domestic violence and driving offences. International research studies have established that alcohol is significantly associated with crime, especially violent crime. According to reviews carried out by health safety authorities, alcohol consumption rates and related harms, domestic abuse, road deaths and street violence increase in states or countries where people consume more alcohol (McDonagh, 2008). These links have been well documented over the years with the majority of the assaults occurring from 7p.m. onwards and hitting a peak between midnight and 3a.m. The most common types of assaults include common assault, actual bodily harm, grievous bodily harm, assault of an officer and shooting with intent other than to murder (Briscoe and Donnelly, 2001; O'Donnell, cited in Donnellan, 2002). See Chapter 7 for more on the interrelated issues involved in this area.

Workplace problems

Professor Joyce O'Connor, who chaired a World Health Organisation expert group on alcohol and drugs, believes there is conspiracy of silence around the issue of alcohol in the workplace. O'Connor notes that companies are taking employees out for nights of free drinking as a reward for work done and deadlines met. She believed that companies should have clear policies on alcohol use, rather than on alcohol abuse (Donnellan, 2003). Returning to work after consuming a couple of drinks appears to be still tolerated in many societies. But what about the implications? The effect on companies can be significant, from sloppy workmanship to missed deadlines and absenteeism. Excessive alcohol consumption can lead to loss of concentration in the workplace, which can lead to work related accidents and loss of productivity. Some national governments have been lobbied in recent years to change the legislation which deals with the issue of 'passive drinking' in the workplace and to treat drinking like smoking, which in recent years has been dramatically reduced. Industry must adopt a zero tolerance policy for their workers who enter the workplace after drinking. McCabe cited in Donnellan (2003) suggested that the aspiration would be that it does not become necessary to test workers for alcohol before they come onto the workplace, as this could be a very final and brutal instrument. Most companies already have detailed alcohol policies and employment-assistance programme officers to whom anyone suspected of having an alcohol problem – or any other problem can be referred. As long as employees are willing to go for treatment, the initial counselling sessions are usually paid for by the company in question. In some circumstances companies will also organise interest-free loans for staff to pay for additional counselling which they are given time off work to attend.

The issue of alcohol in the workplace was confronted by most European governments who signed up to a European action plan under which they collectively agreed to reduce harm that can be done in the workplace by alcohol, particularly in the area of accidents and violence before 2005. Alcohol workplace policies and strategies to assist in developing an alcohol and drug policy for a workplace are covered in detail in Chapter 6.

Economic costs involved in treating alcohol related illnesses

Anderson and Baumberg (2006) argue that there is now strong evidence to propose that alcohol conveys certain health benefits – particularly when consumed at low levels by older people, despite the large burden of disease it creates overall. This evidence is increasingly being taken into account in cost studies. Single et al (2003) maintain that the WHO costing guidelines should present the net costs, which take into account health benefits, alongside the gross cost estimates. Alcohol related illnesses and accidents do however impose great costs on health care systems around the world, and these impacts are acutely experienced in many hospitals. Since the 1970s the majority of developed countries have published estimates of the costs involved, usually based on the following components:

■ cost to the health care system of alcohol related illnesses

■ cost of alcohol related suicides

■ cost of alcohol related road accidents

■ cost of alcohol related crime

■ cost of output lost due to alcohol related absence from work

■ cost of alcohol related accidents at work

■ cost of alcohol related premature mortality

  (Byrne, 2010).

In England, in 2012-13 alone, there were an estimated 1,008,850 hospital admissions, where an alcohol-related disease, injury or condition was the primary reason for admission or a secondary diagnosis (HSCIC, 2014). Harwood (2000) adds that alcohol related illnesses costs the US $26.3 billion dollars annually. These costs place a significant economic strain on health care providers around the world, in addition to the costs borne by the drinkers themselves and the emotional distress of the families involved.

1.4   Alcohol and social problems

It is very difficult to live with anyone whose drinking misuse is causing problems. The drinker is also usually full of conflict and mood swings, and often blames others when things go wrong. Wegscheider (1976) pointed out some of the ways in which the other family members can be affected. These include feelings of hurt, shame, fear and an overwhelming sense of failure. Sometimes family members will take on extra responsibilities, trying to mask the mess but they are fighting a losing battle. Abusive drinking patterns practiced by parents have a direct impact on children, and increase the likelihood that their children will develop similar drinking disorders (Latendresse et al, 2008).

Shin et al, as cited in McMurran (2013), reports that the mistreatment of children, including sexual and physical abuse and neglect, may lead to childhood psychopathology and later to problem drinking. Partners and work colleagues often question themselves and doubt if they can get their loved ones and or colleagues help, as they battle to hide the problem from other family members and neighbours, and to protect their children (Drugs.ie, 2014). Excessive alcohol consumption can also contribute to some of these problems:

■ **legal**: loss of licence due to drink driving, litigation brought about through road related accidents and deaths.

■ **family**: breakdown of the family unit leading to such things as separation, negligence and communication breakdown

■ **financial**: spending entire or bulk of income on alcohol, which may lead to gambling related problems

Case example: Drink driver kills five people

A young couple living in north-eastern France, were summoned to court for 'non-prevention of a crime or misdemeanour that causes bodily harm'. These charges were lodged because they allowed their male cousin to leave their home at 4 am in a drunken state. He drove down the A31 road between Metz and Nancy colliding head-on with the car of a young family of five who were all killed in the crash. The driver was also killed at the scene. Toxicology reports indicated that he was four times over the legal alcohol limit. The court found that the couple were at fault for failing to call the paramilitary gendarmes. This case follows another of a café owner near Dijon who received a two month suspended sentence for selling alcohol to an inebriated client, who then killed three young people in a car crash (Marlowe, 2004).

1.5   Minors and under-age drinking

Children and adolescents are particularly vulnerable to alcohol-related harm (Mäkelä and Mustonen, 2000). Under-age drinking is one of the major concerns of the community and all governments. In most countries, minors are in breach of the law if they purchase, receive or consume alcohol in licensed premises or in a public place. Grant (1998) maintains that alcohol use before 14 years of age is a predictor of impaired health status, because it is associated with increased risk for alcohol dependence and abuse at later ages. To meet the challenge of restricting access to alcohol by children and adolescents, the majority of establishments have regulations and guidelines which include specific authorised areas and evidence of age criteria.

■ **Authorised areas**: areas within licensed premises that can be accessed by minors, who must at all times be in the company and immediate presence of a responsible adult. These may include bistro area, beer garden, lounge and function areas.

■ **Evidence of age**: in most counties, any person who supplies or sells alcohol is under obligation to ask for evidence to ensure the patron is of legal age. If the supplier has reason to believe that the patron is not of legal age, or has doubts that the documentation provided is not authentic, the supplier has reason to refuse alcohol and/or entry to licensed premises. For a wider discussion on minors and under-age drinking, plus the acceptable forms of identification please refer to Chapters 8 and 9.

1.6   Education related problems

Information regarding the effects of alcohol and its related risks to young people is a common component of alcohol education in schools. Babor et al (2010) conclude that exclusive approaches to alcohol education are ineffective. Jones et al (2007) maintains that in secondary schools (age eleven onwards) young people should be given further information about the risks of alcohol, its damaging effect on the family, friends, the community and the wider society, plus information regarding risk aversion and coping strategies. Research studies indicate that alcohol abuse and misuse can cause numerous education related problems at third level (i.e. colleges and universities) which results in many students suffering poor academic performance as a result of their inability to function to the best of their ability. Wechsler et al (1998) maintain that frequent binge drinkers are more likely to miss a class and fall behind in their schoolwork. Alcohol Edu (2008-09) add that the number of drinks consumed correlates positively with the number of classes missed. Wolaver (2002) informs us that alcohol consumption has a negative predictive effect on study hours under all definitions of drinking – binge, frequent binge, drunkenness, and frequent drunkenness. There is also a negative relationship between heavy episodic alcohol use and the time students spend on academic study (Porter and Pryor, 2007). The relationship between heavy or binge drinking and grade point average was explored by Pascarella et al (2007) who concluded that binge drinking two or more times in a typical two week period is linked to significantly lower semester grades.

Figure 1.2: Alcohol and academic performance (fau.edu).

Preseley (1993) reported that the heaviest drinkers obtain the lowest grades; Engs et al (2001) added that those students with a higher GPA (Grade Point Average) of 4.0 consumed a third fewer drinks compared to those with GPAs under 2.0. There is indeed a significant decline in the GPA of learners when comparing abstainers to heavier drinking categories (Rau and Durand, 2000).

Conclusion

The problem of alcohol abuse and misuse in society is a concern for all. This challenge to the tourism, hospitality and retail sectors currently selling and supplying alcohol requires them to continue to work together towards developing best practice procedures to help reduce the impacts of abuse and misuse of alcohol in society.

Web resources

A history of drug and alcohol abuse in America
    www.udel.edu/soc/tammya/pdf/crju369_history.pdf
Alcohol consumption and academic achievement
    www.ncbi.nlm.nih.gov/pmc/articles/PMC3843305/
Alcohol overdose: dangers of drinking too much
    pubs.niaaa.nih.gov/publications/AlcoholOverdoseFactsheet/Overdosefact.htm
American Beverage Association
    www.abanet.org
Alcohol intervention programme - Let it hAPYN! (EU)
    www.eurocare.org/eu_projects/let_it_hapyn
Estimating the costs of alcohol (WHO)
    www.euro.who.int/__data/assets/pdf_file/0009/112896/E93197.pdf?ua=1
Identifying and treating alcohol problems (US)
    www.integration.samhsa.gov/clinical-practice/sbirt/a_sound_investment.pdf
National Institute of Alcohol Abuse and Alcoholism
    www.niaaa.nih.gov
The link between stress and alcohol
    pubs.niaaa.nih.gov/publications/AA85/AA85.htm
World Health Organisation (WHO) – alcohol publications
    www.euro.who.int/en/health-topics/disease-prevention/alcohol-use/publications

2 Alcohol's Origins and its Role in Modern Society

Aims and learning outcomes

This chapter aims to introduce the areas central to the origin of alcohol and its role in modern society. It also explores the rates of consumption. After reading this chapter you should be able to:

■ Outline the origins of alcohol and drinking from its earliest written reference to the early twentieth century.

■ Explain the evolution and development of beer, wine and distilled alcohol.

■ Describe the past legal methods used to prevent the availability and consumption of alcohol plus the effects of banning alcohol consumption.

■ Identify the role and consumption rates associated with alcohol in society.

2.0   The origins of alcohol and drinking

Alcohol can be traced back to the dawn of time. It is beneficial when it is consumed in recommended amounts but dangerous when taken in excess. Professor Robert Dudley of the University of California, Berkeley suggests in his 'drunken monkey hypothesis' that the human attraction to alcohol may have a genetic basis due to the high dependence of early primates on fruit as a food source. For 40 million years, primate diets were rich in fruits and in the humid tropical climate where the early evolution of human took place, yeasts on fruit skin and within fruit converted fruit sugars into ethanol (alcohol). When the alcohol molecules diffused out of the fruit, its smell identified the food as ripe and ready to consume. Natural selection favoured primates who had a keen appreciation for the smell and taste. Dudley (2004) adds that as human evolution continued, fruits were mostly replaced by roots, tubers and meat. Although our ancestors stopped relying heavily on fruit, it is possible that the taste for alcohol arose during our long shared ancestry with primates.

The archaeological evidence indicates that the production of alcoholic beverages dates back to the late Stone Age or Neolithic period. Patrick (1952) contends that samples of 'beer jugs' help to establish that intentionally fermented beverages existed at least as early as 10,000 BC. Dr. Patrick McGovern of the Applied Science Centre for Archaeology, University of Pennsylvania, and colleagues in America and China performed chemical analysis on traces absorbed and preserved in ancient pottery from the Neolithic village of Jiahu, in the Henan province of northern China. This was shown to be the residue left behind by the alcoholic beverages they had once contained (McGovern et al, 2004). Further analysis of this residue confirmed that the fermented drink was made of grape and hawthorn fruit. Wine, honey mead and rice beer were being produced in 7000-5600 BC (McGovern, 2003). Prior to the modern era, fermented alcoholic beverages were known in all tribal and village societies except in Australia, Oceania and North America. Evidence of alcoholic beverages (a pictograph of wine) has also been found from 3150 BC in ancient Egypt (Cavalieri et al, 2003). Other evidence has been found and dated from 3000 BC in Babylon, 2000 BC in pre-Hispanic Mexico, and 1500 BC in Sudan (Dirar, 1993; Pedersen, 1979). In India, alcoholic beverages started appearing in the Indus Valley civilization in the Chalcolithic Era – 3000 BC-2000 BC.

Early written references to alcohol

The first written reference to alcohol records a daily beer allowance for workers on a temple in Mesopotamia in the year 5000 BC. Recipes for making alcoholic beverages have been found on clay tablets from around that time, and art in Mesopotamia shows people using straws to drink beer from large vats and pots. Around 1750 BC, the famous Code of Hammurabi, from the 6th King of the first dynasty of Babylon, devoted attention to alcohol; Popham (1978) notes that this concentrated around fair commerce in alcohol. The Old Testament contains many references to drink, often with advice, which is as relevant today as it was then. For example, it recommends giving alcoholic drinks to those who are dying or depressed, so that they can forget their misery (Book of Proverbs 31:6-7).

Alcohol from the middle ages to the eighteenth century

The Swiss Alchemist Paracelsus (1493-1541) was the first European to use the word 'alcohol' in the Middle Ages. Babor (1986) maintains that throughout history all ancient cultures had their own form of alcohol, and it played its role in each society, be it religious or cultural. Where alcohol was traditionally consumed, production of alcoholic beverages commonly occurred on a small scale as a household or artisanal activity, particularly when and where agricultural surpluses were available. Room et al (2002) maintain that drinking alcohol was thus often an occasional and communal activity, associated with particular festivals. Willis (2006) adds that there are many places in the world where versions of these patterns, originating from tribal and village societies, still persist today.

In Medieval Europe, consuming alcoholic drinks was a way of avoiding water-borne diseases such as cholera when quenching thirst. The small concentration of alcohol in these beverages would have had only a limited effect, but the really dangerous microorganisms would be killed during the boiling of the water and the growth of yeast.

In Europe between the 16th and 18th centuries, alcohol was perceived and consumed as a gift of God, created to be consumed in moderation for pleasure, enjoyment and health, while drunkenness was viewed as a sin. In this period, Jennigan (2000) reports that new beverages, new modes of production, distribution and promotion, and new drinking customs and institutions were created, and as distilled spirits became available and transportation improved, alcoholic beverages became a market commodity which was available in all seasons of the year, and at any time during the week. Colson and Scudder (1988) contend that these supplies and the availability of alcohol often proved disastrous for indigenous economies and subsequently, as Coffer (1966) indicates, for 'the local public health'. Room et al (2002) add that these impacts were experienced on a global scale.

Nineteenth and early twentieth century

The nineteenth century and early twentieth century brought a complete change to alcohol consumption, and the perception, Hanson (1995) argues, that self discipline was needed in place of self expression, and task orientation replaced relaxed conviviality. Every type of problem, moral, social, personal or even religious, was blamed on alcohol and consumption came to be viewed as unacceptable. Temperance was in and abolitionist successfully lobbied for total prohibition, which not only failed but actually created additional new social problems. Nonetheless these early attempts to control alcohol consumption gained broad membership and eventually political strength and a new and fairly stable alcohol control structure was put in place (Aaron and Musto, 1981; WHO, 2011a).

From fermented mare's milk to brewing beer

Home brew came in almost immediately with the raising of grain, though Clark Wissler (famous anthropologist of the American Museum of Natural History and Yale University) contends that people did not wait for cereals to sprout to get a drink. The plainsmen of Siberia discovered that fermented mare's milk was a stimulant. This was probably the world's first intoxicating drink. It is called *kumiss* and is still drunk in parts of Russia today (Wissler, 1932). Brewing has taken place since around the 6th millennium BC, and archaeological evidence suggests that it was used in most emerging civilizations, including ancient Egypt and Mesopotamia (Arnold, 2005). The process involved in brewing beer made drinking it a safer option than drinking water or mare's milk, for many generations. Babylonians regularly used beer as an offering to their gods. Hartman and Oppenheim (1950) contend that in Mesopotamia the brewer's craft was the only profession which derived social sanction and divine protection from female deities/goddesses, specifically Ninkasi, who covered the production of beer, Siris, who was used in a metonymic way to refer to beer, and Siduri, who covered the enjoyment of beer. Throughout the Egyptian, Greek, Roman and Christian eras, right through medieval times and onwards from the 1400s up to the developments of the Industrial Revolution, beer has evolved to become one of the most popular alcoholic beverages consumed today.

Beer has been a drink of and for the common people throughout the centuries. Marciniiak (1992) maintains that it was always brewed on an everyday basis. Brewing nowadays is a global business, consisting of several dominant multinational companies and many thousands of smaller producers, known as microbreweries or regional breweries, depending on size. Although brewing at home is subject to strict regulation or prohibition in many countries, relaxation of the laws on home brewing by some has encouraged some individuals to learn the craft and to experiment with modern techniques and ingredients, to produce classic recipes and some new flavours. The global interest in beer continues to grow, with speciality beers in ever-greater demand. These were developed in direct response to the mass produced carbonated and pasteurized key beers that had dominated pubs around the world. This renaissance brought about the surge of designer lagers and boutique beers. Large-scale breweries have now recognized this segment of the market, and have responded by hiring technical consultants to create new beers.

Wine – the alcohol of the elites

Vouillamoz et al (2006) contend that wine first appeared around 6000 BC in Georgia. The Babylonians, as early as 2700 BC, worshipped a wine goddess and other wine deities. Wine clearly appeared in Egyptian pictographs around 4,000 B.C. (Lucia, 1963). It was consumed in classical Greece at breakfast and at symposia. Wine in those early days seems to have been always reserved for the elites of society; according to Dasgupta (2011), this situation did not change until around 30 BC when wine became available to common Romans, due to the expansion of vineyards. The Greeks and the Romans traditionally drank diluted wine (the strength varied between one part wine and one part water, to one part wine and four parts water). Robinson (2006) maintains that the Roman Empire had an immense impact overall on the development of viticulture and oenology. These developments included wine storage rooms, smokehouses to mimic aging, different grape varieties and appellation systems – but barrels were invented by the Gauls and glass bottles by the Syrians. She adds that virtually all of the major wine-producing regions of Western Europe today were established during the Roman Imperial era.

During the Middle Ages in Europe cider and pomace wine (made from the skins, pulp and seeds of grapes or other fruit after pressing) were widely available, though the better grape wine was still the prerogative of the higher classes (McGovern, 2003). By the 15th century, when the Europeans reached the New World, numerous local civilizations there had already developed alcoholic beverages. According to a post-conquest Aztec document, consumption of the local wine 'pulque' was generally restricted to religious ceremonies, but was freely allowed for consumption to people aged over 70 years.

From life water to the water of life - distilled alcohol

Distilled water has been known since at least c. 200 AD, when Alexander of Aphrodisias described the process (Sherwood, 1945); Middle Eastern scientists used distillation extensively in their alchemical experiments. Stephens and Dudley (2004) maintain that ancient beers and wine probably contained only 5% alcohol until alcohol distillation was invented. The first clear dated evidence of the distillation of alcohol comes from the School of Salerno in the 12th century (Forbes, 1970), with fractional distillation being developed later by Tadeo Alderotti in the 13th century (Holmyard, 1990). In 1500, the German alchemist Hieronymus Braunschweig published *Liber de arte destillandi* (*The Book of the Art of Distillation*), the first book solely dedicated to the subject of distillation. The link between water and distilled alcohol continued throughout the centuries to be the inspiration for numerous types of alcoholic beverages, for example eau-de-vie (France), uisce beatha (Ireland), akvavit – aqua vitae (Scandinavia). The higher alcohol content of distilled beverages allowed them to be stored safely for long periods in simple wood containers, and so could be carried on the long haul voyages of the early modern period.

Distilled alcohol consumption throughout most of the sixteenth century was still largely for medicinal purposes. Braudel (1974) reports of distilled alcohol 'that the sixteenth century created it; the seventeenth century consolidated it; the eighteenth popularized it' (p. 170). As drinks with a higher alcohol content became available worldwide unfortunately so too did alcohol abuse, and that has continued right up to the present day.

2.1   Banning alcohol consumption - the noble experiment

Countries with widespread alcohol problems, or those where the idea that alcohol abuse is part of their nation's tradition, have gained an unfair and unwelcome image of hard drinkers. Waters (2003) contends that alcohol has enabled some countries to endure change and mask the darkness of their past, and in some circumstances their troubled history. Nonetheless in the past some governments and rulers had sought to prevent the availability and social consumption of alcohol through legal means or 'prohibition'. Some attempts at prohibition were made in Aztec society and in feudal Japan. Rong (2014) states that 'the earliest records of prohibition of alcohol in ancient China date back to the Xia Dynasty' (c. 2070 BC – c. 1600 BC). Yu the Great, the first ruler of the Xia Dynasty, prohibited alcohol throughout the kingdom, though it was legalized again during the reign of his son Qi.

In America, when the evils of intemperance began to attract the attention of the ministry, Cherrington (1920) maintains that John Wesley 'denounced the sin of distilling and declared for its prohibition in 1773'. Lee (1963) states that Massachusetts went so far as to prohibit the drinking of toasts in 1638, but this early prohibition law was soon abandoned for obvious, albeit unrecorded, reasons. He argued that the 'liquor laws could do more than control consumption: they could provide a source of revenue'. By the turn of the 18th century in the USA the regulatory impulse was concentrated on fines, excise taxes and license fees. Krout (1967) reports that these fines were imposed for 'drunken behaviour, unlawful sales to a drunken tippler or to Indians, and for selling without a license'; court records indicate that these laws were enforced with reasonable regularity. Brownlee (2002) adds that in the United Kingdom in 1859 a prototype prohibition bill was overwhelmingly defeated in the House of Commons. In the early 1900s, much of the increased activity for the prohibition movement in the Scandinavian countries (where there had been a strong temperance movement since the 1800s) and North America came from 'moralistic convictions of pietistic Protestants' (Jensen, 1971).

The rise of the temperance movement - taking the pledge

Furnas (1965) contends that this new temper of the movement was typified by the travels of Father Theobald Matthew of Cork, Ireland, who toured America from 1849 to 1851, 'administering the pledge of total abstinence to some 600,000 persons in 25 states'. Temperance was popular again, and Furnas maintained that it actually drifted into a new phase, with its enthusiastic spokesman U.S Congressman Gerrit Smith, crying that:

> I would that no person were able to drink intoxicating liquors without immediately becoming a drunkard. For, who then would drink the poison that always kills, or jump into the fire that always burns? (p.15).

At the start of the 1900s, the temperance campaign had penetrated the American school system. Sinclair (1962) informs us that 'Arizona was the only state without compulsory education'; he reminds us also that temperance literature was packed with huge amounts of misleading information about alcohol, for example:

> alcohol sometimes causes the coats of the blood vessels to grow thin. They are then liable at any time to cause death by bursting. (p.43)

In the West the prohibition process also coincided with the advent of women's suffrage, with newly empowered women as part of the political process strongly supporting policies that curbed alcohol consumption (Benjamin, 1991; Heath, 1995). Timberlake (1963) maintains that there was scientific support in this period to 'declare alcohol as a poison'. This support eventually led to 'whiskey and brandy being removed from the list of recognised medicinal drugs contained in the United States Pharmacopoeia'.

Prohibitionists

Numerous techniques were taken on to encourage sobriety. Timberlake (1963) states that these included 'lectures, literature and job preferences for teetotallers'. He adds that businessmen expressed the opinion that 'sobriety expanded productivity, increased bank deposits and stimulated the retail trade'. Supporters of prohibition, filled with anger, had identified the saloon and its products with the urban, immigrant working class. Gusfield (1963) contends that 'the saloon appeared as the symbol of a culture which was alien to the ascetic character of American values', therefore Americanism became a principle act in the temperance movement. This fear is best captured in the words of one temperance spokesperson cited by Timberlake (1963, p.118):

> the influx of foreigners into our urban centres, many of whom have liquor habits, is a menace to good government. The foreign born population is largely under the social and political control of the saloon. If

the cities keep up their rapid growth they will soon have the balance of political power in the nation and become storm centres of political life.

World War I brought American prohibitionists new ammunition; literature depicted brewers and licensed retailers as treacherously stabbing American soldiers in the back. Wheeler cited in Odegard (1928) argued that liquor was a menace to patriotism because 'it puts beer before country'.

Prohibition spreads globally

In the first half of the 1900s alcohol prohibition was introduced across the following countries:

- 1907 - 1948 in Prince Edward Island, and for shorter periods in other provinces in Canada (Heath, 1995)
- 1907 - 1992 in Faroe Islands; limited private imports from Denmark were allowed from 1928
- 1914 - 1925 in Russia and the Soviet Union, a limited version of a Dry Law was introduced which continued through the turmoil of the Revolution and Civil War into the period of Soviet Russia and the Soviet Union (Vvedensky, 1915)
- 1914 - 1955 Sweden adopted a rationing system, referred to as the Bratt System (liquor ration books); a referendum in 1922 rejected an attempt to introduce a total ban.
- 1915 - 1933 in Iceland, ban on wine and spirits was lifted in 1935 but beer was actually still prohibited until March 1989 (New York Times, 1988)
- 1916 - 1927 in Norway (fortified wine and beer also prohibited from 1917 to 1923)
- 1919 - Hungary (in the Hungarian Soviet Republic, March 21 to August 1; called szesztilalom)
- 1919 - 1932 in Finland (called kieltolaki, "ban law"). Smuggling, increased violence, and increased crimes rates turned public opinion against prohibition and it was ended in 1932 (Sariola, 1954; Wuorinen, 1932).

In Mexico the sale and purchase of alcohol is prohibited on the day and the night before certain national holidays, such as Natalicio de Benito Juárez (birth date of Benito Juárez) and Día de la Revolución, which are meant to be dry (Leyton, 2003). Prohibition generally came to an end across North America and Europe in the late 1920s or early 1930s, although a few locations continued prohibition for many more years (IBN Live, 2009). National prohibition today is still maintained across most of Asia, where alcohol is strictly prohibited by the Islamic faith. These countries include Bangladesh, Brunei,

India, the Maldives, Pakistan, the Philippines, and most of the Middle East (IBN Live, 2009; The Age, 2003; U.S. Passports & International Travel, 2014).

2.2   The effects of banning alcohol consumption: Prohibition in the USA

The Anti-Saloon League, founded in 1893, led the USA state prohibition drives of 1906–13. During World War I a temporary Wartime Prohibition Act was passed to save grain for use as food (Odegard, 1928). In 1917 the resolution for submission of the Prohibition Amendment to the states received the necessary two-thirds vote in the Congress; Lee (1963) informs us that Nebraska was 'the last of the 36 states to ratify the new Amendment'. The National Prohibition Act, popularly known as the Volstead Act (after its promoter, Congressman Andrew J. Volstead), was enacted on October 28th 1919 and came into effect on January 17th 1920 (McGrew, n.d.). Hu (1950) maintained that this new act sought to turn the U.S into 'enforced teetotallers', to 'end all the evils associated with drinking' and to eradicate the habits and customs of people through 'outlawing the business that ministered to its satisfaction'.

Prohibition enforcement

The initial impact of Prohibition gave the US government a sense of what was to come. Sinclair (1962) informs us that 'in the three months before the 18th Amendment became effective, spirits worth half a million dollars were stolen from Government warehouses' and before the middle of the summer of 1920, Federal Courts in Chicago were overwhelmed with some '600 pending liquor violation trials'. He also notes that in the first three years of prohibition, '30 prohibition agents were killed in service'. The law was evaded by several means during prohibition. The practice of obtaining a medical prescription for illegal substances was also abused; McGrew (n.d) argues 'that doctors earned $40 million in 1928 by writing prescriptions for whiskey'. Illegal manufacture and sales of liquor went on in the USA on a huge scale; the internal revenue figures offer us an insight into the level of seizures and arrests during the era;

1921: 95,933 illicit distilleries, stills, still works and fomenters seized and 34,175 persons arrested (p. 95).

1925: 172,537 illicit distilleries, stills, still works and fomenters seized and 62,747 persons arrested (p. 6).

1928: 75,307 persons arrested

1930: 282,122 illicit distilleries, stills, still works and fomenters seized (p. 73).

Internal Revenue, Service (1921, 1966, 1970)

Federal government support of enforcement of Prohibition varied considerably during the 1920s. In the US western and southern rural areas support was strong and remains so to this day. Dobyns (1940) however maintains that the legal system was 'evasive' in the 1920s; he contends that the courts only convicted about 'seven percent of those charged with liquor violations'.

Prohibition in general seemed to be enforced wherever the inhabitants supported it. The National Commission on Law Observance and Enforcement (1931) highlighted that prohibition enforcement 'failed in large cities where the law was flagrantly defied' and 'in the smaller towns, populated by miners and industrial workers, where the law was simply ignored'.

Criminality and the rise of speakeasies and blind pigs

Prohibition brought into being a new kind of criminal, the bootlegging gangster, and a population who craved for alcohol in an exciting environment. Smuggling was widespread; rum-runners frequently smuggled liquor from Canada. Sinclair (1962) contends that the Department of Commerce estimated in 1924 'liquor valued at approximately $40 million was entering the United States annually'. The career of gangster Al Capone was a particular example of the development of bootlegging on a large scale; his annual earnings were estimated at $60 million from alcohol sales alone (History and Learning, 2014). In this period, legislators could not quell the never-ending demand for alcoholic products. Lee (1963) argues that this demand lead to an illicit traffic development 'from the point of manufacture to consumption'. He states that 'the institution of the speakeasy replaced the institution of the saloon'. Speakeasies, also referred to as blind pigs or blind tigers, were numerous and popular during the Prohibition years. Lee (1963) suggest that the numbers ranged from 200,000 to 500,000 across the United States. Ceyana and Jen (2013) state that they were 'places designed to be hidden from law enforcement, and were usually run by gangsters, shop owners, and common people'. Speakeasies were usually hidden behind local stores, shut down bars or salons

Most speakeasies went unknown in their early stages, but grew rapidly over the months. Even though police and agents of the Bureau of Prohibition would often raid them and arrest their owners and patrons, Ceyana and Jen (2013) state that 'they were so profitable that they continued to flourish'. MacRae (1870) suggests that the term' speakeasy' is reported to have originated around the late 1800s with saloon owner Kate Hester who ran an unlicensed bar in the McKeesport neighbourhood on the outskirts of Pittsburg. Cheney (1889) adds that, 'unlicensed saloons in Pennsylvania were also known as 'speak-easies'. Harper (2012) reminds us that they were 'so-called because of the practice of speaking quietly about the place in public, or when inside it, so as not to alert the police or neighbours'. Speakeasies had many defences to protect their business, which included doormen, multiple locking doors and guards (Ceyana and Jen, 2013). Most defences were there to defend against raiding police, but were used occasionally for the common drunk person.

Blind pigs or blind tigers applied to lower-class establishments that sold alcoholic beverages illegally. The operator of such an establishment would charge customers to see an attraction (such as an animal – pigs or other curious animals) and then serve a 'complimentary drink – such as a gin cocktail', thus circumventing the law (Shay, 1934). Grimes (2009) reports that although blind tigers were mysterious places, they also distributed for consumption 'the very bad whiskey for which Prohibition is indirectly responsible'.

In many rural towns, small speakeasies and blind pigs were operated by local business owners. These family secrets were often kept even after Prohibition ended. Major supporters of prohibition became gradually disillusioned with the Volstead Act by these developments and often cited the increase in criminal liquor production and sale, plus the development of the speakeasy, as their primary reason for supporting the repeal of Prohibition (McGrew, n. d). Speakeasies largely disappeared after the Prohibition era ended; the term is now used to describe retro style bars. Diamond (2012) contends that the name 'speakeasy' was revived in the late 2000s in the United States, to refer to a legal, prohibition-themed cocktail bar, generally serving only classic cocktails. The term has now expanded, to include all retro bars, and to non-Prohibition countries such as Australia and the United Kingdom by 2012 (Sweeny, 2007).

Repeal of prohibition

In spite of the apparent weak enforcement of the US National Prohibition Act, Gusfield (1963) believes that 'the Depression and the need for tax revenues and increased employment' killed the Act. In contrast, Sinclair (1962) believes that Prohibition was 'a by-product of the stress and excess of war' and 'could not have survived in peacetime'. Dobyns (1940) however contends that selfishly motivated U.S. businessmen brought about the 'same pressure and tactics which were cleverly adopted by the temperance movement in the previous decades'. Whatever the motivation, the repeal movement was financed and driven by the Association Against the Prohibition Amendment. In 1932 the Democratic Party adopted a platform calling for repeal, and the Democratic victory in the presidential election of 1932 sounded the death knell of the Eighteenth Amendment. In February 1933 Congress adopted a resolution proposing the Twenty-first Amendment to the Constitution to repeal the Eighteenth.

Lessons learned from the US National Prohibition

Much has been written about American Prohibition and its 13 year duration, and lessons be learnt from the ban of alcohol in the US. Hu (1950) argues that prohibition failed because it sought to 'destroy the manufacturing and distributive agencies through which the demand for liquor had been legally supplied, but the demand remained'. The Wickersham Commission, as cited by Hu (1950), concluded that 'the country had prohibition in law but not in fact'. Data to support a favourable outcome for Prohibition is scarce; perhaps Figures 2.1 and 2.2 will help to explain why.

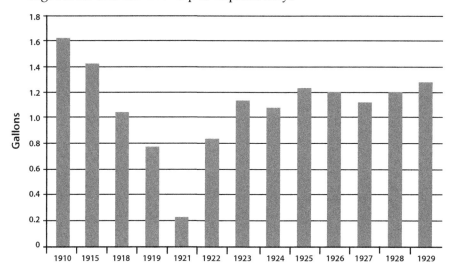

Figure 2.1: Per capita consumption of alcoholic beverages (gallons of pure alcohol) 1910-1929.

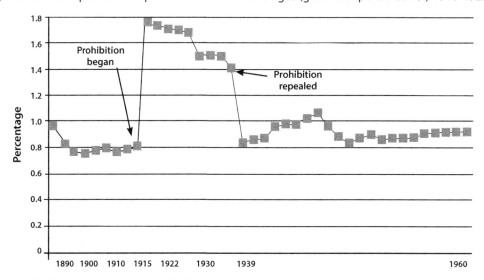

Figure 2.2: Expenditure on distilled spirits as a percentage of total alcohol sales, 1890-1960. (History of the Alcohol and Tobacco Division, n.d)

The data in Figure 2.1 above appears promising. In the early years of prohibition alcohol consumption began to slope downwards, while the individual US states begin to enact prohibition legislation, spiking in a major decline when National Prohibition was passed. Unfortunately by 1922 alcohol consumption has doubled and continued to increase through the next thirteen years. Tillitt (1932) reported that the 'per capita rate for the Prohibition years when computed amount to 1.63 proof gallons', which he claims was '11.64% higher than the pre-prohibition rate'. The data in Figure 2.2, which shows the total amount for alcohol sales from 1890 to 1960, also demonstrates how sales raised significantly to their highest point during Prohibition and decreased after it ended. Brown (1932) indicates that people were actually drinking at a younger age during Prohibition, adding that 'several state mental hospitals reported large group of high school patients admitted for alcoholic psychoses'. Malzburg (1949) also points to the increase in mental disorders and deaths from alcoholism in the wider population during Prohibition. Dobyns (1940) highlights that one of the great ironies of Prohibition noted by the Wickersham Commission was that 'women happily took to drink during the experimental decade, and did so in public'.

Figure 2.3: (Left) A woman adds alcohol to her drink, poured from a hollow walking stick. (Right) Women concealing alcohol during the prohibition era. (Wikicommons, 2014).

2.3   Alcohol's role in modern society

Social and convivial aspects

Alcohol has contributed towards a more sociable and convivial atmosphere between locals, invited guests and travellers for many centuries around the world. Murphy (2013) contends that over the centuries, alcohol has also helped change the political and economic landscape in most countries. Its evolution and development have been closely linked with the widespread introduction of hospitality establishments such as inns, alehouses, bierkellers, and hotels. The pub, for example, is the focal point in most villages, often doubling up as a meeting place for local sporting and voluntary organisations. In some cultures, the consumption of alcohol is closely associated with other social activities, such as holidays, dining out, entertainment, and business and of course celebrations. It provides for most consumers a great deal of pleasure and causes little or no harm. Alcohol is considered to be society's most prevalent and accepted legal recreational drug; it is generally accepted as a component of our daily life. The majority of adults around the world celebrate, relax and commiserate with alcohol. Waters (2003) however sheds a fresh perspective on our fascination with alcohol; he proposes that we need to stop thinking about drink the instant we think about ways of enjoying ourselves. National drink problems have their roots in some form of collective psychiatric condition, and so the use and abuse of this lethal drug must, as a matter of urgency, be intellectually and otherwise separated from our concepts of leisure, pleasure and relaxation.

The USauthor and addiction expert Dr. Stanton Peele, suggests in his book *The Joy of Drinking* that a positive model than can promote successful drinking patterns. He maintains that most people, when asked individually about their views of alcohol and its effects, place pleasure foremost. Yet public health groups place harm foremost, particularly as they relate to young people. Dr Peele argues that 'ignoring health and pleasure benefits while referring only to danger and harm associated with alcohol may delay even permanently impair people's ability to adopt sensible and pleasure drinking practices'. The real goal here should be to learn moderate drinking. The development of moderate drinking habits is both possible and beneficial, and people should learn as an ethical tenet that excessive drinking and anti-social behavior while drinking is wrong. MacAvoy (2002) reminds us also that at the heart of any debate of alcohol's role in a modern society is the inability to form a balanced view of what an ideal society in which alcohol is present might look like. 'History has taught us the folly of many attempts to prohibit alcohol, particularly where there are no compelling cultural, religious or moral beliefs to support such an approach'. He adds that 'alcohol will remain an intrinsic part of most societies in which it has found a niche and that we should therefore really debate how to live harmoniously with alcohol rather than how to battle to live without it'.

2.4   Consumption rates of alcohol

Babor et al (2010) maintain that a variety of factors have been identified at the individual and societal levels, which affect the magnitude and patterns of consumption, and can increase the risk of alcohol use disorders and other alcohol-related problems in drinkers and others. The WHO (2007) proposes that these factors include environmental elements such as economic development, culture, availability of alcohol and the level and effectiveness of alcohol policies. These are all relevant factors in explaining differences in vulnerability between societies, historical trends in alcohol consumption and alcohol-related harm. Where there is unequal access to health care or other treatment resources, the subsequent patterns of drinking are most likely to be more severe for those with less resources (Shi and Stevens, 2005; Blas and Kurup, 2010). Schmidt et al (2010) adds that although no single risk factor is dominant, research indicates the more vulnerability a person has (i.e. physical, mental and social outcomes which include alcohol related issues) the more likely the person is to develop alcohol problems. Blas and Kurup (2010) add that it has also been shown that vulnerable individuals are often at greater risk of having more than one individual risk factor, for example an unhealthy diet, lack of physical activity and tobacco use, which together compound the challenges involved.

In most countries, as alcohol consumption continues to grow, trends in the brand and types of alcohol consumed change. This next section looks at the levels and patterns of alcohol consumption. It is based on the World Health Organisation's regions and member countries as at 2014.

The levels of alcohol consumption worldwide are usually measured using several indicators, but the two major indicators are alcohol per capita (APC) consumption in litres of pure alcohol per annum, and alcohol consumption in grams of pure alcohol per person per day.

Total per capita consumption

Individuals above 15 years of age drink on average 6.2 litres of pure alcohol per year, which translates into 13.5 grams of pure alcohol per day. However the WHO (2014) report that there is wide variation in total alcohol consumption across WHO regions and member states. The highest consumption levels continue to be found in the developed world, in particular in Europe and the Americas. Intermediate levels of consumption are found in the Western Pacific and African Regions, while the lowest consumption levels are found in South-East Asia and the Eastern Mediterranean. Differences in the levels of total consumption between regions and countries are the result of complex interactions between a wide range of factors which include socio-demographic factors, prevalence rates of abstention, level of economic development, culture, such as the predominance of Islam, and the preferred beverage types.

Unrecorded alcohol consumption

The figures above do not include the percentage of unrecorded alcohol consumption worldwide which is estimated to cover 24.8% of all the alcohol consumed. Unrecorded alcohol is that consumed but not accounted for in official statistics on alcohol taxation or sales. In some countries, particularly South-East Asia and the Eastern Mediterranean, unrecorded alcohol consumption accounts for more than 50% of the total alcohol consumption. Interestingly, in some countries where alcohol is banned, as in some Islamic states in the Eastern Mediterranean, unrecorded alcohol amounts to 100% or almost 100% of total APC.

Most consumed alcoholic beverages

Although geographical differences exist regarding the type, internationally 50.1% of the total recorded alcohol is consumed in the form of spirits. The second most consumed beverage type is beer, which accounts for 34.8%; beer is also the most consumed type of beverage in the Americas at 55.3%. Significantly only 8.0% of the total recorded alcohol is consumed in the form of wine, but wine represents one fourth (25.7%) of total consumption in Europe. Other alcoholic beverages (fortified wines, rice wine or other fermented beverages made of sorghum, millet or maize) constitute the most popular types in Africa, at 51.6% of the total recorded consumption.

Heavy episodic drinking (HED)

HED is an indicator of the pattern of alcohol consumption and is defined as 60 or more grams of pure alcohol (six plus standard drinks in most countries) on at least one single occasion at least monthly. The volume of alcohol consumed on a single occasion is important for many acute consequences of drinking such as alcohol poisoning, injury and violence, and is also important wherever intoxication is socially disapproved of. HED is associated with detrimental consequences even if the average level of alcohol consumption of the person concerned is relatively low. HED levels vary widely between countries at present and the WHO (2014) report that there is no consistent association between total alcohol consumption and HED figures among drinkers.

Quality of the alcohol consumed

Preedy and Watson (2005) argue that the quality of alcoholic beverages can have an impact on health and mortality, Rehm et al (2010) add that although home-made or illegally produced alcoholic beverages may be contaminated with methanol or other very toxic substances, such as disinfectants, the consumption of unrecorded alcohol cannot be conclusively linked to health and mortality figures. Consumption of alcoholic drinks produced illegally or informally is relevant for estimation of alcohol-attributable burden of disease. As unrecorded products are often available outside the regulated market, resulting in cheaper prices, different controls, or no controls on availability, they may increase overall consumption and have also been linked to more heavy drinking occasions (Rehm et al, 2010).

Conclusion

People have been making and consuming alcohol from ancient times to the modern day, and throughout these beverages have played a significant role in each society, be it religious, cultural or economic. Drinking alcohol was traditionally an occasional and communal activity, and in some eras it was also a way of avoiding water borne diseases.

Unfortunately because of its addictive properties and the effect of abusive drinking patterns have had on some societies, some governments have attempted, with varying degrees of success, to completely ban its sale and consumption through experiments like prohibition. The most famous prohibition period in the world took place in the US between 1920 and 1933. It failed to reduce the sales and consumption of alcohol, and actually helped to create bootlegging gangsters and increased levels of criminality.

Alcohol is still considered to be society's most prevalent and accepted legal recreational drug and it is generally accepted as a component of our daily life. The majority of adults around the world celebrate, relax and commiserate with alcohol and when enjoyed responsibly it has contributed towards a more sociable and convivial atmosphere between locals, invited guests and travellers for many centuries. However high and intermediate levels of consumption which we are currently experiencing in Europe, the Americas, Western Pacific and the African countries can increase the risk of alcohol use disorders and other alcohol related problems especially in vulnerable societies. These consumption trends must be closely monitored into the future.

Web resources

A history of drinking in the US

    www.youtube.com/watch?v=WxpMFlnMGAE

Alcohol research (UK)

    www.alcoholresearchuk.org

Alcohol focus (Scotland)

    www.alcohol-focus-scotland.org.uk

Alcohol prohibition (US)

    www.druglibrary.org/schaffer/library/studies/nc/nc2a.htm

Brief history of alcohol in Europe (EU)

    btg.ias.org.uk/pdfs/alcohol-in-europe/alcoholineu_chap2_en.pdf

National Institute on Alcohol Abuse and Alcoholism (US)

    www.niaaa.nih.gov/

National Drug & Alcohol Research Centre (Australia)

    ndarc.med.unsw.edu.au/resource/consumer-issues-australia-and-asia

The foundation for alcohol research

    www.abmrf.org/

Indiana University (US)

    www.indiana.edu/~engs/articles/ar1096.htm

Social issues research centre

    www.sirc.org/publik/drinking_origins.html

World Health Organisation (WHO)

    www.who.int/substance_abuse/publications/alcohol/en/

3 The Nature of Alcohol

Aims and learning outcomes

This chapter aims to provide the knowledge necessary to understand the nature of alcohol. It explains its scientific composition and how it is produced, plus the general effects and strengths of alcoholic beverages. After reading this you should be able to:

- Explain how alcohol is produced and know the general effects of alcoholic beverages.

- Outline the scientific composition of ethanol and the role which aldehyde dehydrogenase plays in its breakdown.

- Identify the systems used for determining the strength of alcoholic beverages and apply formulas for calculating the grams and units of alcohol they contain.

3.0 Introduction

Alcohol has a long and chequered history, as we witnessed in Chapter 2, and over the centuries it has been used for many purposes around the world. Ethyl alcohol or ethanol is a chemical and in its primary form is found in most alcoholic beverages. It is used as fuel, and also has many scientific, medical, and industrial uses. In its natural form (i.e. without ageing or additives), it is a clear liquid which dissolves easily in water.

The human body contains a high percentage of water and blood streams act as a super highway for alcohol to roam freely. The body also contains powerful enzymes and organs which help to break down ethanol and to eliminate its by-products. The strength of alcoholic drinks varies and is based on how much ethanol they contain. It is crucial that people involved in the sale and service of alcoholic drinks understand these strengths. They can be easily calculated using the formulas supplied in this chapter. People consume alcohol because of the general effects it offers to their bodies. These effects are dependent on the amount of alcohol consumed and the outcomes can differ between different individuals, genders and ethnic backgrounds. They can sometimes cause harmful behavioural patterns and unpleasant alcohol hangovers.

3.1   What is alcohol and how is produced?

The word 'alcohol' derives from the Arabic *al-kuhul* and is applied to the many members of the family of alcohols. The Persian physician and scientist Rhazes (ca. 865 – 925) discovered this substance, but because he wanted his book to be published in most of the then-known world, he used the Arabic language instead of Persian (although he made copies in Persian). The word was introduced into Europe, together with the art of distillation and the substance itself, around the twelfth century by various European authors who translated and popularized the discoveries of Islamic and Persian alchemists.

The term 'alcohol' originally referred to the ethyl alcohol (ethanol), the dominating alcohol in beverages like beer, wine and spirits. Ethanol is the only alcohol safe for human consumption. It is a simple molecule with the chemical formula C_2H_5OH, often abbreviated as EtOH. It is the presence of the –OH combination (the hydroxyl group) attached to a carbon atom that makes a molecule a member of the alcohol family (IUPAC, 1997). The simplest form of alcohol is methanol (methyl alcohol, CH_3OH), sometimes also called 'wood alcohol', because it can be produced by fermentation of wood. Other members of this family include glycol (found in anti-freeze for cars), propanol or propyl alcohol (rubbing alcohol), and cholesterol, a complicated molecule vital for many bodily functions and which, in excess, can cause serious illnesses such as heart disease (Charnley et al, 1995). For more on the family of alcohols, see Appendix I.

The nature of pure 100% alcohol as a chemical is such that:

- at room temperature it is a clear liquid
- it easily dissolves in water
- it can be used as a fuel and it is quite flammable

Alcohol is primarily made by fermentation, distillation and brewing. For the fermentation process, carbohydrate-containing plant materials are allowed to ferment, producing a dilute solution of ethanol in the process. The dilute solution can be separated by distillation, thus achieving a higher concentration level of alcohol, to create hard liquors or spirits.

Fermentation

Fermentation occurs in yeast and bacteria. It is employed for preservation in a process that produces lactic acid as found in such sour foods as pickled cucumbers, kimchi and yogurt (fermentation in food processing), as well as for producing alcoholic beverages such as wine and beer. Fermentation can even occur within the stomachs of animals, including humans. Fermentation in its widest sense is also used to refer to the bulk growth of microorganisms on a growth medium. French microbiologist Louis Pasteur is often remembered for his insights into fermentation and its microbial causes (Pasteur, 1879), see *Pasteurisation* below.

Fermentation is required for the production of ethanol in alcoholic beverages. Yeasts already contained in or introduced to grain or fruit juices or mixes, convert sugars such as glucose, fructose, and sucrose, into ethanol and carbon dioxide. The result is a dilute solution of ethanol. There are two types of fermentation relevant to the poduction of alcoholic beverages.

Ethanol fermentation

More commonly known as alcoholic fermentation, this is the biological process in which sugars such as glucose, fructose, and sucrose are converted into cellular energy and produce ethanol and carbon dioxide as metabolic waste products. Because yeasts perform this conversion in the absence of oxygen, alcoholic fermentation is considered an anaerobic process. All ethanol contained in alcoholic beverages (including ethanol produced by carbonic maceration) is produced by means of fermentation induced by yeast. The major types of alcoholic drinks produced by ethanol fermentation include:

- **Beer, whiskey, and vodka** are produced by fermentation of grain starches that have been converted to sugar by the enzyme amylase, which is present in grain kernels that have been malted through germination. Additional sources of starch, for example potatoes and un-malted grain, may be added to the mixture, as the amylase will act on those starches as well. Whiskey and vodka are distilled; gin and related beverages are produced by the addition of flavouring agents to a vodka-like feedstock during distillation.

- **Mead** is produced by fermentation of the natural sugars present in honey.

- **Rum** and some other beverages are produced by fermentation and distillation of sugarcane. Rum is usually produced from the sugarcane product molasses.

- **Rice wines** (including sake) are produced by the fermentation of grain starches converted to sugar by the mould Aspergillus Oryzae. Baijiu, Soju, and Shōchū are distilled from the product of such fermentation (see Sake below).

- **Wine** is produced by the fermentation of the natural sugars present in grapes. Cider and perry are produced by similar fermentation of natural sugar in apples and pears, respectively. Other fruit wines are produced from the fermentation of the sugars in the fruit.

In all cases, alcohol fermentation must take place in a vessel that allows carbon dioxide to escape but prevents outside air from entering. Exposure to oxygen would prevent the formation of ethanol, while a build-up of carbon dioxide creates a risk that the vessel could rupture or fail, which could cause serious injury and property damage (Stryer, 1975).

Lactic acid fermentation

This refers to two means of producing lactic acid (homolactic and heterolactic fermentation). They are biological processes by which glucose and other six-carbon sugars and disaccharides of six-carbon sugars (for example sucrose or lactose) are converted into cellular energy and the metabolite lactate.

- *Homolactic* fermentation (producing only lactic acid) is the simplest type of fermentation. One molecule of glucose is converted to two molecules of lactic acid.
- *Heterolactic* fermentation in contrast yields carbon dioxide and ethanol in addition to other acids.

Lactic acid fermentation is used in many areas of the world to produce foods and alcoholic beverages that cannot be produced through other methods. The most commercially important genus of lactic acid-fermenting bacteria is Lactobacillus, though other bacteria and even yeast are sometimes used (Campbell and Reece, 2005).Two of the most common applications of lactic acid fermentation are in the production of foods (yogurt and sauerkraut) and in alcoholic beverages (sour beers – Lambic and Berliner Weisse, see below).

Lactic in beer

The percentage of acids, primarily lactic and acetic, in a beer determines its sourness. Some beers have just a hint of tartness; others are overpoweringly sour. German Berliner Weisse and several Belgian beer styles are characterized by their sourness. Each style has a different level of sourness, and even within the same beer style this level varies. Fermentation with lactic acid bacteria is not an exact science, and one brand of beer may have different levels of sourness from batch to batch or from year to year (Nummer, 2012).

Aerobic respiration

Fermentation does not necessarily have to be carried out in an anaerobic environment. Dickinson (1999) maintains that even in the presence of abundant oxygen, yeast cells greatly prefer fermentation to aerobic respiration, as long as sugars are readily available for consumption, a phenomenon known as the Crabtree effect. Voet and Voet (1995) maintain that sugars are the most common substrate of fermentation, and typical examples of fermentation products are ethanol, lactic acid, carbon dioxide, and hydrogen gas (H_2). However, more exotic compounds can be produced by fermentation, such as butyric acid and acetone. Yeast carries out fermentation in the production of ethanol in beers, wines, and other alcoholic drinks, along with the production of large quantities of carbon dioxide.

Brewing

This is the method used for the production of beer and sake. To make these distinctly different beverages, the sugar required to produce the alcohol must first be converted from a starch source (commonly cereal grains or rice) into a sugar and added to water. The resulting sweet liquid is then fermented using yeast. It is done in a brewery by a brewer, and the brewing industry is part of most western economies.

Beers

The basic ingredients of beer are water and a starch source, such as malted barley, which is able to be fermented. Most beer is fermented with a brewer's yeast and flavoured with hops (Murphy, 2013). Secondary starch sources (adjuncts), such as maize (corn), rice, or sugar, may also be used, as may less widely used sources such as millet, sorghum and cassava (Bright, 2005). The amount of each starch source in a beer recipe is collectively called the grain bill. Steps in the brewing process include malting, milling, mashing, lautering, boiling, fermenting, conditioning, filtering, and packaging. There are three main fermentation methods, warm, cool and spontaneous. Fermentation may take place in an open or closed fermenting vessel; a secondary fermentation may be encouraged in the cask or bottle.

Pasteurisation

Pasteurisation of beer is carried out by flash-heating canned or bottled beers. The object is to stabilise the beer. Pasteurisation slows down, but does not halt, the ravages of time and lengthens the shelf life of the product. Pasteurisation is the main difference between draft and bottled or canned beers.

Sake

Sake is made from five main ingredients (water, rice, technical skill, yeast, and land/weather). More than anything else, sake is a result of a brewing process that uses rice and lots of water. The brewing process for sake differs from the process for beer, in that for beer, the conversion from starch to sugar and from sugar to alcohol occurs in two discrete steps. But when sake is brewed, these conversions occur simultaneously. Furthermore, the alcohol content differs between sake, wine, and beer. Robinson (2006) states that wine for example generally contains 9% to 16% ABV (alcohol by volume), while most beer contain 3% to 9%, and undiluted sake contains 18% to 20%, although this is often lowered to about 15% by diluting with water prior to bottling.

Distillation

This is a method of separating the chemical substances based on differences in their volatilities in a boiling liquid mixture. The word distillation comes from the Latin *destillare* meaning 'to drip'. It is the extraction of higher alcohols from fermented drinks by using the action of heat to vaporize them (Murphy, 2013). Alcohol has a lower boiling point than water (78.5°C compared to 100°C for water), so the alcohol vaporizes into steam some time before the water content in the wine, wort or young beer starts to boil. When the alcohol laden steam hits a cool surface, it condenses and forms a liquid of which the alcohol constitutes a much higher proportion than it did in the wine, wort or young beer. The liquid produced is colourless and tasteless.

Example: A wine of 8% alcohol by volume condenses into distillate of 20% volume after being boiled off in a pot still. If it is boiled a second time the strength goes up to about 60% ABV. If, when vaporising wine you take the wholesome middle-cut of the run, missing out the poisonous first part and the watery final part, as distillers learned to do, you have grape spirit, eau de vie, or brandy of about 70% ABV.

This method is scientifically the best separation method for spirits and research figures indicate that the distillation method accounts for 98% of the world's spirits produced. It is the method most widely officially recognized by governments to separate alcohol for creating spirits on which taxes and duties are levied (Murphy, 2013). Spirits such as rum, cognac and whiskey are prepared by distilling dilute solutions of ethanol (see below). Components other than ethanol are also collected in the condensate, including water, esters, and other alcohols which account for the flavour of the beverage.

Types of distillation

There are two types of still used for distillation, the pot still and the continuous still. The pot still looks like a large copper kettle and is heated by direct heat, in a small batch process (see Figure 3.1). The vapours collect in the head and are led off through a narrow tube at the top, called the swan's neck, from where they go to the condenser. Here they are liquefied.

This is an expensive and labour intensive method. Redistilling, often several times, is necessary to achieve the appropriate alcohol level. Most spirits made with a pot still are double distilled, but sometimes it is done in three or even four stages (e.g. Irish whiskey, distilled three times). Several spirits are produced using the pot still including cognac, brandy, Scotch malt whisky, Irish whiskey, American bourbon whiskey and some darker rums.

The Copper Alambic

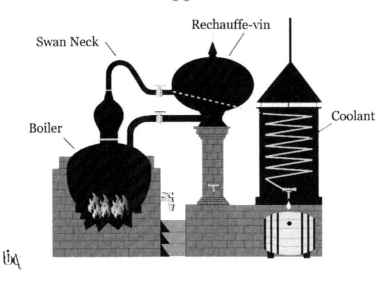

Figure 3.1: Pot still process (© BNIC).

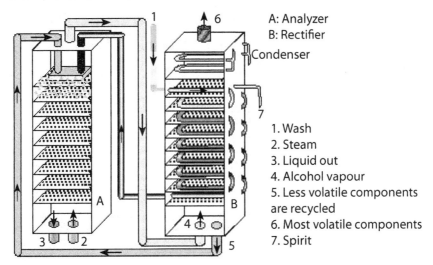

Figure 3.2: Continuous still process (Still Cooker.com).

The continuous still, also referred to as the Patent, Column or Coffey Still, basically consists of two tall columns, each about sixty feet in height, called the analyser and the rectifier. The alcoholic wash is broken down into its constituent vapours, or analysed, in the analyser, and the vapours are selectively condensed, or rectified, in the rectifier (see Figure 3.2). The various vapours are condensed and drawn off the still at different alcoholic strengths, according to where in the still the spirit plate is placed.

The spirit can have a high degree of alcohol and purity, so only one distillation is needed. The result of using the continuous still is a more neutral spirit than that obtained from a pot still. Spirits made using the continuous still include vodka, grain scotches, light rums and gin.

Congelation (cold extraction)

Congelation was originally used in the 8th century in Poland before distillation was discovered. It involved the cooling of the fermentable liquid (called the alcoholic wash) below 0°C. This is a dangerous method of alcohol separation, because the poisonous fusel oils molecules tend to stick more closely together under cold conditions and can be left in. It is for this reason that most countries have made this method of alcohol separation illegal, but some operators use it to avoid paying taxes. It is sometimes used in Canadian homes to make Applejack. Cider is put out to freeze on a winter night, and in the morning the ice formed is discarded. This process is repeated for three to four nights and the resulting residue is increased in alcoholic strength. Less than (2%) of the world's beverage spirits are made using this method.

3.2   The scientific composition of ethanol

The ethanol molecule is very small compared to the other molecules with which it interacts in the human body, and it carries a small electrical charge, which is crucial to its behaviour. Lodgsdon, cited in Kroschwitz (1994), suggest that each one of these tiny molecules has the power to affect the body's biochemistry.

Its slight negative charge causes ethanol to react with the slight positive charge on a water molecule, allowing it to dissolve. Since ethanol mixes well with water, it can easily penetrate our water-filled bodies and pass into the blood stream. Ethanol is also soluble in oils. This means that ethanol can easily pass through the membranes of cells, which are made largely of fat molecules. In effect, ethanol can roam freely throughout the human body. Ethanol has the chemical ability to enter the bloodstream and various organs in the body very quickly. In fact, in the four or five seconds it takes for a mouthful of beer to reach the stomach, ethanol is already being absorbed by the lining of the mouth and gullet; however most of the absorption takes place in the stomach and small intestine. From there, alcohol passes to the brain, where it acts on the neurochemical pathways that control many of your functions. Whether in beer, wine or spirits, the ethanol in the drink has the same effect on the body.

The breakdown of ethanol and the role of aldehyde dehydrogenase

The body contains powerful enzymes that are responsible for breaking down ethanol and for eliminating its by-products. As ethanol enters the stomach, it stimulates increased secretion of acid and the enzyme alcohol dehydrogenase, which is the first line of attack in the breakdown process. This enzyme converts ethanol into an inactive form called acetaldehyde. While this molecule does not have the effects of ethanol, it can damage cells. Therefore, to make sure that acetaldehyde is also eliminated from the body, a second enzyme takes over — aldehyde dehydrogenase — and turns acetaldehyde into the inactive and innocuous acetic acid (IUPAC, 1997). Only some of the ethanol ingested is broken down in the stomach. Most of it passes into the small intestine and from there into the blood stream, which sends it on to the liver.

The liver is the organ that breaks down most of the ethanol consumed. It is therefore also the organ that will take the largest toll from alcohol, especially from the toxic effects of acetaldehyde. This is the reason why people who drink heavily and over long periods of time often develop liver damage called *cirrhosis*. Upon consuming alcohol, the liver accelerates fatty acid synthesis. Fat accumulates in the liver which interferes with the distribution of nutrients and oxygen to the liver cells. If this condition persists, liver deteriorations called *fibrosis* occurs (Murty, 2004).

Not all people have the same amounts of the two enzymes that break down ethanol. Women generally have less alcohol dehydrogenase in their stomachs, which makes them more susceptible to the effects of alcohol. Since it cannot be broken down as quickly, more ethanol passes into the blood and body, where it lingers longer than in men. Some people, in particular Asians, often have a genetically different form of aldehyde dehydrogenase that is not active. This leads to the so-called 'flushing reaction', where the person becomes hot and sweaty, dizzy, nauseous, and turns red in the face. In addition, many Asians also have an inactive form of alcohol dehydrogenase (Eng et al, 2007; Scott and Taylor, 2007), and are much less able to eliminate the molecule from their bodies.

3.3   Strength of alcoholic beverages

The strength of an intoxicating drink depends on how much alcohol it contains. Pure alcohol is impossible to obtain as alcohol has a great affinity for water. Even the 'pure alcohol' sold for clinical purposes will contain at least five percent water. The amount of alcohol contained is expressed as the percentage of alcohol by volume, ABV for short. The format for expressing ABV is alc.% vol or % vol. This means that for a liqueur such as Southern Comfort, labelled as alc. 35% vol., 35% of any given quantity is pure alcohol. If a wine is labelled as alc. 13% vol. or 13% vol., then 13% of any given quantity of it is pure alcohol. Wines can vary from 8 to 16% ABV. Beers range from 3 to 8.5% ABV. Most spirits are between 35 and 50% ABV.

Systems for determining alcohol strengths

Alcometer

The concentration of the distillate can be determined by measuring its density using a special alcohol hydrometer also known as an alcoholmeter, usually calibrated at 20°C with readings in % v/v. The formula to calculate density is:

$$\text{Density} \quad = \quad \frac{\text{Weight}}{\text{Volume}}$$

Alcohol being less dense than water means that the decrease in density, relative to water, will directly correlate to the volume of alcohol present. If the temperature of the alcohol solution is greater or less than 20°C, the density reading will be less or greater than the true value. The true alcohol concentration at temperatures other than 20°C can be read on a correction table chart, using the temperature and alcohol concentration range. The hydrometer method of determining alcohol concentration in distillate is one of the cheapest and simplest to perform with the least chance of errors. This alcoholmeter with the aid of a copper parrot spout, which is attached to the distillate outlet of the condensing recipient, will provide constant and accurate readings of the exiting distillate.

Sykes hydrometer system (1816-1980), Sykes proof law

Invented by an English customs official named Sykes, this hydrometer offered the first accurate method for testing the strength of spirits or beer. The Sykes hydrometer is based on a very simple law – the law of flotation. It measures alcoholic strength in term of 'proof'.

This states that a floating body displaces its own weight of liquid. Pure alcohol is lighter than water. If we therefore place a floating body in pure alcohol and then in water it will be found that more of the former is displaced. As mentioned earlier, pure alcohol is impossible to obtain, and this presented a problem for Sykes when he first used the hydrometer. Instead of using 100% alcohol as his standard, he took advantage of the difference in the specific gravity of water and alcohol. He fixed his standard weight at twelve thirteenths of the weight of an equal quantity of distilled water. After calculating it out, by an involved process of mathematics, this means that 100 proof is equal to 57% ABV or 175 proof is equal to 100% ABV.

The Gay Lussac system

The French scientist Gay-Lussac applied himself, in 1821-1822, to the study of the relation between liquid density and alcohol concentration. He perfected a new alcoholmeter which was easy to use and gave directly, due to its calibration, the alcoholic rate at a given temperature. He then manufactured them under his name and reputation. The precision of this new system was at the root of a new law about wines and spirits in 1824. The Gay Lussac (GL) system also expresses percentage volume but measures it by hydrometer at 15°C giving a reading slightly higher than the OIML system.

Percentage of pure alcohol by volume (ABV)

On the 1st January 1990, the Sykes hydrometer system was abolished under EEC directive 76/766 and a new system was adopted under which strengths of alcoholic drinks would be expressed as a percentage of alcohol by volume. The Organisation Internationale de Metrologie Legale (OIML) system measures this by hydrometer at 20°C. The new hydrometers are made of glass, and those to be used by the Customs and Excise bear the EU verification (the letter 'e'). Thermometers made to the EU requirements are available through trade channels. Strength tables can also be purchased from the Government Publications Sales Office. In America it was decided that 'proof spirit' should be half water and half alcohol. 'Pure' alcohol, 100 over proof, can be expressed as 200 proof. Table 3.1 may be of some help to make comparisons.

Table 3.1: Alcoholic strengths of distilled spirits: comparison table – OIML (Murphy, 2013)

alcohol by volume ABV (%)	UK proof degrees	USA proof degrees	Gay Lussac G.L (%)
100	175	200	100 (pure alcohol)
57	100 (proof)	114	57
50	88	100 (proof)	50
44	80	90	45
40	70	80	40
37	65	74	37
0	0	0	C (water)

Conversions between measures of spirit strengths

To convert US proof degrees to ABV: US proof° ÷ 2 = ABV%

To convert ABV percent to US proof: ABV × 2 = US proof°

Duty and taxes are paid according to ABV strengths on alcohol products in most countries. Listed below are the current duty bands for the United Kingdom in this regard:

below 1.14% ABV: no duty

above 1.14% but below 8.5% ABV: beer and cider,

above 8.5% to maximum 15% ABV: light wines,

15-18% ABV: fortified wines (band 1)

18-22% ABV: fortified wines (band 2)

above 22% ABV: liqueurs and spirits taxed per degree of alcohol.

Units of alcohol

Alcoholic beverages vary in their strengths. Beer is a perfect example as this beverage can range from 2% to about 9% ABV. The majority of alcoholic beverages will be also mixed with soft drinks, juices or water to ensure consistency in their measurement. When determining how much alcohol an individual has consumed, consider two pieces of information: the volume held in the glass or container used and how much of that volume is ethanol. It is then possible to calculate the total amount of alcohol in each drink. It is useful to remember that the following contain approximately the same amount of alcohol:

1 small beer = 1 small glass of wine = 1 nip of spirits = 1 unit of alcohol

A standard alcoholic beverage

Turner (1990) argues that there is no common convention to define a standard drink measure among countries or in the scientific literature. Dufour (1999) reminds us that where standard units have been implemented, they may vary according to the type of beverage — spirits, wine, or beer. The ICAP (2003) reports that the international agreed convention for standardising the strength of alcoholic beverages is in grams of absolute ethanol. Basically this means that a 'standard' drink will always contain a given amount of absolute ethanol, regardless of whether it is beer, wine or distilled spirits. Having a standard measure of ethanol enables consumers and service staff to be able to assess the risk levels for consumption. This standard is also useful in assisting consumers with advice on how much they are drinking and what the potential effects are like to be on their general health. Campbell et al (1999) also indicate that such information is useful for providing advice on low-risk consumption patterns, for tracking data on drinking practices, and for the development of prevention measures. Different countries however have different 'standard' drinks, ranging from 8 grams to 14 grams and some countries do not have such a thing as a standard drink. Where serving sizes are defined, these measures depend to a great extent on local culture and customs (see Appendix II). Therefore, if you are involved in the service or consumption of alcoholic beverages, do not assume that each drink, be it a pre-packaged bottle of beer, a standard glass of wine or a measured spirit, to be a standard drink. Most countries will have official advice and relevant guidelines regarding how much alcohol adults can consume with minimum or zero risk to their overall health.

Formula for calculating grams of alcohol in alcoholic beverages:

Amount of drink (ml) × by the strength of drink (ABV)% = mls of alcohol

[10 millilitres = approximately 8 grams = 1 UK unit of alcohol].

3

> **Recommendation:** It is advisable that licensed premises involved in the sale of alcoholic beverages should include a reasonable selection of lower strength or non-alcoholic drinks, and in a range of sizes. This enables customers to make an informed choice in order to help them to stay within healthy guidelines for consumption.

Variations to standard alcoholic beverages

You should keep in mind that there are many variations to the percentage of alcoholic content of certain beverages. Individuals involved in the service of alcoholic beverages should give these particular drinks special attention during service. They include:

- *Spirits with alcohol contents over 40% ABV*: for example over proof rums, strong liqueurs or cask strength spirits.
- *Full strength beers and ciders* which are served in large glasses or pitchers. Many bars tend not to offer these strong drinks in large vessels, but sometimes on festival or promotions days they can be used incorrectly.
- *New bottled beers, canned beers, alco-pops* and some ciders can vary hugely in their alcohol content.
- *Cocktails*, especially when are prepared fresh, can contain more than one type of alcohol which can be more than 10 gms. Another consideration is when cocktails are prepared by the free-pouring method where measures are not used to control the exact amount of alcohol in each mixed drink.
- *Shots / shooters*: these mini mixed drinks can contain two to three different types of alcohol with the total grams of alcohol being more than 10 grams.
- *Wine, champagne or spirits purchased by the bottle*: sometimes the glasses provided are not of the standard glass size (10 centilitres) and when customers top up their own glasses from the bottle, control of consumption diminishes.

The 'Strength of alcohol chart' in Appendix III will show you how to calculate the units of alcohol in an alcoholic beverage, if you know the amount of drink in millilitres and its strength in alcohol by volume. Both are usually stated somewhere on the label or in the accompanying packaging.

The use of standard measures for drinks service

The use of standard measures for drinks service enables servers and customers to keep account of what they are drinking. In most countries the use of these measures is required by the laws of the land. The use of standard measures is an indication of best practice standards of service for pouring alcoholic drinks within most establishments. Standard pouring measures can vary from country to country. They can also differ depending on which drink is served and the strength of the alcohol in question.

Figure 3.3 : Standard measures (top) and glassware (bottom) for drinks service (Murphy, 2014).

It must be remembered that a standard drink and a standard size glass are not the same thing, for example in the United Kingdom, wine is sold in glasses of 125 millilitres (ml), 175ml or multiples of these amounts. Spirits are sold in either 25ml or 35ml or multiples of these amounts. A sign has to be displayed stating the size of measure for wine and the spirits, vodka, gin, whisky and rum in the UK. In Australia, a single measure of spirits is 30ml, in New Zealand, 15ml. In other parts of the world, wine is served in a 200ml glass (20 grams of alcohol or the equivalent of 2 standard drinks). Ready to drink spirits (RTDs) or 'Alco-pops' are usually served in 275ml bottles and cans, so most RTDs will contain 1.5 standard drinks (IBA, 2008).

Case example: Standard measures of wine in pubs and restaurants

3

Some people get a guilty thrill when they get a larger than normal glass of wine in a restaurant, and there is a considerable confusion about what constitutes a 'glass' of wine. Unlike most other alcoholic drinks, in the absence of a clearly defined measure of a glass of wine, the size poured is sometimes left up to the whims of the server. In some restaurants and bars the quantity poured can run as high as a third of a bottle, which is the equivalent of two pints of beer. Some restaurants and bars use a 187.5ml glass which gives a neat four glasses per bottle; catering staff are sometimes instructed to get six glasses per bottle at functions and business events, which reduces the measure to 125ml (this requirement can depend on the function specification which includes budgets); and most pubs also offer 175ml miniature wine bottles. Rolande Anderson of the Irish Council of General Practitioners, cited in Pope (2009), states that a typical bottle of wine should contain seven standard drinks. He gives the measure of a glass of wine as 100ml and states that ignorance of the correct measure is a very serious issue. In response to the calls from experts to introduce a standard measure of wine in pubs and restaurants to help limit excessive drinking, Pope (2009) stated that Britain introduced a mandatory code of practice for bars to force them to offer smaller glasses of wine. The 125ml wine measure was made available to drinkers, although pubs retained the right to sell 175ml and 250ml measures.

3.4   Non-alcoholic beverages

Alcohol consumption is legal in most countries of the world where a drinking culture exists, but in countries where alcohol is illegal, similar non-alcoholic beverages are permitted. The definition of alcohol-free may vary from country to country. The term 'non-alcoholic' (i.e. alcohol-free beer) is often used to describe a beverage that contains 0.0% ABV. Such beverages are permitted by Islam and are popular in countries that enforce alcohol prohibition, such as Kuwait, Iran and Saudi Arabia. However, most beverages advertised as 'non-alcohol' or 'alcohol free' actually contain alcohol, and these beverages are very popular. In most parts of the European Union, to be classified as 'alcohol free' a drink must contain no more than 0.05% ABV, and to be classified as 'low or non-alcohol', no more than 1.2% ABV, and both variations must be labelled accordingly. The labels of beverages containing more than 1.2% ABV must state the actual alcoholic strength in ABV% vol. (ICAP, 2014.F). In the United States of America in order to be called non-alcoholic under Federal Laws, a beverage can contain up to 0.5% ABV. Beverages in the USA containing no alcohol at all must be called alcohol-free. A summary of the strengths of alcoholic drinks as defined by law currently in the United Kingdom is given in Table 3.2.

Table 3.2: Summary of strengths of alcoholic drinks (adapted from BIIAB, 2005).

Drink strength	Subsequent requirement
Not more than 0.05% ABV	Alcohol free, no premises or personal license is required for sale or supply.
Above 0.5% ABV	Legally defined as alcohol.
Not more than 1.2% ABV	Low alcohol.
More than 1.2% ABV	ABV must be shown on the label or displayed at the point of sale.
1 unit of alcohol	8 grams or 10 millitres of alcohol.

People who are forbidden to drink alcohol, like devout Muslims, can't partake of so-called 'non-alcoholic' beer and wine. Nor can people under the legally permitted age for alcohol consumption. In the hospitality, retail and tourism industries, it is crucial that when a customer requests an 'alcohol free' product is not given or sold a 'low alcohol' one. Careful attention must also be given with the sales and service of these beverages in countries which adopt a quite high ABV regulation for 'non-alcoholic' drinks, which would have been classified as alcoholic drinks by most other countries.

Non-alcohol malt beverages

Non-alcoholic malt beer is a fermented beverage produced from cereal grain. Typically, the grain is barley, but malt beverages may also be based on corn or wheat. Malt beverages are usually flavoured with natural or artificial flavours to make them taste like lager or other types of beer. Other flavours vary from cider to wine. Non-alcoholic malt beverages are produced by avoiding fermentation in the early stages of the production process or by removing the alcohol in the final stages. Alternatively, the beverage can be based on a malt extract. An extract is made from a malt beverage, allowing liquids and flavours to be added later (GEC, 2014). We noted earlier that the basic process of traditional brews consists of eight steps; for non-alcoholic beer there are nine, with the extra step between maturation and finishing, when the brew is converted to non-alcoholic beer (Birmingham Beverage Company, 2014)

Low- and non-alcoholic beer production

The conversion from a alcoholic beer to a non-alcoholic beer takes place after the seventh step (as noted above). The un-carbonated beer is brought up to the boiling point of alcohol, which is around 78.3°C (173.5°F) (O'Leary, 2000). This boiling point will vary slightly with altitude and barometric pressure; higher temperature at lower altitude and lower temperature at higher altitude. Another method of removing the alcohol is to decrease the pressure so the alcohol boils at room temperature. This is the preferred method because the addition of heat this late in the brewing process can greatly affect the flavour of the brew. In essence, the beer is placed under a light vacuum to facilitate the alcohol molecules going into gaseous state. If a sufficient vacuum is applied, it is not necessary to cook the beer.

An alternative process called reverse osmosis (or cold filtration) does not require heating. The beer is passed through a filter with pores small enough so that only alcohol and water (and a few volatile acids) can pass through. The alcohol is distilled out of the alcohol-water mix using conventional distillation methods. After adding the water and remaining acids back into the syrupy mixture of sugars and flavour compounds left on the other side of the filter, the process is then complete (Reisch, 2007).

If brewers decide to convert their brew to a non-alcoholic brew they must consider the volume of liquid they have lost from the removal of the alcohol. Typically the volume is reduced by roughly (4%); to compensate the brewer will simply add water. Because water is a key ingredient in beer it does not affect the flavour. Once the alcohol is removed, the non-alcoholic beer is carbonated and bottled.

De-alcoholised, alcohol free and low-alcohol wines

Alcohol free wine is made from real wine which was produced in the traditional wine making fashion. Cousins et al (2014) define these wines as:

- alcohol-free wine: maximum 0.05% ABV,
- de-alcoholised wine: maximum 0.50% ABV,
- low alcohol wine: 1.2% ABV.

These are produced by similar processes used for low and non-alcoholic beers. When evaporation is used, table wine is combined with demineralized water and poured into a centrifugal evaporator where the alcohol is spun off to produce an alcohol free wine base. Grape juice concentrate is then added to make alcohol free wine. Non-alcoholic sparkling wine is made with a secondary fermentation or by the addition of carbon dioxide.

Experts in the drinks industry state that it is very difficult and very expensive to eliminate all the alcohol from wine or beer. This is why non-alcoholic beverages still contain some of the original alcohol from wine or beer.

3.5   Cooking with alcohol

Alcohol is also used in cooking in different ways, depending on the individual dish, recipe or cooking style in question. Dishes such as coq au vin, bratwursts boiled in beer, overnight marinades of beef, chicken or pork in beer and spices, or deglazing a pan with alcohol for a sauce are examples of its use. The categories of alcoholic beverages involved include specialist cooking liqueurs, vermouths, eaux de vie, fortified and table wines plus strong spirits, which are used by chefs to augment the flavours in classic and modern dishes. Specialist cooking alcohols in marinades can help to tenderise the meat and are of particular benefit to game dishes. Cooking with alcohol however poses some interesting questions and concerns for people in the tourism, hospitality and retail industry (especially bakers, cooks and chefs). For example, does all the alcohol used actually burn off during the cooking process? The basic answer to this question is 'no'. Alcohol will indeed boil at a much lower temperature than water (78.3°C compared to water at 100°C), and for example, the alcohol in a sauce will begin to evaporate before the water does. But simply heating the alcohol, or adopting any other cooking liquid or process, for that matter, will not make it all evaporate. The conventional wisdom accepted by just about everyone in the food and beverage world had always been that all the alcohol you add to a dish evaporates or dissipates during cooking. This is wrong; in fact, you have to cook something for a good three hours to eradicate virtually all traces of alcohol. And some cooking methods are less effective at removing alcohol (see Table 3.3 below).

Lapsley (cited in Shioya, 2007), maintains that the amount of alcohol left after cooking will crucially depend on three factors: concentration, heat, and time. He adds that a recipe using a higher percentage of alcohol heated briefly will retain more alcohol than a recipe using a lower percentage of alcohol heated for a long time. This means that a crêpe suzette flambéed with Grand Marnier will retain more alcohol than boeuf bourguignon made with red wine that has been cooked for several hours. A major study conducted by the US Department of Agriculture's Nutrient Data Laboratory and a team of researchers from the University of Idaho and Washington State University in 2007 calculated the percentage of alcohol remaining in a dish based on various cooking methods. They concluded that the amounts of alcohol retained in food can range from 5% to 85%, depending on the preparation method. Baked or simmered dishes will still contain 5% of the original amount of alcohol added even after two and half hours of cooking time, but significantly when the alcohol is added to a boiling liquid and then removed from the heat, 85% of the alcohol will remain (USDA, 2007). Although the amount of alcohol in most dishes would be modest overall, the facts still highlight that some of the alcohol remains even after two and half hours' cooking. These research results could be of significant concern to parents, individuals who have ethical or religious reasons for avoiding alcohol or recovering alcoholics.

Table 3.3: Cooking with alcohol – percent of alcohol retained (adapted from USDA, 2007).

3

Preparation method	Percent of alcohol retained
Alcohol added to boiling liquid & removed from heat	85%
Alcohol flamed	75%
No heat, stored overnight	70%
Baked, 25 minutes, alcohol not stirred into mixture	45%
Baked/simmered, alcohol stirred into mixture:	
15 minutes	40%
30 minutes	35%
1 hour	25%
1.5 hours	20%
2 hours	10%
2.5 hours	5%

Conclusion

This chapter focused on the nature of alcohol. It explained its scientific composition and the place of ethanol in the family of alcohols. It explored how alcohol is produced by fermentation, and how it can be concentrated by distillation. It outlined the role which aldehyde dehydrogenase plays in its breakdown in the human body. The chapter also identified the systems used for determining and for describing the strength of alcoholic beverages and gave formulas for calculating the grams and units of alcohol that they contain. Finally it highlighted that when cooking with alcoholic beverages, some of the alcohol will normally still be present in the finished dish.

Web resources

Alcohol – its nature and effects

www.youtube.com/watch?v=6fhAplFQGOU

Ariel non-alcoholic wines

www.arielvineyards.com/wines.html

Drink Aware

www.drinkaware.co.uk

Ethanol - Royal Society of Chemistry (UK)

www.rsc.org/chemistryworld/podcast/CIIEcompounds/.../ethanol.asp

European School survey project on Alcohol and Drugs (EU)

www.espad.org

ICAP (International Centre for Alcohol Policies)

www.ICAP.org

Use of alcohol

academics.lmu.edu/headsup/forstudents/historyofalcoholuse/

Understanding alcohol

science.education.nih.gov/supplements/nih3/alcohol/guide/info-alcohol.htm

4 The Effects of Alcohol on the Body

Aims and learning outcomes

This chapter introduces the positive and negative effects of alcohol on the human body by providing a good basic knowledge of how it works its way through the body and its vital organs. It explores blood alcohol concentration and their effects on a typical individual, which can include the alcohol hangover. It also highlights safe drinking guidelines and the impact of alcohol consumption on sexual and sporting performance and the subsequent risk taking behaviours associated with alcohol consumption. After reading this chapter you should be able to:

- Demonstrate knowledge of blood alcohol concentration levels and their associated behavioural effects.

- Explain how alcohol works its way through the human body from its absorption through to its final elimination.

- Outline the specific effects of alcohol on women, men, pregnant women, old and young people and individuals with certain genetic predispositions.

- Demonstrate a good basic knowledge of safe drinking guidelines and the impact of alcohol consumption on sexual and sporting performance.

4.0 Introduction

Alcohol is enjoyed by many people globally because of its relaxing properties, its ability to intensify sociability, and as a complement to meals. Although alcohol has positive effects, unfortunately it can also create problems for some individuals who misuse it and drink it to excess. The effects of alcohol on the body are numerous; these effects can however differ in individuals due to their gender, age, their physical and medical condition, their mental health status and their genetic predisposition. Alcohol has different effects on men and women due to differences in their genetic predisposition, their body mass, the way alcohol is broken down in the body and the relative proportions of water and fat in male and female bodies. Women will experience the full effects of consuming alcohol at lower levels than men. Age is also an integral component in determining the effects of drinking in both young people and older adults. The intoxicating properties of alcohol can be very seductive and unfortunately additive. When consumed to excess alcohol can harm the body in many ways including death. In this chapter we explore the effects of alcohol on the body by initially tracing its path through the human body and it effect on the body's vital organs. The factors which mediate alcohol's effect on women, young people and older adults will also be explored. Finally we will highlight the impact of alcohol on sexual behaviour and the association between performance and alcohol in sport.

4.1   Effects of alcohol

Alcohol acts on the brain as an anaesthetic, sedative, and stimulant, depending on how much of it is consumed. The effects of alcohol change the more you consume. Many people drink alcohol for these effects. It is important to know that drinking in excess can also be extremely harmful. Professor George Bakalkin (2008) maintains that the social problems arising from excess drinking are serious, caused by the pathological changes in the brain and the intoxicating effects of alcohol. Some of the more serious problems caused by alcohol abuse include child abuse, domestic violence, rape, burglary, assault and other criminal offences (Isralowitz, 2004), and loss of employment (Langdana, 2009) which can lead to financial problems. Drinking at inappropriate times, and behaviour caused by reduced judgment, can have legal consequences, such as criminal charges for drunk driving or public disorder, or civil penalties for tortious behaviour, and may lead to a criminal sentence (Glifford, 2009).

In relatively small amounts alcohol can:

- impair your overall coordination and slur your speech
- create the need to urinate more than usual
- make you light-headed and dizzy
- dilate blood vessels in the skin, making it look red and flushed as more blood comes to the surface – bloodshots eyes are another example of this
- increase sweating, which is directly associated to the dilation of your blood vessels
- increase body temperature, as your brain is struggling to control levels
- upset your stomach lining

- lower your inhibitions, change your mood and normal behaviour
- increase your heart rate

The outcomes of these experiences can differ from person to person, but the most obvious effect is usually the lowering of inhibitions and changed behaviour which can make some individuals appear to be more friendly and extroverted. This effect is why it is traditionally described as a social enhancer. There are also potentially negative effects, which include increased displays of boldness and an increased desire to be promiscuous. A smaller number of people can become aggressive and violent after consuming even small quantities. Heavy consumption sessions can also lead to experiences of irritability, euphoria, and diminished control of bodily movements leading eventually to unconsciousness. If they have been drinking up to and beyond a certain point, they may fall into a coma. At extreme levels of drinking, people may die of acute alcohol poisoning.

4

Case example: Alcohol death by misadventure

Barman died of alcohol poisoning

In 2011 a 23 year old barman died following an after-hours drinking session. The deceased man, who had been enjoying drinks while playing poker and pool in a social club with friends, died of acute alcohol intoxication. Friends stated that they raised the alarm when they were unable to wake the man who fell asleep on a couch. A post-mortem exam found he had consumed a fatal level of alcohol with 499 milligrams of alcohol per 100 milligrams of blood in his system. The Court Coroner stated that the problem was the proof of some of the drinks consumed on top of other alcohol consumed during the drinking session. These drinks included Chartreuse, a French liqueur with an alcohol content of 55% alcohol by volume. The coroner recorded a verdict of death by misadventure (O'Halloran, 2011).

Methanol, a by-product of the alcohol production process, can be found sometimes in beverages that are not carefully controlled for quality (i.e. home produced, illegal and very cheap spirits). Drinking methanol can lead to intoxication but it also leads to dangerous consequences. Methanol is broken down by an enzyme that converts it into formaldehyde, a chemical used to preserve biological specimens. Since this enzyme is present in the human eye, the formaldehyde 'fixes' the eye tissue, causing permanent blindness (Schep et al 2009). Drinking even small amounts of methanol is extremely dangerous and methanol contamination of alcoholic beverages has been known to poison and kill people.

Case example: Poisonous alcohol

Holidaymakers killed by tainted illegal alcohol

In 2009 a 25 year old female graduate student and a 59 year old man died in Indonesia after drinking homemade liquor laced with a toxic chemical, in a scandal that claimed 25 lives. Both of the deceased passed away after consuming arak palm wine that was spiked with methanol, while holidaying on an islet off the island of Lombok and Bali. Indonesian authorities have responded to the poisonings by cracking down on home distillers of arak, a cheap and potent spirit that is popular with tourists in cocktails. Alcohol is heavily taxed in Indonesia, the world's most populous Muslim nation, and the high prices have spawned a huge black market for wine and liquor (Mail Foreign Service, 2009).

Drink Aware

The Drink Aware trust works at increasing awareness and understanding of the role of alcohol in UK society, enabling individuals to make informed choices about their drinking. It aims to challenge the national drinking culture to help reduce alcohol misuse and minimise alcohol-related harm. If you are supplying alcohol to the public in any way, you should check your own local government agency or relevant trade body's 'Code of Practice' and ensure that you and other staff members are familiar with your responsibilities in your own market.

4.2   Alcohol's path through the body

Absorption

Alcohol has very small molecules, and these are absorbed into the blood. Normally, this takes place in the small intestine, but, in theory, if you were to fill your mouth with, for example, a small measure of brandy without swallowing it, the alcohol would still be absorbed into your blood through the lining of your mouth. The stomach absorbs 20% of the alcohol, and the remaining 80% is absorbed by the small intestine. The speed at which alcohol is absorbed depends on several factors, which include:

- the alcohol concentration in the beverage – the higher the concentration, the faster the absorption,
- the type of drink – fizzy drinks help to speed up the absorption of alcohol
- if the stomach is full or empty – food slows down alcohol absorption.

Cell membranes are highly permeable to alcohol. After absorption, the alcohol enters the blood stream. Blood then carries it throughout the body where it dissolves in the water inside each tissue of the body. The blood alcohol concentration (BAC) will rise significantly 20 minutes after having a drink.

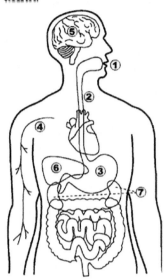

1. Alcohol enters the mouth.
2. Alcohol travels down the throat to the stomach.
3. Alcohol is absorbed into the blood by the stomach and small intestine.
4. Alcohol travels through the blood to the water-containing organs of the body.
5. Alcohol affects many brain functions.
6. Alcohol is metabolized in the liver.
7. Alcohol is excreted from the body after processing by the kidneys.

4

Figure 4.1: Tracing alcohol's path through the body (adapted from Matthews, cited in National Institute of Health, 2014).

The brain

Excess alcohol causes both physical damage to the brain and psychological effects. When alcohol is swallowed it goes first to the stomach, which breaks down food and drink before passing it to the small intestine. If there is no food in the stomach, then the alcohol passes more quickly into the small intestine from where it is absorbed into the blood. The alcohol circulates around the body (in the blood) until it reaches the brain, which takes approximately five minutes. When the alcohol reaches there, it begins to depress the functions interfering with communication between nerve cells and all other cells in the brain. This starts with the part of the brain that controls inhibitions and judgement. Nerve cells talk to each other and to other cells (such as muscle or gland cells) by sending chemical messages, called neurotransmitters. Neurotransmitters can either excite the receiving cell to cause a response or inhibit the receiving cell from stimulation.

Alcohol affects various centres in the higher and lower orders of the brain. Freudenrich, cited in *How Stuff Works* (2014), indicates that these centres are not equally affected by the same BAC. The higher orders are more sensitive than the lower order centres. As the BAC increases, the more centres are affected. The order in which alcohol affects the various brain centres is:

1 **Cerebral cortex** (processes information from your senses, does your thought processing and consciousness)

2 **Limbic system** (controls emotions and memory)

3 **Cerebellum** (coordinates the movement of muscles and balance)

4 **Hypothalamus and pituitary gland** (controls and influences many automatic functions; urine secretion is controlled by the pituitary gland)

5 **Medulla or brain stem** (controls breathing, heart rate, temperature and consciousness.

Dr. Craig Freudenrich as cited in How Stuff Works (2014)

Individuals can suffer from acute alcohol withdrawal commonly referred to DTs (delirium tremens), which can cause brain damage and even death; longer-term consumption also contributes to brain disease. Memory loss is a feature of alcoholic brain disease and is linked to a deficiency of the vitamin, thiamine, in vulnerable individuals. Chronic brain damage from alcohol abuse leads to dementia (a decline in cognitive functioning). The body's peripheral nerves are damaged in up to 15% of individuals, leading to symptoms such as pins and needles and numbness.

The liver

Alcohol reaches the liver approximately 20 minutes after ingestion. The liver processes the alcohol – breaking it down and neutralizing it, then removing it from the body. In general, the liver breaks down alcohol at the rate of around 8 grams of alcohol per hour (see Chapter 3 for how to calculate the grams of alcohol in any drink). Gilmore, cited in Rodgers (2006), states that alcohol is metabolized almost exclusively by the liver. This means that the liver is one of the first parts of the body to suffer the harmful effects of heavy drinking. Symptoms of an underperforming liver include dry skin, headaches, tiredness and indigestion. Alcoholic liver problems affects 46% of heavy drinkers, include hepatitis, which means the inflammation of the liver cells. Continuing to consume alcohol heavily can lead to cirrhosis of the liver, in which cells die and are replaced by new cells that cause a hardening of the liver tissue (fibrosis). The main effect of cirrhosis is to block the smooth flow of blood through the liver. Liver cells normally produce proteins, blood-clotting factors and vital vitamins. When cirrhosis sets in, this factory element of the liver fails and the individual is left with blood-clotting problems and other knock-on effects. As the process of cirrhosis continues, the liver becomes a hard lumpy rock incapable of sustaining life (Houston, 2002).

The bloodstream

The amount of alcohol in the blood is determined by the quantity and type of alcohol consumed, the speed of drinking, whether or not there is food in the stomach, and a variety of other factors. The immediate effects of drinking depend upon the amount of alcohol in the blood stream – the blood alcohol concentration. BAC also varies according to a person's sex, weight and body composition. Women tend to have a slightly higher BAC than men after drinking the same amount because they have less body fluid to dilute the alcohol (Gilmore, cited in Rodgers, 2006).

Breath, sweat and urine

A small amount of alcohol (less than 10%) is eliminated from the body in urine, breath and sweat. The rest is oxidized – this means, like food, it combines with oxygen in the blood to release heat, energy or calories. However, although alcohol has some nutritional value, it is of poor quality because it lacks vitamins, proteins and other nutrients (Ellis, 2005).

Stomach and gullet

Alcohol strips the lining of the stomach, giving rise to a condition called gastritis. Severe gastritis can lead to internal bleeding and the individual may bleed from the back passage or vomit up blood. Alcohol also contributes to the development of both stomach and duodenal ulcers. Varicose veins may develop around the gullet, leading to overwhelming bleeding into the gastrointestinal system (Houston, 2002).

Pancreas

Individuals with alcohol problems often develop both acute and chronic pancreatitis. The pancreas produces insulin and is the source of enzymes that are normally released into the intestine to help digestion. When pancreatitis occurs, these enzymes turn on the pancreas itself, causing cell death and damage to blood vessels. Pancreatitis can have a high death rate. It is estimated that 42% of deaths from acute pancreatitis are associated with alcohol. Diabetes mellitus can also occur if the part of the pancreas which produces insulin is affected.

Sex organs

Heavy drinking causes shrinking of the testicles in a minority of men, while even moderate consumption of alcohol can decrease the capacity for erection.

How alcohol leaves the body

Once absorbed in the blood stream, alcohol leaves the body in three ways: (a) the kidney which eliminates 5% of the alcohol in the urine, (b) the lungs will expel approximately 5%, (c) the liver oxidizes approximately 90% and breaks it down into water and carbon dioxide. The average person can eliminate 8 grams (10ml) of alcohol per hour. So it would take a little over an hour to eliminate the alcohol from a 355ml tin of 4% abv beer. It's important to note that, the BAC increases when the body absorbs alcohol faster than when it can eliminate it.

4.3   The effect of alcohol on humans

Alcohol and women

Alcohol consumption amongst women has been rising in recent years (Bloomfield et al 2006; Suzuki et al 2004; Wilsnack and Wilsnack 1997). This new development has stimulated the need to provide more information and advice in relation to prevention and harm reduction for women. Mumenthaler et al (1999) and Noeln-Hoeksema (2004) remind us that we must remember that alcohol's effects are different for women than they are for men. Women are usually smaller and that their bodies contain less water and more fat, allowing the concentration of ethanol to rise more quickly. Crowe and George (1989) state that a woman's body often takes one-third longer to eliminate alcohol. Lieber (1997) also states that there is also a major difference between men and women in the chemical process that breaks down ethanol and eventually eliminates it from the body (see also Chapter 3).

Research studies indicate that the following health benefits have been associated with low to moderate alcohol consumption in women:

- **Reduced risk for coronary heart disease (CHD)**: particularly for post-menopausal women (Baer et al., 2002; Grobbee, Rimm, Keil, and Renaud, 1999).

- **Reduced blood cholesterol levels:** a reduction of low-density lipoprotein cholesterol, LDL - bad cholesterol, and increases in high-density lipoprotein, HDL - good cholesterol (Koppes et al 2000; Silanaukee et al 2000).

- **Reduction of Type 2 diabetes:** research suggests that moderate alcohol consumption may have a protective effect (de Vegt et al., 2002).

- **Reduction of osteoporosis and bone fractures:** especially for older women, there may be beneficial effects regarding the progression of osteoporosis and the severity of bone fracture (Diaz et al 1997; Williams et al 2005).

Equally the following negative health outcomes have been linked to alcohol consumption in women:

■ **Affective and anxiety disorders:** a strong association between these disorders and problem drinking has been described in women, often increasing with age (Pulkkinen and Pitkanen, 1994; Chander and McCaul, 2003).

■ **Breast feeding:** women who are nursing may transfer alcohol to their child through breast milk, which may adversely affect the infant's sleep and development (De Araujo Burgos, Bion, and Campos, 2004; Mennella, 2001).

■ **Breast cancer:** alcohol consumption, even at low doses, may increase the risk, especially if there is a family history of the disease (Aronson, 2003; McPherson et al 1999)

■ **Eating disorders and compulsive shopping:** heavy and problematic drinking in women has been associated with these problems (Plant, 1997; Plant, Miller, and Plant, 2005).

■ **Infertility:** heavy drinking may also be a contributing cause (Eggert et al 2004; Olsen et al 1997).

■ **Foetal alcohol syndrome, spontaneous abortions and related disorders in offspring:** certain maternal drinking patterns during pregnancy may present these risks (Plant et al 1999).

■ **Sexual assault and violence:** certain patterns of drinking and situations increase this vulnerability for women (Kaufman Kantor and Asdigian, 1997; Mohler-Kuo et al 2004).

Women must also consider additional personal safety issues which surround alcohol consumption (Abbey, McAuslan and Ross 1998). These concerns also include date rape drugs (Rohyphnol, Ketamine Hydrochloride, and Gamma Hydroxy Butyrate (GHB), which are used to interfere (spike) their drinks.

Although in recent times products have been released which detect the presence of these substances in drinks, the fact remains that the wisest approach for women is to actively monitor their drinking behaviour and that of their colleagues and friends. Table 4.1 below highlights the safe drinking guidelines for women and men. For the most up-to-date version of this table go to www.icap.org, or consult your local government agency to find the local safe drinking guidelines for women and men.

Table 4.1: Safe drinking guidelines (adapted from ICAP, 2003, 2014).

Country	Source	Standard Drink	Recommended limits	
			Women	Men
Australia	National Health & Medical Research Council	10 g	2 units/day; 14 units/week	4 units/day; 28 units/week
Canada	Centre for Addiction & Mental Health	13.6 g	2 units/day; 9 units/week	2 units; 14 units/ week
Czech Republic	National Institute of Public Health	-	16 g/day	24g/day
Denmark	National Board of Health	12 g	14 units/week	21 units/week
France	National Academy of Medicine	12 g	3 units/day	5 units/day
Hong Kong	Department of Health & Social Security	1 glass wine or pint beer	2-3 units/day; 14 units/week	3-4 units/day; 21 units/week
Italy	Ministry for Agriculture & Forestry and National Institute for Food & Nutrition	12 g	1-2 units/day; 12-24g/day	2-3 units/day; 24-36g/day
Ireland	Department of Health	8g	14 units/week	21 units/week
Poland	State Agency for Prevention of Alcohol Related Problems	10 g	1 unit/day; 50g/ week	2-3 units day; 100g/week
South Africa	National Council on Alcoholism & Drug Dependence	12 g	14 units/week	21 units/week
United Kingdom	Department of Health	8 g	2-3 units/day; 14 units/week	3-4 units/day; 21 units/week
USA	Department of Health and Human Services & Department of Agriculture	14 g	1 unit/day; 7 units/week	1-2 units/day; 14 units/week

You should also consider reading the following two reports which were prepared for the European Union, published by Euro Care (The European Alcohol Policy Alliance), to enhance your understanding of the issues involved in this area: *Alcohol Problems in the Family* (1998), *Reducing and Prevention alcohol related harm – a shared responsibility* (2010). The two reports are available at http://www.eurocare.org/resources/eurocare_publications .

Activity

Using the information and guidelines in this and previous chapters compile a 'drinks diary' of your weekly alcohol consumption and compare your consumption to the safe drinking guidelines for your area, region or country.

Listed next is a small sample of some individuals who have carried out this activity in Ireland over a two week period and the advice they received from health care professionals based on their weekly intake.

- 29 year old single female: 35 units consumed.

    Medical feedback: firmly in the medium to high risk category, drinking pattern indicates tendency to binge drink, she needs to intersperse her drinks with some water and insist that her wine glasses are only filled to half each time, cut out the binging at weekends (Sweeney, 2010).

- 47 year old married female: 24 units consumed.

    Medical feedback: drinking too much for her age, consider taking a break from consumption and reconsider her drinking habits (McCaffery, 2008).

Pregnant women and alcohol

The consumption of alcohol by pregnant women and its associated problems have received a lot of attention in recent years. Gilmore, cited in Rodgers (2006), states that early in pregnancy women may not realise that they are carrying a child, but should be abstaining. There is no known minimum safe level, but Abel (1998) adds that a safe limit should be defined. Falgreen Eriksen et al (2012) and Patra et al (2011) however report that there is no association between maternal drinking and foetal effects. Lewis et al (2012) differ, maintaining that among children with particular genetic variants, low to moderate levels of maternal alcohol consumption were associated with lower IQ. If mothers do not allow sufficient time between their alcohol consumption and nursing sessions, infants may ingest alcohol, which can be harmful to their development (Giglia and Binns, 2008). A woman's drinking pattern also plays a crucial role in relation to foetal development; binge drinking is associated with severe foetal harm (Abel, 1998). Some of the other medical considerations of alcohol for pregnant women, other parents and women trying to get pregnant include:

- Women over 30 years of age have increased risks, including infertility issues (Jacobson et al, 1993; Eggert et al, 2004).
- Abuse of alcohol is linked to stillbirth and spontaneous abortion (Patra et al, 2011; O'Leary et al, 2012).
- Differences in weight, IQ levels and immune system problems (Abel, 1990).
- Heavy drinking by the father has been linked to FAS in some children (May et al, 2008; Disney et al, 2008).
- Increased risk of cardiovascular defects, such as ventricular septal defect, in the offspring (Savitz et al, 1991).

To reduce the harmful outcomes which are associated with alcohol consumption during pregnancy, there is a need to provide government issued guidelines (via healthcare agencies, social workers) to women of childbearing age and especially to those who are pregnant or who are trying to get pregnant. ICAP has the local guidelines for many countries. For more information, go to http://www.icap.org/Table/InternationalGuidelinesOnDrinkingAndPregnancyor contact your local healthcare provider or government agency.

Old people and alcohol

Old people become more sensitive to the effects of alcohol and its by-products, because of their decreased ability to break it down, and their medication intake if they are in poor health. As their bodies age they experience decreases in their total body water levels and increases in their body fat levels, which affects their ability to absorb and metabolize drink (Onder et al., 2002; Meier and Seitz, 2008). Yuan et al (2001) suggest that this also heightens the risk of injury.

They are also likely to experience the benefits of consuming alcohol in moderation, which include a reduction in coronary heart disease, heart failure, and myocardial infarction, particularly in older men (Paganini et al, 2007; Rehm et al 2003; Trevisan et al, 2004; Djousse and Gaziano, 2007), and in type two diabetes mellitus (Djousse et al 2007). The additional benefits reported include improved cognitive functioning (Bond et al, 2005; Simons et al 2006; Xu et al, 2009), reduced stress and improved mood and sociability (Bond et al, 2005; Turner, Bennett, & Hernandez, 1981). Although these benefits are welcomed, medical experts argue that older individuals should not be encouraged to increase their alcohol consumption purely for health reasons.

Research has indicated that people who do drink, drink less as they get older, while consumption amongst non-drinkers or light drinkers remain stable (Liberto et al 1992). Abuse and misuse of alcohol is less common among old people when compared to young people (Moore et al 2003; Moos et al 2005). However recent studies conclude that heavy drinking among the old is on the increase (Kim et al 2007; Meier and Seitz, 2008). Abuse of alcohol by old people is closely linked with a wide variety of illnesses which include diabetes (Riserus and Ingelsson, 2007), liver disease (Meier and Seitz, 2008), depressive/anxiety symptoms (Kirchner et al, 2007) and gastric cancer (Song et al, 2008). Elderly people will sometimes use alcohol for stress relief to cope with the challenges which include the death of loved ones, loss of friends, loss of employment, lowered income levels and increased health problems (Blow and Barry, 2002).

Case example: Policy options for the elderly

The International Centre for Alcohol Policy developed approaches to help address the challenges involved for old people and alcohol. They suggest that although some of these options might be difficult to implement, they are worth considering. The options include guidelines and specific information which relates to the risk and benefits of alcohol, recommendations by physicians and healthcare providers and social workers on drinking, sensitive to the changing physiology, social context, and psychological needs of older adults, plus access to prevention services and screening treatment for elderly people. They also recommend the training of health workers to recognize problematic drinking patterns among the elderly, and interventions through alternative channels (social workers, etc.) for individuals who may be difficult to reach (ICAP, 2014).

4

Young people and alcohol

Young people are also very sensitive to alcohol consumption, due to their inexperience and the many on-going changes in their young bodies. Governments around the world have developed policies, health plans and minimum age limits to help promote responsible consumption and to reduce the risks involved for young people (WHO, 2004). For a comprehensive listing on the minimum ages to legally purchase and consume alcohol, in over 100 countries please refer to http://icap.org/Table/MinimumAgeLimitsWorldwide. Consuming alcohol prior to adulthood is traditionally deterred by most countries, but young people are introduced to alcohol quite early in some societies. This usually takes place at family gatherings for meals, or special functions. Heath (2000) contends that this integrative and relatively permissive approach to drinking is commonly found in cultures with a 'Mediterranean' drinking style.

Young men consume more alcohol than young women, though this difference is narrowing with young women now catching up (Currie et al, 2012). Culture and other factors play a prominent role in setting the norms and expectations around how young people consume alcohol (Hibell et al, 2004). These factors, which also help to fashion young people's attitudes toward drinking alcohol, include:

- The influence of their parents, and their drinking habits and behaviour (Ryan et al, 2010).
- The family structure and the presence or lack of adult support and supervision (Milgram, 2001).
- The influence of peers and friends (Martino et al, 2009).

- Faith and active religious involvement appear to have a protective effect (Borynski, 2003).

- Involvement in extracurricular activities reduces the desire to drink (Eccles amd Barber, 1999), though Wichstrom and Wichstrom (2009) report that young people involved in sports can be prone to risky drinking practices.

- For social motives (Kuntsche et al, 2005).

- To cope with their emotions (Kuntsche et al, 2008).

Although abuse and misuse of alcohol by young people is concerning, Chassin et al (2002) argues that the majority of youths grow out of their harmful and reckless drinking patterns over time. O'Malley et al (2004) maintain that this change in drinking pattern is usually brought about when the responsibilities linked with employment, marriage, and children take on a larger role in their life.

Young people and binge (episodic) drinking

Heavy (binge) drinking amongst young people is an area of major concern around the world (Gmel et al, 2003; Windle, 2003), and Higuchi et al (2004) believe that this is a major public health problem and social issue needing our immediate attention, as it is unfortunately getting out of control. Wechsler et al (2002) argue that some young people see binge drinking and drunkenness as 'desirable' goals of drinking occasions, which can include risk-taking and dangerous drinking patterns. Binge drinking is often linked to harmful outcomes for young people (Jennison, 2004), which can include alcohol dependence (Vickers et al, 2004) and risk-taking behaviours (Fromme et ak, 1997). To meet these challenges, in recent years governments have introduced minimum drinking and purchase age legislation, alcohol education programmes, responsible advertising and marketing laws and strategies which highlight the role of parents in addressing alcohol consumption amongst young people (see also Section 1.5 *Minors and under-age drinking*).

Case example: The relationship between teenage and parental attitudes to alcohol

A study carried out by Behaviour and Attitudes Ltd for the Mature Enjoyment of Alcohol in Society (MEAS) examined the relationship between teenage and parental attitudes to alcohol, and revealed some interesting features of modern family life. The main findings were:

- Under-age drinking was comparatively widespread especially between 15-16 years of age.

- There has been an escalation in the relationship between under-age drinking and involvement in random violence.

- Access to alcohol is not problem for teenagers, through a combination of theft from home, uses of fake IDs, and some bars and off-licenses turning a blind eye.

- Parental attitudes and styles have changed, and in homes where the parents drink under-age alcohol experimentation is widespread. Parents allow their children to drink in their company at a young age striving for a more open friendly relationship with their children.

- Evidence of dishonesty amongst young people about their drinking, which teenagers will use as a core 'boundary tester' activity.

- A decline in the communication between parents of peer group members, making it easy for teenagers to flout their parents rules in the homes of their friends,

Behaviour and Attitudes Ltd, as cited in Holden (2004).

4.4   Blood alcohol concentration (BAC)

Blood alcohol concentration (BAC) levels decribe the amount in milligrams per every 100 millilitres of blood. There are many ways to evaluate a person's BAC level; Jones (1990) indicates it can be taken via an exhaled sample of breath. This method is best favoured by the police because it can be undertaken quickly and at the scene in question. The amount of alcohol in the blood stream and urine samples are both excellent indicators regarding the amount of alcohol an individual has consumed. These evaluations are traditionally used for legal reasons to estimate the individual's level of intoxication, especially in relation to drinking driving cases, but as Currier et al (2006) highlights although they are both reliable, both evaluations are less practical and do not provide immediate results. Stockley and Saunders (2010) and Grant et al (2007) also highlight the fact that an individual's BAC level may drop in the time needed to reach a clinic or testing site.

The most commonly used measurements are grams of ethanol per decilitre of blood (g/dl=g/100ml), used in the United States, and milligrams of ethanol per millilitre of blood (mg/ml), used in much of Europe. For example, 0.05 g/dl = 0.5 mg/ml. BAC levels will rise when alcohol is consumed, and they will continue to rise for up to one hour afterwards. BAC levels can vary with not only the amount of alcohol consumed, but also the physical and psychological differences between each drinker, for example weight, gender, size, genetic make-up, overall state of health and considering whether or not food was consumed with the alcohol. We are all aware of the legal limits on BAC levels for car drivers, but operators of other forms of transport (airline pilots, bus drivers, taxi drivers, ships captains, and the like) are governed by strict BAC levels which are usually a lot lower than those for motorists (zero sometimes) because these individuals are directly responsible for their passengers. Irrespective of the severity of the BAC levels and the laws of the land in place, BAC policies in general when applied by themselves will not change behaviour and reduce accidents. Kaplan and Prato (2007) suggest that raising public awareness can however enhance the effectiveness of the local legislation. Education campaigns are also effective in raising awareness in relation to BAC levels (Blomberg, 1992). These campaigns in recent years have been organised through safety groups, trade organizations, government agencies and support groups. Table 4.2 outlines the effects of alcohol on a typical individual. However, it must be recognized that different people react to alcohol differently as mentioned above.

Table 4.2: BAC Levels and their effects for a typical individual (ICAP, 2014).

BAC level (mg/ml)	Effects
0.2 – 0.9	mood changes, acting inappropriately, impaired coordination, slowed reaction time, diminished response to pain
1.0 – 1.9	lack of coordination, inability to correctly interpret what is happening, impaired judgment, difficulty in walking and standing steadily
2.0 – 2.9	nausea, vomiting
3.0 – 3.9	serious intoxication, lowered body temperature, partial amnesia ("blackout") likely
≥ 4.0	alcohol poisoning, coma, risk of death (about 50% of people who have a BAC ≥ 4.00 will die of alcohol poisoning)

Broadly speaking, one standard alcoholic beverage (spirits, beer or wine) will raise the blood alcohol concentration level approximately 0.2 mg/ml. Alcohol will metabolize in the body as soon as it is consumed, but the rate of the process differs from person to person, traditionally a healthy liver will reduce BAC by approximately 0.15 mg/ml per hour.

Blood alcohol concentration thresholds in different countries

The World Health Organisation (2009) report that most countries have taken actions to help minimize the potential harm which results from drink driving by setting maximum legally permissible BAC levels for all drivers. The levels set by local governments incorporate international research and identify best practice guidelines in relation to the risk factors involved with the effects of alcohol on the ability of individuals to perform certain tasks (which includes driving). These levels can range from zero (0.0 mg/ml) up to one (1.0 mg/ml). The communication of BAC levels and information in relation to how BAC limits are enforced also differs worldwide (WHO, 2009). An extensive survey conducted by the WHO in 2004 reported that 28% set their BAC limit at a lower level at 0-3 mg/ml, 39% set their level at a middle level 0.4-0.6 mg/ml and finally 26% reported setting their level at the higher limit 0.6 mg/ml and above. A small number of countries (7%) have no legal BAC limit. You should consult your local government or state agency to find BAC levels for your area. The International Centre for Alcohol Policies offers examples of BAC levels in operation across a large number of countries around the world (http://www.icap.org/Table/BACLimitsWorldwide).

4.5   The alcohol hangover

Stephens et al (2008) contend that a hangover is the experience of various unpleasant physiological and psychological effects following consumption of alcoholic beverages and is generally characterized by a feeling of severe discomfort that may last more than 24 hours. It is caused by the combined effects of the congeners (see below) and the products of the breakdown of alcohol. The typical symptoms of a hangover may include headache, drowsiness, concentration problems, dry mouth, dizziness, fatigue, gastrointestinal distress, sweating, nausea, hyper-excitability and anxiety (Vester et al, 2010). Penning et al (2012) suggest that alcohol hangover symptoms develop when blood alcohol concentration falls considerably and peaks when it returns to almost zero.

Signs and symptoms of a hangover

Although the causes of a hangover are still poorly understood, Prat et al (2009) maintain that several factors are known to be involved including acetaldehyde accumulation, changes in the immune system and glucose metabolism, dehydration, metabolic acidosis, disturbed prostaglandin synthesis, increased cardiac output, vasodilation, sleep deprivation and malnutrition.

Stephens et al (2008) add that beverage specific effects of additives or by-products such as congeners also play an important role. Penning et al (2010) suggest that these effects takes place typically after the intoxicating effect of the alcohol begins to wear off, which is usually the morning after a night of heavy drinking. The body can suffer some the following conditions from a hangover:

■ **Dehydration**: the first effect of alcohol is dehydration because although you're taking in more fluids, you're also expelling them more quickly, altering the water balance in the cells and tissues. This is probably the major cause of hangover headache. Alcohol is a potent diuretic. It blocks the release of a hormone responsible for recycling water in the blood stream through the kidneys. This is the anti-diuretic hormone (ADH). Water that would usually be reabsorbed into the blood stream is now channelled out of the body to flush out the alcohol and its metabolites. The body needs water to break down alcohol, and it is important that water be replenished.

■ **Dry mouth and headaches:** which are a direct result of dehydration and changes in pressure within blood vessels.

■ **Fatigue, lethargy, and weakness:** these conditions will accompany hangovers is the result of a build-up of lactic acid, which is normally cleared from the body through the liver. Lactic acid is familiar to all those who have had sore muscles from exercising. When high levels of alcohol are present in the body, the liver's first priority is to eliminate it from the system, allowing other toxins (including lactic acid) to build up.

■ **Irritation of the stomach lining:** alcohol stimulates acid to be released into the stomach; these increased acids can result in queasiness.

■ **A degree of poisoning:** methanol, a type of alcohol found as a congener in most alcoholic drinks, is not broken down by most people's bodies until the morning after. It's then that the unpleasant toxins responsible for many hangover symptoms are produced, (see Congeners below).

■ **Vessels relax (bloodshot eyes):** Alcohol relaxes blood vessels, which then expand to let more blood through, causing tell-tale bloodshot eyes.

■ **Nervous system (sensitivity):** The body combats the sedative effects of alcohol by making the nervous system more sensitive - hence difficulty in sleeping, sensitivity to lights and noise.

■ **Low blood sugar.**

Rohsenow and Howland (2010) add that some symptoms, such as changes in sleep pattern and gastrointestinal distress, are attributed to direct effects of the alcohol intoxication, or withdrawal symptoms. Drowsiness and impaired cognitive function are the two most dominant features of a hangover.

Congeners

Congeners are found in the majority of alcoholic drinks, and are a by-product of fermentation and the aging process. Although congeners do help to give flavour to alcoholic drinks they can also potentially aggravate the hangover. Rohsenow and Howland (2010) state that congeners include substances such as amines, amides, acetones, acetaldehydes, polyphenols, methanol, histamines, fusel oil, esters, furfural, and tannins, many but not all of which are toxic. Alcoholic beverages contain various amounts of congeners. The dark spirits and wine categories (i.e. whisky, brandy, dark rum, red wine) contain higher concentration levels compared to clear spirits (i.e. vodka, gin, white rum, white wine). Rohsenow and Howland (2010) give the example that bourbon has a total congener content 37 times higher than that found in vodka. Numerous research studies have concluded that dark spirits which contain higher levels of congeners produce the worse alcohol hangovers (Pawan, 1973; Wiese et al, 2000; Verster, 2006). Methanol is another congener found in alcohol. It is formed naturally in tiny amounts during the fermentation process and sometimes it may be mistakenly concentrated by poor distillation techniques. Rohsenow and Howland (2010) and Verster (2009) report that ethanol actually slows the conversion of methanol into its toxic metabolites so that most of the methanol can be excreted harmlessly in the breath and urine without forming its toxic metabolites. This delayed action explains why some people like to consume more alcohol to relieve the symptoms of a hangover.

Additional factors which can influence the harsh effects of the hangover

The severity of an alcohol hangover can be influenced by such factors as personality, age, genetics, gender, health status and the activities linked to drinking, such as smoking, the use of other drugs, dancing and other physical activity, as well as sleep quality and duration (Penning et al, 2010).

- **Gender**: females are more prone to hangovers when compared to males. This is because women attain a higher blood alcohol concentration than men at the same number of drinks. However Piasecki et al (2010) maintains that at equivalent BACs, men and women appear to be indistinguishable with respect to most hangover effects.

- **Cigarette smokers:** Min et al (2010) argue that acetaldehyde which is absorbed from cigarette smoking during alcohol consumption is regarded as a contributor to hangover symptoms.

- **Age**: the data suggests that as we age some individuals will experience more severe hangovers. Jalan, cited in the *Daily Mail* (2009), maintains that this is caused by declining supplies of alcohol dehydrogenase, the enzyme involved in metabolizing alcohol. Verster et al (2010), disagree with this conclusion and suggest that heavy drinking episodes that may result in hangover are much less often experienced as age increases.

- **Genetic make-up**: Piasecki et al (2010) suggest that drinkers with genotypes known to lead to acetaldehyde accumulation are more susceptible to hangover effects. Verster et al (2010) adds that when we consider the data which indicates that 25% of heavy drinkers claim to have never experienced a hangover, this is also an indication that genetic variation plays a role in individual differences of hangover severity.

Hangover remedies

It is possible to prevent the symptoms of the hangover by drinking plenty of water and other non-alcoholic fluids after drinking alcohol (Penning, 2010). This will allow the body to regain its balance and more efficiently clear alcohol and its breakdown products from the system. In recent years a large number of other possible remedies and antidotes have been proposed, though Pittler et al (2005) and Verster and Penning (2010) maintain there is no compelling evidence to suggest that any are effective for preventing or treating alcohol hangovers. Pittler et al (2009) add that avoiding alcohol or drinking in moderation are the most effective ways to avoid a hangover. We must also consider that there are wider problems and health risks caused by alcohol hangovers, which include weaker work performance, reduced productivity, poor academic achievement and workplace absenteeism. Hangovers can also compromise potentially dangerous daily activities such as driving a car or operating heavy machinery (Verster et al, 2010).

See also Appendix IV - Hangover remedies.

4.6   Sexual intercourse

The WHO (2005) contends that the consumption of alcohol has a direct impact on sexual behaviour. These effects can vary between suppressive effects on physiology, which decreases sexual activity, and the suppression of inhibitions, which can increase the desire for sex (Crowe and George, 1989). When alcohol is consumed, it will cause the body's systems to slow down and because alcohol is a mood altering drug, the consumer can experience mixed feelings which can range from happiness to anger or depression.

Male sexual behaviour and performance

The sexual behaviour of males can be affected dramatically by alcohol (Mendelson et al, 1978) Frias et al (2002) contend that both chronic and acute alcohol consumption have been shown in most (but not all, Sakola and Eriksson, 2003) studies to inhibit testosterone production in the testes. Testosterone is critical for the libido and physical arousal, but alcohol tends to have a detrimental effect on male sexual performance. Halpernfesher et al (1996) add that intoxication can also decrease pleasure ability and intensity of orgasm, and increase difficulty in attaining orgasm.

Female sexual behaviour and performance

Sarkola et al (2000) highlight that acute alcohol consumption tends to cause increased levels of testosterone which tends to increase the strength of libido in women and their interest in sex, though Beckman and Ackerman (1995) contend that it does lower the physiological signs of arousal. They propose that an increase in BAC levels is associated with longer orgasmic latencies and decreased intensity of orgasm for females. Women who were intoxicated believed they were more sexually aroused than before consumption of alcohol. Although alcohol can influence the capacity of females to feel more relaxed, and in turn be more sexual, Beckman and Ackerman (1995) state that alcohol is considered by some women to be a sexual dis-inhibitor.

Sexual promiscuity and sexually transmitted diseases

Halpernfelsher et al (1996) state that during intoxication some people will engage in risky sexual behaviour, such as unprotected sex. The evidence is however unclear as to whether the two are linked, or if the types of individuals who regularly consume large amounts of alcohol are more tolerant of risk-taking. Hanson et al (2005) report that alcohol is also linked to a large proportion of unwanted outcomes associated with sex such as date rape, unwanted pregnancy and sexually transmitted diseases. Reducing the spread of human immunodeficiency virus (HIV), the virus that causes acquired immunodeficiency syndrome (AIDS), involves reducing the risky sexual behaviour which intoxication can cause in some individuals. The World Health Organisation (2002) state that unsafe sex is one of the ten leading risk factors for harm worldwide and is the most common mode of HIV transmission. Further research studies have proposed a correlation between heavy and harmful drinking patterns and an increased likelihood of sexual risk-taking behaviours, including engaging in unprotected sex (Standerwick et al, 2007; Baliunas et al, 2010; Wen et al, 2012).

Recent studies however have indicated that the relationship between alcohol and sexual conduct is context and community-specific (Baliunas et al, 2010). Wen et al (2012) maintain that the intended outcomes will therefore vary, depending on the situation, gender, sexual and alcohol experiences, cultural norm, drinking patterns, and the individual physiological responses to alcohol. Heath (2000) reminds us that the implications of these studies across different traditions, cultures and social environments will vary according to the contextual factors of each region or nation.

4.7   Alcohol and sport

Alcohol enjoys a strong association with sport worldwide and at all levels. Athletes, coaches and associated officials are often captured in the media celebrating a win with alcohol. Major drinks companies often sponsor sporting events and many high-profile sporting teams are affiliated with these companies via sponsorship agreements. In this section we will consider why athletes should not disproportionately misuse alcohol compared with their non-athlete counterparts. Professor David Cameron-Smith of the University of Auckland, as cited in *The Guardian* (n.d.), examined the effects of alcohol on the finely tuned biological processes that all athletes are looking to optimise. In his extensive studies he concluded that alcohol can make you far more prone to injury, and that happens in a variety of ways:

- **Altering your sleep cycle:** this decreases your body's ability to store glycogen (needed for endurance) and increases levels of the stress hormone cortisol, which slows down healing, and reduces levels of human growth hormone by up to 70%.

- **Triggering multiple chemical processes:** for example the release of toxin from your liver which attacks the hormone testosterone, needed for muscle growth and regeneration.

- **Powerful diuretic:** alcohol promotes the production of urine, which can severely dehydrate the body for up to a week.

- **Injuries:** while dehydrated, musculoskeletal injuries such as cramps, muscle pulls and strains can occur.

- **Alters your water balance:** alcohol has a negative effect on the water balance in muscle cells. The combination of this and alcohol inhibits gluconeogenesis, which produces a compound known as adenosine triphosphate (ATP), that provides the energy your muscles need to contract. Without this, you would never improve and you would be constantly injury-prone

- **Muscle protein:** alcohol has an enormous impact on muscle protein synthesis, reducing it by up to a third.

4.8   Psychological and social factors which influence alcohol purchases

Psychological and social factors influence consumer behaviour. These include environmental and marketing factors, the situation, personal factors, family, and culture. Drinks businesses will constantly try to figure out trends so they can reach consumers who are most likely to buy their alcohol products, using variables such as the layout of a store, music, grouping and availability of alcohol products, pricing and advertising. While some influences may be temporary and others are long lasting, different factors can affect how consumers behave (White and Jackson, n.d.). These factors have been examined in numerous research studies, which show that consumers are influenced to purchase alcohol for the following reasons:

■ **Alcohol expectancies:** Schulenberg and Maggs (2002) suggest individuals expect benefits from drinking and become less convinced of the risks. Carey and Correia (1997) maintain that heavier drinkers endorse an overall greater number and variety of reasons for drinking. While Jackson et al (2005) argue that drinking for social purposes is associated with greater consumption, and drinking for escape or relief is associated with problem drinking.

■ **Family influences:** White et al (2000) maintain that parental drinking patterns have been shown to affect drinking by offspring over the life course. Family members, including young people, model their own behaviour on their parents' patterns of consumption (including quantity and frequency), situations and contexts of use, attitudes regarding use, and use expectancies. Jackson et al (2005) argues that findings have been inconsistent about whether drinking patterns differ between children of alcoholics and others.

In addition to the influence of parents, Schulenberg and Maggs (2002) add that siblings can also influence drinking through modelling, direct social influence, and access.

■ **Impulsivity, sensation-seeking, and risk-taking:** Arnett (2005) indicates that the most consistent predictors are sensation-seeking and the pursuit of novel and intense experiences. Impulsivity and sensation-seeking have also been related to higher frequency and quantity of drinking, and to experiencing more negative alcohol-related consequences (Jackson et al, 2005) and deviant behaviour (Baer, 2002). Goldberg et al (2002) maintain that the decision to drink is more influenced by the perceived benefits of drinking (i.e. positive expectations of the effects) than by the perceived risks which might occur.

■ **Negative affect:** Jackson et al (2005) point to high levels of negative affect, as seen in anxiety disorders which are associated with problem drinking especially in college students. Some people drink to regulate emotional distress (Cooper et al, 2000). Read et al (2003) however add that emerging adults are more likely to drink for positive or celebratory reasons than to drink to cope with negative feelings.

■ **Peer influences:** Borsari and Carey (2001) suggest that peer influence is exerted directly (e.g. open drink offers or urges to drink) and indirectly (e.g., modelling perceived social norms) or via the perceived cultural norms (Jackson et al, 2005). Bullers et al (2001) add that young people are just as likely to select a peer group based on the group members' drinking behaviour because they can be influenced by peers to change their own drinking behaviour.

Consumers can also be influenced by the media and advertising for a wider discussion of these factors see Chapter 8, *Selling and Marketing Alcohol Responsibly*.

Conclusion

Alcohol can offer many benefits but equally it can create many problems for people who consume it irresponsibly. The amounts and frequency by which alcohol is consumed will increase the short term and long term health risks to the main organs of the body. Alcohol will affect men and women differently, and women typically feel the initial effects of alcohol more quickly and are more susceptible to the potential for harm of alcohol. To achieve a reduction in this, we must consider advising women to take more control over their drinking patterns and to seek further information in relation to the effects of alcohol on their bodies, especially pregnant women to help ensure there are no lasting effects for the child. For some people, not drinking at all can be advisable. These include those who are unable to metabolize alcohol easily, those with a family history of alcohol dependence, and those who have trouble controlling the amount they drink. The establishment of blood alcohol concentration limits should be perceived as a means of reducing the harm associated with alcohol consumption. Setting levels to ensure compliance has been shown to reduce serious accidents and deaths caused by drink drivers. Education campaigns, implemented through a variety of public and private organizations including support groups, are critical in raising awareness about the dangers of excessive consumption.

The elderly can benefit from the positive health outcomes of moderate alcohol consumption, but the health and social factors associated with ageing also place the older drinkers at particular risk for harm. Treatment and harm prevention strategies must be appropriate and sensitive to the particular needs of the elderly, and policy makers and healthcare agencies must ensure that the elderly are informed of the issues involved. The majority of young people will have experiences with alcohol before they reach adulthood or the legal age for consumption. Those who abuse or misuse alcohol face considerable risks for health, injury, neurological and social problems, heavy patterns of drinking and risk-taking behaviours expose young people to the risk of violence, sex attacks and drink driving. A series of psychological and social factors can influence the reasons why individuals purchase and consume alcohol. To meet these challenges national governments, policy groups and families have worked together to understand the processes which shape young drinkers' consumption and to introduce prevention and intervention courses for young people. The consumption of alcohol has a direct impact on sexual activities which includes risky sexual behaviour which can lead to unwanted pregnancies and sexually transmitted diseases; alcohol can also increase arousal and desire but reduce performance. During sports activities, consumption can also lead to reduced endurance levels and injuries.

Web resources

Alcohol and Australian Sport - Australian Sports Commission
   www.ausport.gov.au/ais/nutrition/factsheets/basics/alcohol_and_australian_sport
Alcohol screening
   www.alcoholscreening.org
Alcohol effects on the brain
   www.youtube.com/watch?v=GruK1SXhPJk&feature=related
Alcohol effects your body
   www.alcohol.org.nz/alcohol-you/your-body-alcohol/body-effects
Alcohol and your brain
   www.youtube.com/watch?v=zXjANz9r5F0
BUPA – How alcohol effects the body
   www.youtube.com/watch?v=PA1gDo4OXp4&feature=related
Pathway of alcohol through the body
   www.scramsystems.com/static/videos/product/how-does.html
Teacher's guide – understanding alcohol
   science.education.nih.gov/supplements/nih3/alcohol/guide/guide_lessons_toc.htm
The drinkers check-up
   www.drinkerscheckup.com
Test your drinking
   www.alcohol.org.az/hadenough/questionnaire/concern.html

5 Alcohol and Health

Aims and learning outcomes

This chapter introduces the areas central to understanding the relationship between alcohol, health and well-being. It also explores in detail the harmful and beneficial outcomes associated with alcohol consumption and the adverse reactions of consuming alcohol with prescribed medications or illegal drugs plus the health benefits of individual alcohol beverages. After reading this chapter you should be able to:

■ Describe the short (acute) and long term (chronic) risks associated with alcohol consumption as they relate to particular diseases and to general health and well-being.

■ Demonstrate a knowledge of the adverse reactions which occurs in individuals who consume alcohol with prescribed medications or illegal drugs.

■ Establish the general and more specific benefits from moderate alcohol consumption and how it plays a positive role in the life of many individuals.

5.0 Introduction

Research conducted over recent decades has highlighted a firm association between alcohol consumption patterns and a variety of health outcomes both harmful and beneficial. The more dangerous outcomes are traditionally linked with heavy consumption, but these are dependent on the inter-related elements of how people consume alcohol and the types, amount and frequency of their consumption. The outcomes are also influenced by the gender, age, general health, genetic makeup and other factors, for example alcohol triggers different physiological effects on men when compared to women. Consuming alcohol in moderation has many health benefits, which include extending and improving the quality of life, but for individuals with medical conditions and those who are taking prescribed medications it can lead to adverse reactions. Alcohol has known medicinal, antiseptic, and analgesic properties, and facilitates relaxation, but research studies have highlighted its role in the development of a wide series of illnesses and harmful conditions, including cancer, type two diabetes, cognitive and neurological function, coronary and vascular diseases.

5.1 Alcohol – medicinal in moderation and poisonous in excess

The medicinal use of alcohol was mentioned in Sumerian and Egyptian texts dating from about 2100 BC. David J Hanson, Ph.D., Professor Emeritus of Sociology of the State University of New York at Potsdam, states that the Hindu ayurvedic texts also describe both the beneficial effects of alcoholic beverages and the consequences of intoxication and alcoholic diseases. He concludes that in these texts alcohol was a medicine if consumed in moderation, but a poison if consumed in excess, adding that Hippocrates (ca 460-370 BC) had identified numerous medicinal properties of wine (Hanson, 1995). Alcohol has had a traditional role in many forms of medicine in China where various remedies containing alcohol are over 2,000 years old. The *Compendium of Materia Medica* in the Ming Dynasty listed 79 different alcohol containing drinks (Xiao, 1995).

5

The world of medicine today still uses alcohol to treat kidney disorders, digestion problems, and gastroenteritis where it can reduce pathogenic intestinal flora. It is also used as an analgesic after injuries while resetting broken or fractured bones, and it forms part of modern medicinal mixtures, including iron supplements and cough syrups. Even though alcohol has many health benefits, it is also the third leading risk factor for disease and death in Europe, and currently is the cause of over sixty types of disease which include lung diseases, pre-natal harm, cancers, liver, cardiovascular skeletal and muscular diseases, gastrointestinal conditions, and immunological and reproductive disorders. The amounts and frequency of drinking alcohol are significant factors which increase the risk of alcohol related harm (Euro Care, 2014).

5.2 The associated risks of alcohol consumption

The risks associated with alcohol consumption usually relate to general health or to particular diseases, and can be categorised as long-term (chronic) or short-term (acute). The harmful risks are generally linked to heavy drinking patterns and, of course, alcohol abuse. Cunningham et al (2003) maintains that the results of these drinking patterns can cause long-term health problems and or serious accidents and injuries. Amongst the more chronic health consequences are liver cirrhosis and certain cancers. Houston (2002) reports that the two main life threatening conditions that can be sparked by alcohol are cancer and heart disease. Although some medical studies have shown that moderate amounts of alcohol can reduce the risk of developing some types of cardiovascular disease, the long-term effects of excessive consumption can be devastating. In this section we will explore these risks in detail. Please also consult Chapter 4, *The Effects of Alcohol on the Body*.

■ **Short term health risks include**: anxiety, impaired judgement leading to accidents and injuries, loss of consciousness, slowed breathing and heart-beat, potentially fatal poisoning, and sexual difficulties such as impotency.

■ **Long term health risks include:** brain damage, liver disease, osteoporosis (thinning of the bones), pancreatitis, stomach ulcers, heart disease, raised blood pressure, stroke, dementia, infertility, and damage to unborn child.

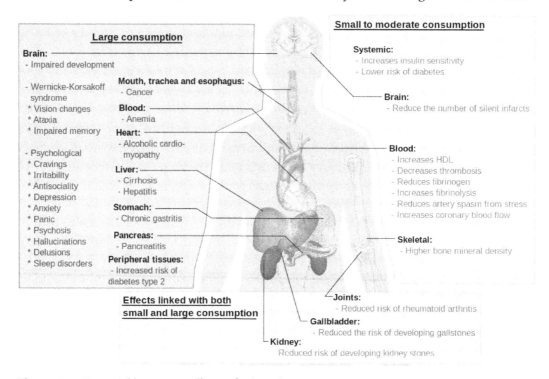

Figure 5.1: Potential long term effects of ethanol consumption (Häggström, 2009).

The impact of alcohol related diseases on health and well-being

Coronary and vascular diseases

Nicolas et al (2002) and Rotondo et al (2001) report that heavy consumption of alcohol is linked with vascular diseases, atrial fibrillation, haemorrhagic stroke and congestive heart failure. These conditions are brought about because of the strong link of alcohol consumption with high blood pressure, which is in turn linked to coronary heart disease and stroke. Binge drinking is also associated with the development of an abnormal heart rhythm. A condition known as cardiomyopathy, in which the heart muscle is damaged, is linked to chronic heavy drinking. The affected muscle cannot pump as well as before and eventually the chambers of the heart enlarge to the point where the valves cannot function properly and heart failure occurs. Alcoholic myopathy (painful and swollen muscles) can also occur. Chronic drinking can also decrease the production of white blood cells, leading to an increased risk of infection.

Liver disease

Meister et al (2000) and Mann et al (2003) state that harmful drinking patterns are associated with cirrhosis of the liver, and Szabo (2007) contends that this risk increases with heavy consumption, especially in women who are more vulnerable at lower levels of consumption then men (Becker et al, 1996). Individuals who practice moderate alcohol consumption have also been affected with the early stages of cirrhosis (Kondili et al, 2005; Luca et al, 1997).

5

Type two diabetes and metabolic syndrome

Kao et al (2001) and Nakanishi et al (2003) state that modern research studies have indicated that moderate alcohol consumption can offer protection against metabolic disorders like type 2 diabetes (sometimes referred to as 'adult-onset' diabetes) and metabolic syndrome (Freiberg et al, 2004). Puddey et al (1985) add that moderate consumption delivers benefits for patients suffering with hypertension. These benefits are not experienced by everyone, and Emanuele et al (1998) maintain that moderate consumption by some individuals with type 2 diabetes can speed up low blood sugar levels and other related health consequences. A significant Dutch research study of 11,959 incident cases of type 2 diabetes in 369,862 participants, who on average were followed for 12 years, discovered that healthy adults who drink one to two glasses per day have a decreased chance of developing type 2 diabetes, compared to those who don't drink at all. 'The results of the investigation show that moderate alcohol consumption can play a part in a healthy lifestyle, to help reduce the risk of developing type 2 diabetes' (Kroppes et al, 2004).

Cancer

Certain cancers occur more often in people with problem drinking, with a cancer rate up to ten times higher than that of the general population. Harmful drinking patterns have been directly linked with the following cancers: oesophagus, larynx and pharynx (Ashley et al, 1997) breast cancer, renal cancers (Lee et al, 2007) and colorectal cancers (Moskal et al, 2007). Researchers in the USA revealed that middle aged women who drink just seven units of alcohol per week have a much greater chance of developing lobular cancer (Gilmore, cited in Rodgers 2006; Smith-Squire, 2008).

Ethanol found in alcohol has therefore been assigned to the category of Group 1 carcinogen. Seitz and Meier (2007) adds that ethanol's metabolic by-products, including acetaldehyde and urethane (IARC, 2007), have been similarly classified. Boffetta et al (2006) report that 5% of all cancers are associated with alcohol consumption.

Case example: Woman develops breast cancer at 25

A 25 year old woman from England was diagnosed with breast cancer although there was no family history of the disease. The woman stated that prior to entering college that she was an occasional drinker, but upon entry to college she was exposed to the booze culture with the local town selling booze cheaply. She continued her drinking habits throughout her studies and into the workplace and at 24 she was an alcoholic. After being admitted to hospital for treatment, a cancerous lump was discovered and she endured a lumpectomy followed by chemotherapy and radiotherapy which caused her to lose her hair. The woman is now clear of the disease. Paul Wallace, Chief Medical advisor to the charity Drinkaware, stated that only 19% of adults are aware that breast cancer can be a serious consequence of drinking to excess (Smith-Squire, 2008).

Cognitive function

The benefits of alcohol consumption on brain activity can differ. A major research study containing 365,000 participants gathering data dating back to 1977, reported in the *Journal of Neuropsychiatric Disease and Treatment* that moderate drinkers were 23% less likely to develop cognitive impairment or Alzheimer's disease and other forms of dementia. Dr. Edward J Neafsey, co-author of the study, stated that small amounts of alcohol might, in effect, make brain cells more fit, as alcohol in moderate amounts stresses cells and thus toughens them up to cope with major stresses that could cause dementia. The authors added that they don't recommend that nondrinkers should start drinking, but moderate drinking can be beneficial (Neafsey and Collins, 2011). Other studies indicate that moderate consumption helps to delay the onset and development of vascular dementia and other neurone-degenerative disorders (Brust, 2002; Galanis et al, 2000), and may have overall improvements in cognitive function in older individuals (Brust, 2002, Zuccala et al, 2001). On the other hand, harmful drinking patterns have been closely linked with alcohol-related brain damage (Thomas & Rockwood, 2001; Whelan, 2003).

Stress reduction

Many people, including clinicians, researchers, and social and problem drinkers believe that alcohol is somewhat effective as a temporary stress reliever. Peele and Brodsky (2000) and Rodgers et al (2000) add that it may also reduce the emotional effects of stressful situations that may lead to depression.

5.3   Consuming alcohol with medical conditions, prescription medications or illegal drugs

Research studies have highlighted the risks involved and adverse reactions of drinking alcohol with medical conditions and/or the use of certain medications. Emmanuelle et al (1998) report that even moderate consumption can affect patients with some conditions. Beilin (1995) and Wakim-Fleming and Mullen (2005) highlight diabetes, hypertension, and hepatitis C. People with panic and anxiety or bipolar disorders or depression are at increased risk of alcohol abuse (Paschall et al, 2005). Another study carried out by Schubiner (2005) reported that attention-deficit hyperactivity disorder (ADHD) in children could be an indicator for alcohol abuse and misuse in later years.

Mixing alcohol with certain medications can cause nausea and vomiting, headaches, drowsiness, fainting, or loss of coordination. It also can put you at risk of internal bleeding, heart problems, and difficulties in breathing. In addition to these dangers ,when alcohol interacts with medications it can raise the risk factor and reduce their effectiveness. Ramskogler et al (2001) maintains that in some circumstances these interactions can be dangerous or fatal.

Figure 5.2: Mixing drugs with alcohol, warnings on labels.

Some medicines that you might never have suspected can react with alcohol, including many which can be purchased without a prescription. Even some herbal remedies can have harmful effects when combined with alcohol. Weathermon and Crabb (1999) indicate that reports of these adverse interactions have been linked with antihistamines, analgesics, anticoagulants, antibiotics, psychoactive and anti-hypertensive drugs. Your pharmacist, doctor or other health care provider can help you determine which medications interact harmfully with alcohol For a more detailed list please refer to 'Mixing alcohol with medicines' (NIH, 2014).

Mixing alcohol and with illegal drugs

When alcohol is mixed with illegal drugs there are many factors which can lead to death. These include the person's psychological history, mood and body chemistry, and any medications they take or illnesses they have. The most dangerous thing to mix with alcohol is another sedative. This combination can lead to extreme depression of the central nervous system and be fatal. Listed below are a list of the most common illegal drugs and the possible outcomes which can occur when they are mixed with alcohol.

- *Acid (LSD):* when LSD is combined with alcohol, the visual hallucinations common in a trip often decrease, and users may find themselves able to drink more than normal without experiencing the same level of inebriation.

- *Cocaine/crack:* in low doses cocaine increases blood pressure and heart rate. When it is combined with alcohol, cocaine increases the heart rate three to five times as much as when either drug is given alone. This can lead to heart attacks and heart failure. Research shows that mixing cocaine with alcohol can have either an additive (the user experiences the highs of both drugs) or antagonistic effects (the effects of the drugs cancel one another out). However, when cocaine is used in high doses, the effects are usually additive, and overdose from either drug is more likely.

- *Ecstasy:* drinking alcohol while using ecstasy can be very dangerous because it increases dehydration. Ecstasy also decreases the body's ability to regulate body temperature, and alcohol can raise body temperature, increasing chances of death by hypertension.

- *GHB:* when added to alcoholic drinks it can cause black-out periods to the person who drinks it (hence its use as a date-rape drug). GHB is a CNS depressant and is thus dangerous when used in tandem with alcohol. The combined effect can slow respiration and heart rate to a dangerous level.

- *Heroin:* the heroin high is characterized by the depression of the central nervous system. In an overdose, breathing stops. Because alcohol is also a CNS depressant, it is dangerous to drink alcohol while using heroin as the compounded effect can potentiate a heroin overdose.

- *Marijuana:* can suppress feelings of nausea. When a person has drunk so much alcohol that poisoning is a concern, the body needs to vomit. Pot suppresses this, so excess alcohol is not expelled, making overdose more likely.

- *Methamphetamine:* use of methamphetamine masks the effects of alcohol, which is dangerous because the user will be less aware of the effect that the drug is having on their body. Even though the high is lessened, the physical effects such as heart rate are not affected. Hence, the user's sense of when their body needs them to stop will be skewed.

■ *Mushrooms:* there are no known dangerous physical interactions between alcohol and mushrooms. However, mushrooms are unpredictable, and mixing them with anything makes them more unpredictable.

■ *PCP/Special K:* the most dangerous substances to mix with these are alcohol and other sedatives. Make no mistake, this combination can kill you.

■ *CNS Depressants:* using alcohol with other depressants and narcotics compounds the depression of the CNS and can be fatal. These include heroin, morphine, opium, and barbiturates.

(adapted from SCU Wellness Centre, 2014).

You could also refer to Chapter 6 under 'Illegal drugs in the workplace' to enhance your awareness of the nature of these drugs, techniques regarding how to identify abuse and the outcomes of illegal drug taking.

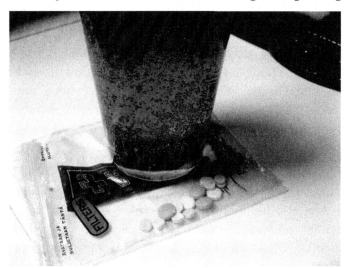

Figure 5.3: Alcohol, drugs and cigarettes a lethal mix (Wiki Commons, 2014).

Case example: man dies after acute alcohol consumption

A 35 year old man was found lifeless outside a telephone box near one of the exits of a city hospital. He had been dead for a number of hours. A post-mortem found that the man died of acute alcohol intoxication with 364 milligrams of alcohol per 100 milligrams of blood in his system at the time of death. Any level over 350 milligrams can be fatal for males. The inquest heard that the man had a difficulty with alcohol and heroin in the past and was known to hospital staff. The coroner recorded a verdict of death by misadventure (O'Halloran, 2009).

Drink-testing kit aims to prevent drug rape

Drink Detective is a drink-testing kit retailing at £3.95. It is designed in a match-book style; it tests for the three most common groups of drugs used in drug rape and other spiking crimes GBH, benzodiazepines (including Rohypnol and Valium) and ketamine. To perform a test, the drinker uses a pipette to apply drops of the beverage to three chemically sensitive pads on the kit and observes the reaction, which only takes a couple of minutes. The aim is to have the kit available for sale in bars. Unattended drinks have become a big problem since the introduction of smoking bans, if customers are not allowed to take their drink with them when they go outside to smoke (Tyrell, 2004).

5.4   The benefits of moderate alcohol consumption

People who consume alcohol in moderation are different from non-drinkers or heavy drinkers. They benefit from consumption and alcohol plays a positive role in their life. In this section we explore these benefits under the headings of happiness, health, relaxation, sleep improvements, social and food intake.

Happiness

In a major survey of US alcohol consumption habits, nearly half of all moderate consumers reported as feeling happy and cheerful, Cahalan (1970) states that the data also highlighted that these experiences rose to approximately 80% amongst problem drinkers and alcohol dependent individuals. Pliner and Cappell (1974) add that individuals who consumed alcohol in simulated bar or home settings, and in experimental laboratories, reported elevated mood changes and euphoric feelings. These experiences were also discovered in the work of Lowe and Taylor (1997) who stated that individuals who had consumed alcohol were happier and laughed more than a comparable group who had not consumed any alcohol. This experience of euphoria is brought about by the chemical action of alcohol, and occurs during the upward curve of the blood alcohol concentration (BAC) levels. It should be remembered that as these BAC levels drop, the euphoria feelings are usually replaced by experiences of malaise and dysphoria amongst alcohol dependent persons.

Health

- **Gallstones:** In a ten year study completed in 2009, involving over 25,000 men and women, in which 267 patients developed gallstones, researchers discovered that those who reported consuming two UK units of alcohol daily had a one-third reduction in their risk of developing gallstones. Dr Andrew Hart, Senior lecturer in gastroenterology at UEA's School of Medicine, Health Policy and Practice, stated that the findings significantly increase the understanding of the development of gallstones (University of East Anglia, 2009).

- **Cardiovascular disease (CHD):** The idea that moderate drinking protects against cardiovascular disease makes sense biologically and scientifically. Research studies carried in out in over 25 countries across the world concluded that moderate consumption of alcohol, for some individuals, can act as a protective element against CHD. Ashley et al (2000) and Rehm et al (2003) propose that these positive results are very strong for middle aged and older males and for postmenopausal women, especially when the consumption is regular (Rimm and Moats, 2007). CHD suffers have also recorded reduction in the progression of the condition (Niroomand et al, 2004). These positive effects have also been recorded for individuals suffering with other vascular diseases including peripheral arterial disease (Meister et al, 2000). Booyse et al (2007) propose that moderate amounts of alcohol raise the levels of high-density lipoprotein (HDL, or 'good' cholesterol), which is associated with greater protection against heart disease. Moderate alcohol consumption has also been linked with beneficial changes ranging from better sensitivity to insulin, to improvements in factors that influence blood clotting, such as tissue type plasminogen activator, fibrinogen, clotting factor VII, and von Willebrand factor. Such changes would tend to prevent the formation of small blood clots that can block arteries in the heart, neck, and brain, the ultimate cause of many heart attacks and the most common kind of stroke (Booyse et al, 2007). This finding is applicable to both men and women who have not been previously diagnosed with any type of cardiovascular disease.

- **The common cold:** In a study conducted in 1993 with 391 adults at the Department of Psychology at Carnegie Mellon University, it was found that while susceptibility to the common cold was increased by smoking, moderate alcohol consumption led to a decrease in cases for nonsmokers (Cohen et al, 1993). A report published in the *New York Times* in 2002 highlighted a Spanish research study in which it was discovered that consuming eight to fourteen glasses of red wine a week reduced the risk of developing a cold. The scientists suspected that this had something to do with the antioxidant properties of wine (O'Connor, 2007).

- **Rheumatoid arthritis (RA):** A US study which ran from 1980 to 2008 involving 116,430 female registered nurses of the NHSII uncovered only 580 incident cases of RA in the cohort. Women who consumed beer two to four times a week had a 31% decreased risk compared to women who never drank beer. Based on the overall results the research team highlighted that a modest association between long term moderate alcohol drinking and reduced risk of RA did exist, proposing that future studies would also be required to confirm their findings in other populations (Bing et al 2014). Further studies conducted amongst women in Scandinavia, concluded that non-drinkers had a 40% higher risk of contracting RA when compared to regular drinkers who had a 45% lower risk (Edwards, 2013). Jin et al (2013) explored dose-response association between alcohol consumption and the risk of rheumatoid arthritis examining eight prospective studies which included 195,029 participants and 1,878 RA cases. The research team reported that low to moderate alcohol consumption, regardless of the gender, yielded a preventive effect on RA development. Analysis of the dose response (amount of alcohol consumed) in relation to the reported relative risks (RR) concluded that the RR was 0.93 for 3 g/day of alcohol consumption, 0.86 for 9 g/day (which is equivalent to just under a small glass of wine), 0.88 for 12 g/day, 0.91 for 15 g/day, and 1.28 for 30 g/day (two medium glasses of wine daily). The overall results indicate that the most effective RA preventing dosage appears to around 9 grams of alcohol a day with the risks increasing for individuals consuming 30 grams or more daily. Edwards (2013) highlights further studies conducted by Sheffield University in 2010 which examined the alcohol consumption habits of 800 RA patients. Participants who consume alcohol up to 10 days a month reported that they experienced pain levels reduced by approximately 25 per cent, with more frequent drinkers reporting reduction levels of 30 per cent. Edwards also added that X-rays showed reduced damage to joints and reduced levels of swelling and inflammation amongst participants.

- **Osteoporosis**: Regular moderate alcohol consumption is directly linked with the delay and onset of osteoporosis in older women (Bainbridge et al, 2004; Williams et al, 2005). Recent studies published in the American journal Menopause conducted by researchers at Oregon State University Skeletal Biology Laboratory examined the effects of alcohol withdrawal on bone turnover in 40 early-postmenopausal women who consumed one to two drinks daily several times a week. These women were not receiving any hormone replacement therapies and had no history of osteoporosis-related fractures. The team discovered a significant increase in blood markers of bone turnover in women after they stopped drinking for short periods. Past studies have shown that moderate drinkers have a higher bone density than non-drinkers or heavy drinkers, but these have provided no explanation for the differences in bone density (Berg et al, 2008; Wosie et al, 2007). The US researchers reported that alcohol appears to behave similarly to oestrogen in that it reduces bone turnover. The team found evidence for increased bone turnover – a risk factor for osteoporotic fractures – during the two week period when the participants stopped drinking. Significantly the researchers reported that that less than a day after the women resumed their normal drinking patterns, their bone turnover rates returned to previous levels (Corvallis, 2014).

■ **Macular degeneration**: This is a major cause of blindness. A study by Obisesan et al (1998) at the University of Washington explored the drinking habits of their patients with failing eyesight. The team reported that moderate consumption of wine amongst these patients was clearly linked to the reduced probability of developing age-related macular degeneration. Stevens et al (2004) also reported a reduction in macular degeneration and pancreatic disease from alcohol consumption.

■ **Dementia**: Please refer to the 'Cognitive function' in section 5.2.

■ **Diabetes**: Please refer to 'Type two diabetes and metabolic syndrome' in Ssection 5.2.

5

Relaxation

The consumption of alcohol has complex effects on many parts of the brain and these are not fully understood. It is believed that the disinhibiting and empowering effects on social impulses of alcohol on the central nervous system aid relaxation. This experience was initially recorded by the Mass Observation studies of bars in Britain in the late 1930s (Mass Observation, 1943). Conger's seminal research in 1951 built on these observations and explored the relationship between alcohol use and tension; he concluded that the findings supported an element of the Tension Reduction Hypothesis (TRH) that is that alcohol mitigates aversive states, such as fear or tension (Conger, as cited in Thombs, 2006). Further studies by Langenbucher and Nathan (1990) support the validity of the TRH. The sensation of relaxation was also reported in numerous research studies from North America (Pernanen, 1991), Europe (Mäkelä and Simpura 1985; Mäkelä and Mustonen 1988) and Australia (Hall et al. 1992). In Saunders's 1998 survey amongst clinicians, it was reported that relaxation was one of the main psychological benefits of drinking. If individuals consumed alcohol after work or after a stressful event, they would be less likely to generate stress in or demands of others.

Sleep improvements

Stone (1980) suggests that low doses of alcohol (i.e. one 360 ml beer) appear to increase total sleep time and reduce awakening during the night. The sleep-promoting benefits of alcohol dissipate at moderate and higher doses of alcohol. Previous experience with alcohol also influences the extent to which it positively or negatively affects sleep. Roehrs et al (1999) found that in insomniacs, moderate doses of alcohol improved their sleep maintenance.

Social

Alcohol consumption in most cultures is associated with the wider elements of social activities; these can include consumption with family members, peer groups, friends, ceremonial occasions, or work colleagues. Alcohol consumption is predominantly a solitary activity is very few societies.

- **Sociability**: Heath (1995) maintains that the psychological dimensions of happiness and relaxation gained by consuming alcohol have been identified as a predominant reason for drinking by people from a range of cultures around the world. These benefits included alcohol's function as a social lubricant, increasing someone's courage in approaching a person of the opposite sex. In some circumstances it increased the truthfulness of people. Lowe (1994) states that sociability is the main reason for alcohol consumption by college students, young adults, and older people. Respondents in research studies also highlighted the need for individuals drinking in these situations to ensure their safe transport home and to protect themselves from unwanted attention.

- **Social networks**: Consuming alcohol tends to bring people together in a shared experience, usually in drinking environments (i.e. bars or nightclubs), and can form part of acceptance into a social grouping. The drinking establishments which facilitate these gatherings are referred to by Oldenburg (1997) as 'the third place' where individuals can gather and enjoy the company of others. Lyons et al (1995) studied social well-being in the UK and discovered that the social benefits of moderate alcohol consumption included discovery of common interests, identification of previously distant acquaintances as a good person, and widening of business contacts. The negative effects of consumption, which were linked with harmful drinking patterns, included a reduced social circle, which usually consisted exclusively of regular consumers.

- **Celebratory events**: Alcohol consumption forms a central component in celebrations and special events. Sporting teams will gather after the event to discuss and celebrate the outcome. Research studies which included clinicians highlighted that 90% of the respondents stated that it was a significant benefit, especially around New Year, after examinations and birthdays (Lowe, 1994).

- **Social credit**: Drinks enjoyed in hospitality establishments help to create a boundary between work and leisure time. In certain countries, like Japan, this activity helps junior colleagues to express themselves to their superiors in a fashion that would be unthinkable in the office. Heath (1998) reports that in these drinking situations, the reciprocal hospitality shown by people and companies, when they offer drinks and dinners to friends and employees, forms a 'social credit', in so far as the expectation is that the hospitality and drinks will be repaid in the near future, although as he adds this is neither inevitable nor obligatory.

Figure 5.4: Enjoying alcohol together in a commercial environment is a popular social activity.

Food intake

Gustatory / nutritional deficiencies: The taste and texture of alcohol depends on the context of the drinking occasion, for example the bitter flavour of a beer is favoured by individuals after undertaking heavy physical work; an aperitif cocktail enhances appetite before a meal; and the unique characteristics and benefits of wine consumption throughout the meal experience have been well documented. Alcoholic drinks are regarded in many cultures as an invaluable aid to digestion. A research study reported that 83% of respondents valued alcohol as a good complement to particular foods (Single et al 1998). These included beer with meat pies, salted peanuts and pizzas; red wine with certain cheese and meats; white wine with Asian food or cocktails with Mexican or Caribbean foods.

Figure 5.5: Alcohol paired with water and food.

B.R Murty of the Department of Biochemistry based at Coimbatore in India offers a cautionary note, stating that nutritional deficiencies are virtually inevitable consequences of harmful drinking patterns, not only because alcohol displaces food but also because alcohol directly interferes with the body's use of nutrients, making them ineffective even if they are present (Murty, 2004). Yeomans et al (2003) propose that 'alcohol is a complex component of the diet, and appears to have multiple effects on appetite. Failure to reduce food intake in response to energy from alcohol makes moderate alcohol consumption a risk factor for obesity'. Research conducted by McCrickerd et al (2014) also points to the beliefs about the consequences of consuming a beverage can affect the impact of its nutrients on appetite regulation and provide further evidence that a beverage's sensory characteristics can limit its satiating power.

5.5   The health benefits of alcoholic beverages

The following guide to some of the most popular drinks in the world, adapted from Carey (2010), gives an indication of their individual benefits. The health benefits of moderate alcohol consumption have not been generally endorsed by physicians over the years, for fear that heavy consumers may consider any message as a license to drink in excess. Remember that one of the reasons why moderate consumption offers benefits could be that, within safe limits, it helps alleviate to stress, which is one of the biggest contributors to ill health.

Red wine

The principle benefits of consuming red wine are that it fights cancer, raises good cholesterol, boosts brain power, helps insomnia and protects against hearing loss and tooth decay. Robinson (2006) maintains that the majority of these benefits of red wine are down to resveratrol, a plant chemical in the skins and pips of grapes. Robinson adds that the production and concentration of resveratrol is not equal among all the varieties of wine grapes. Differences in clones, rootstock, vitis species and climate conditions can affect the production of resveratrol, for example the US Muscadinia family of vines and the European vitis vinifera grapes, derived from the Burgundian Pinot family, have substantially higher amounts of resveratrol than others. Salicylate, an antioxidant in red wine, can help to prevent deafness by protecting the tiny hairs in the inner ear that are vital for hearing. American researchers discovered that chemicals in the seeds and skins of grapes blocked the ability of corrosive bacteria to bind with tooth enamel, protecting teeth from decay. Dr William McCrea of the Great Western Hospital in Swindon prescribed two glasses of Chilean Cabernet Sauvignon to 400 patients for two years and discovered that it reduced the risk of heart attack by 50% (Mitchell, 2003). Researchers at the University of Milan reported that consuming red wine regularly can also help individuals suffering from insomnia. They discovered that grape skins contain melatonin, a hormone which maintains the body's harmony and induces sleep. Neurological studies conducted at the Columbia University in New York showed that moderate red wine drinkers scored higher in their mental agility tests when compared to non-drinkers.

Beer

Dowden (2002) reports that the main benefits of beer are vitamins and minerals needed to protect the heart and bones, plus fibre. A pint of ale contains more than a quarter of an adult's recommended daily dose of vitamin B folate, which stops the build-up of homocysteine, which is directly linked to heart attacks. The antioxidant content of beer is equivalent to that of wine, but the specific antioxidants are different because the barley and hops used in the production of beer contain flavonoids different from those in the grapes (Denke, 2000). Beer also contains boron, a trace mineral needed for healthy bones. Research at the King's College and St. Thomas Hospital in London found that an individual's intake of the mineral silicon is directly linked to bone strength, and beer is one of the richest sources of silicon with a pint a day supplying 20% of the daily intake. Beer can also deliver one tenth of your body's fibre needs, and it contains niacin which also helps to release energy from food. Beer is high in magnesium and low in calcium which are crucial in avoiding the development of kidney stones; one pint of beer a day can help to reduce the risk of developing kidney stones by 40%. The issue of increasing waistlines and high calorie content has had a negative impact on beer consumption, especially amongst the female population. Epidemiologist Martin Bobak explored this area and compared 2,000 beer drinkers with non-drinkers. Interestingly, he reported that there was little difference in their waist-hip ratios. One final consideration which should also be noted is that non-alcoholic beers are just as good.

Whiskey and brandy

The main benefits of these distilled spirits is that they can protect you against cancer, heart attacks and blood clots. Both spirits contains antioxidants and plant compounds (derived from the wooden oak barrels they are matured in) which help to clear up damaging free radicals in the human body. A study conducted at the University of Bordeaux reported that a small measure of brandy delivers the same effect as aspirin in that it contributes towards averting heart attacks and blood clots. Whiskey and brandy also contains high levels of ellagic acid, which inhibits the growth of tumours caused by carcinogens and kills cancer cells without damaging healthy cells. The Hollings Cancer Institute at the University of South Carolina carried out clinical trials on 500 cervical cancer patients over nine years and found that ellagic acid stopped cancer cells dividing.

Cider

The main benefits include protection against high blood pressure and heart disease. According to researchers, cider contains the same level of antioxidants as red wine, green tea and blackcurrant juice, helping to fight disease. Dowden (2002) maintains that cider contains high levels of potassium which are needed for nerve function, muscle control and to regulate blood pressure. Low levels of potassium are linked to hypertension, diabetes, stroke and heart disease. Cider can also reduce your chance of developing iron-deficiency anaemia (with its attendant symptoms of fatigue, lack of concentration and dizziness). One pint of cider supplies one fifth of the recommended daily allowance of iron.

Guinness

Research shows that a pint of Guinness a day is good for your health. It may work as well as a low dose of aspirin to prevent heart attacks. Researchers at the University of Wisconsin discovered that when they gave Guinness to dogs with narrowed arteries, it worked as well as aspirin in preventing clots forming. They informed a convention of the American Heart Association in Orlando, Florida, that a pint taken at meal time had the best impact. They believe that antioxidant compounds in Guinness are responsible for the health benefits, as it decreases harmful cholesterol gathering on the artery walls. This has been attributed to antioxidants, like those in fruit and vegetables, which slow down the deposit of cholesterol. Guinness contains 190 calories per pint, so if you have lost weight due to illness, it can also help to build you back up.

Vodka

Analysis from one scientific study discovered that vodka had only one-six thousandth of the content of the toxic alcohol methanol when compared to bourbon. Vodka is good for a sensitive gut and avoiding a heavy hangover. Being so highly distilled means that it may be deemed suitable (in small amounts) for people on sugar-free, yeast-free diets designed to tackle conditions such as thrush, candida and irritable bowel syndrome. According to the USDA Nutrient Data Laboratory, it contains only 64 calories per ounce and is totally free of carbohydrates which are perfect for anyone trying to lose weight or those individuals following a low-carb diet (USDA, 2004).

White wine

White wine lowers cholesterol, benefits lungs and acts as an anti-inflammatory. Daglia et al (2007) suggests that it is an effective antibacterial agents against strains of Streptococcus. The grape flesh used in white wine contains the chemicals tyrosol and hydroxytyrosol, which lower artery clogging LDL cholesterol. A paper in the October 2008 issue of *Cancer Epidemiology, Biomarkers and Prevention* reported that moderate consumption (one to two glasses taken daily) may decrease the risk of lung cancer in men (ACCR, 2008), because its antioxidants protect against the molecules that damage lung tissue. Research conducted by the University of Milan reported that white wine contains caffeic acid, which can help to partially suppress inflammation and ease the pain encountered by individuals suffering with rheumatoid arthritis. Recent studies conducted by the University Of Connecticut School Of Medicine, the University of Milan and several other research institutes across Italy reported in the *American Chemical Society Journal of Agricultural & Food Chemistry*, challenges the idea that red wine is more heart-healthy than white wine. Scientists say they have found evidence that the pulp of grapes appears just as heart-healthy in laboratory experiments as the skin.

Conclusion

Small quantitiies of alcohol consumed regularly and in line with health guidelines confer many benefits and protective effects, especially for middle-aged men, as alcohol can assist the heart and circulatory system and reduce the build-up of cholesterol in blood vessels. This can reduce heart attacks and strokes. For older women, moderate consumption can prevent weakening of the bones (osteoporosis) and for some assist in reducing some types of diabetes. Moderate alcohol consumption can also alleviate stress and increase happiness, relaxation, sleep and food intake. It can contribute to the quality of life and general well-being, helping to increase awareness levels and improve sociability. For people who abuse alcohol or practice harmful drinking patterns, the long term health risks can be chronic, including brain damage, liver disease, coronary and vascular disease and various types of cancers. When alcohol is consumed with prescription medications or illegal drugs, it can either reduce their intended effect or deliver a lethal dose. The scientific world and drinks industry must work together to deliver more rigorous research to move this debate to the middle ground, where moderate alcohol consumption patterns can prevail, thereby enhancing the health status of everyone.

Web resources

Alcohol Concern (UK)
   www.alcoholconcern.org.uk

Alcohol Action (Ireland)
   alcoholireland.ie/facts/health-and-alcohol/

Centre for disease control and prevention (US)
   www.cdc.gov/alcohol/fact-sheets/alcohol-use.htm

The link between stress and alcohol
   pubs.niaaa.nih.gov/publications/AA85/AA85.htm

Health Behaviour in School-aged Children (EU)
   www.hbsc.org

Health Education Board (Scotland)
   www.healthscotland.com

Health Promotion Division (Wales)
   www.hpw.wales.gov.uk

Institute of Occupational Safety & Health (UK)
   www.iosh.co.uk

6 Alcohol and the Workplace

Aims and learning outcomes

This chapter introduces the key elements involved in the recognition of harmful drinking patterns in the workplace. It aims to create awareness amongst management and employers regarding their legal and moral responsibilities, which includes setting out specific workplace policies and assisting employees suffering from alcohol addiction problems to receive the necessary treatment and support. After reading this chapter you should be able to:

■ Describe alcohol's role in the workplace from the 17th century up to the modern era.

■ Explain the unique challenges which alcohol present in the hospitality, tourism and retail workplaces.

■ Determine the role and responsibilities of managers and employers in the workplace in relation to intervention, treatment and assistance programmes for employees who abuse or misuse alcohol.

■ Outline the rationale for adoption by employers of alcohol and drug policies for the workplace, and describe the key elements involved in creating them.

■ Describe the most common illegal drugs and identify the symptoms which indicate their use in the workplace environment.

6.0 Introduction

Alcohol is the single most used and abused drug in the workplace. The OPM (2014) estimate that the cost to industry in the U.S. alone ranges from 33 to 68 billion dollars annually. This cost can manifest itself in many ways, including lost productivity, increased health care costs, absenteeism, workplace accidents, and fatalities. This chapter will outline the significant factors involved in the recognition of alcohol addictive problems and their subsequent health effects in the workplace. It is aimed at fostering a better awareness amongst supervisors, managers, and human resource personnel of their respective roles and responsibilities surrounding the issues of alcohol in the workplace. It is not intended to cover all aspects of alcoholism and alcohol abuse, but to give you enough information to understand and recognize the problems and know where to go to get assistance for colleagues. We also highlight how an employee, identified as having a problem or if they disclose that they are suffering from an alcohol addiction, should be treated by the management and work colleagues. It also addresses the appropriate treatment which must be offered at an early stage, reminding us that an employee cannot be in the workplace under the influence of alcohol or drugs. Whilst this chapter is primarily aimed at the hospitality, tourism and retail industries, it may be of benefit to other public and private sector organisations and private industries who wish to set out their own policies for alcohol in the workplace.

6.1   The workplace environment

Gamella (1995) argues that throughout history alcohol has been an integral part of the workplace. Spanish workers drank a small glass of aguardiente in the morning to prepare them for work; sailors in the British Royal navy in the 17th century were given a pint of dilute rum a day, plus a gallon of beer and a double ration of rum before battle. Brewery and distillery workers received daily allowances of their alcoholic products. *Brewery Workers* (2000) reports that amongst the union demands for better conditions in the late 1900s was the inclusion of free beer for the employees. In those days in many places around the world employers used alcohol in lieu of wages especially when they were short of cash (Scully, 1992), but in more recent years this practice was outlawed by the International Labour Organization (ILO, 1949). The nature of the workplace in the 1800s and 1900s changed, with the Industrial Revolution and the introduction of machinery, which increased the possibility of accidents and harm brought about though alcohol consumption. Heath (2000) contends that alcohol in this period became part of the private realm, often symbolizing the transition between work and leisure time. The middle 20th century brought further changes to the attitudes to alcohol in the workplace. Alcohol was viewed as a disease which required intervention schemes and approaches like the employee assistance programmes. Sloan et al (2000) add that employers' legal liability for the health and safety of their employees at work in many countries also brought about significant changes to restrict alcohol in the workplace environment. In the 21st century there are still particular professions and practices with high occurrences of alcohol-related problems. These problems can include the following:

- **Accidents and injuries:** in workplaces where heavy machinery is involved (Frone, 2009).

- **Reduced safety, stressful climate and poor relations in the workplace:** alcohol abuse by some can result in low morale, higher absenteeism, less productivity amongst the whole staff (drinkers and non-drinkers) and poor workplace safety (Frone, 2008).

- **Exhaustion, burnout and poor workplace conditions:** which can include long working hours, can lead to alcohol abuse (Ahola et al, 2006)

- **Specific occupational challenges:** mortality rates appear to be higher where alcohol is regularly available, for example seafarers, bar owners, restaurant and bar staff, and drinks companies (Romeri et al, 2007).

Alcohol consumption in the workplace is related to social norms (i.e. expectations of the local or the company culture) during work hours or break times. Frone and Brown (2010) propose that these norms are either *injunctive* (which incorporates the degree to which other colleagues would approve of working while intoxicated) or *descriptive* (which covers the frequency and amount of alcohol consumed by colleagues before or during work). Both norms have been shown to predict alcohol consumption and impairment at work.

6.2   The unique challenges of the hospitality, tourism and retail workplace

The hospitality, tourism and retail industries encompasses a wide range of work environments where alcohol is widely available and viewed positively. Leigh et al (1993) report that as a consequence of this availability, the figures of liver cirrhosis mortality and other alcohol problems are higher in these industries when compared to many other industries and professions. Workplace policies aimed at reducing consumption amongst employees in these industries have been in operation since the 1920s; Kjaerheim et al (1995) highlight that the Hotels Association of British Columbia in Canada prohibited its beer parlour members from drinking on the job. Kjaerheim (1995) adds that a recent hotel and restaurant research study in Norway noted that alcohol consumption amongst these workers was restricted to celebrations and special events. Sloan et al (2000) remind us that the legal liability towards customers allowed to engage in harm-related activities due to intoxication has been a major influence which encouraged these industries to adopt policies for their respective workplaces.

The introduction of training programmes for the responsible sale, marketing and serving of alcohol which help employees to recognise potentially harmful consumption patterns among their customers have been a great success. The International Centre for Alcohol Policies (2002) maintains that these training programmes also cover standard serving practices, information regarding alternative beverages, how to deal with intoxicated customers and monitoring techniques to ensure crowd control. ICAP (2002) also report that 15% of countries around the world use the responsible sale and serving of alcohol training programmes as a component of their national or local policies for alcohol. They add that a series of initiatives are in operation which are run by the hospitality, tourism and retail industries themselves or support groups which surround these industries. For a further discussion and details regarding these programmes please refer to Chapter 9.

6.3   Absenteeism and productivity loss

Abuse and misuse of alcohol pose a major threat and incur significant costs to the workplace, fundamentally as a result of lost productivity (Rehm et al 2006; Saar, 2009). These costs, which include those arising from accidents and injuries, absenteeism and alcohol associated deaths, were calculated to be in the region of €59 billion in the EU for 2003 (Anderson & Baumberg, 2006) and $134 billion in the US for 1998 (Harwood, 2000). The majority of these arise from alcohol consumption outside the workplace (i.e. after work or at lunchtime), and moderate drinkers, who sometimes consume excessively, are directly responsible for a large amount of productivity losses from absenteeism (Salonsalmi et al, 2009). Abuse and misuse of alcohol will normally result in temporary illness (i.e. severe hangovers) which subsequently leads to employees taking off half or full days (Pidd et al, 2008). The immediate effect of this absenteeism is not only experienced by companies but also by their employees, who as Dale and Livingston (2010) argue, have to take on additional work to compensate for absent colleagues.

Employees who report to work following a heavy drinking episode may be less productive than usual, an effect sometimes referred to as *presenteeism*, categorized as below par performances in the workplace. This is believed to cost industry and organizations a lot more in losses when compared to the losses from absenteeism (Goetzel et al, 2004). Suffering from the effects of an alcohol hangover usually results in lower output, poor quality of work, increased conflict, possible injuries and falling asleep (Ames et al, 2000). Cook (1997) reminds us that the quality of work in some tasks will be affected for a while after the alcohol has been eliminated from the employee's body.

6.4 Intoxication in the workplace – intervention and treatment

The majority of public and private employer organizations, which include all the industries across the wider hospitality, tourism and retail sector, will rightly argue that an employee's decision to drink is that individual's personal business. However, when their employees' use or abuse of alcohol interferes with their ability to perform their duties, or when their conduct is unacceptable, employers have a legal and moral obligation to take action.

The role of managers and supervisors

Managers and or supervisors have an important role in dealing with alcohol problems in the workplace. Along with other team members, they have the daily responsibility to actively monitor the workplace and performance of employees, especially if the employee is required to perform safety sensitive duties, for example using heavy equipment, patient care, or driving vehicles. The early recognition of alcohol problems is complex, and managers and supervisors need training and support to recognise these problems and to help them to deal with them effectively.

It is not for managers and supervisors to diagnose alcoholism in their colleagues, but their responsibilities do include assigning, monitoring, reviewing and appraising workplace standards and performance, and taking the necessary corrective and disciplinary actions when problems do arise. They are also responsible for setting appropriate workplace schedules, approving or disapproving leave requests and, crucially, referring colleagues to the company employee assistance programme when appropriate. In some circumstances the employee might admit to being an alcoholic, or the problem is self-evident, for example, when a colleague may become intoxicated while on duty. The manager's role will include referring their colleague to the EAP and in some situations taking the appropriate disciplinary action. Looking after a colleague who suffers from alcoholism is challenging, and the best method to adopt is to initially inform the individual of the gravity of their condition (e.g. likely loss of job) and its effect on their workplace performance and conduct. Some of the initial signs of alcohol abuse in the workplace would include:

- **Workplace relationships:** the individual could be short-tempered, engage in aggressive behaviour which causes conflict, argumentative (Ames et al, 2000) particularly after the weekends or in the mornings, have poor relations with colleagues, and/or prefer to be alone. Other symptoms can include financial problems (the individual borrows money from colleagues and could be pursued by credit companies at work).

6

- **Problems with performance:** the quality and detail of their work drops (incomplete or imperfect reports, poor presentation, missed submission dates) and the employee might initially try to hide or cover these problems, for example excuses for missed deadlines (Mangione et al, 1999)

- **Leave and attendance:** the individual is constantly missing from their workplace area or station without permission, and also appears to be afflicted by the absence immediately before or after weekends, higher than normal use of sick leave or unplanned absences due to 'emergencies', constant tardiness, and high ratio of unauthorized or unexplained absences.

- **Workplace behaviour:** These signs can include sleeping on duty, excessive use of mouthwash or breath mints, smell of alcohol on the breath, bloodshot eyes, mood and behavioural alterations – inappropriate loud conversation and laughter, hand tremors and unsteady on their feet or staggering (OPM, 2014)

Some of the other signs will include accidents and unusual incidents, fluctuating work performance, unkempt appearance, excessive sweating and confusion or drowsiness (WHB, 2003).

What managers and supervisors should not do

Managers and supervisors might believe that they are being supportive by not reporting individuals who are regularly intoxicated in the workplace, but this continues to support the person's intoxicated behaviour and does not hold them responsible for their actions. This lack of accountability can have a disastrous effect on the individual's other colleagues' morale and workplace efficiency. Some other examples of management or supervisory behaviour which is counterproductive to the overall well-being of the individual include:

- Allocating the employee's work to fellow colleagues
- Adjusting the employee's work schedule, (i.e. facilitating the employee to continually come in late and to make up the hours later in the day or during the week).
- Covering up for their behaviour
- Failing to refer the employee to the EAP
- Attempting to counsel the employee on their own
- Allowing spouses or other family members to inform the company about their absence
- Making excuses for the employee's behaviour or performance
- Supplying them with loans of money
  (OPM, 2014)

Employee Assistance Programme (EAP)

EAPs are developed to cope with various kinds of problems which arise in and outside the workplace for the employee. They help to provide short-term counselling, initial assessment and sometimes referral of employees with financial, marital, health, personal or alcohol and drug abuse problems. The service is confidential and the relevant programmes are normally operated by qualified external counsellors, but sometimes may be run in-house with EAP agency personnel. The European Alcohol and Health Forum (2011) maintain that the privacy laws which protect information about employee use of EAPs make it hard to perform a rigorous evaluation of a particular EAP approach, especially in relation to drinking patterns, which the International Labour Office (2009) suggest could be collected through questionnaires. Irrespective of the method, an EAP counsellor will usually meet up with the employee to assess or diagnose the problem, and, if necessary, refer the employee to a treatment programme or resource (see *Treatment approaches*, below). With the permission of the employee, the EAP counsellor will keep the employer informed as to the nature of the problem, what type of treatment may be needed, and the progress of the employee in treatment.

Before releasing this information to a manager, or anyone, the counsellor would need a signed release from the employee, which would state what information may be released and to whom. The EAP counsellor will monitor the employee's progress and provide follow-up counselling if required. Sometimes, employees will contact the EAP on their own. In other cases, employees will be referred by a manager who has noted a decline in their conduct, attendance, or performance and/or seen actual evidence of alcohol use or impairment at work.

Alcohol testing

Most industries and organizations don't have legal mandates to carry out alcohol testing in the workplace, and normally it is done voluntarily. Testing is usually done via a breathalyser, but can also be done by taking blood or saliva samples. The breathalyser is most favoured because it tends not to encroach on the individual's privacy and it is the method used most widely by the police. Individuals involved in motor vehicle or traffic offenses, including serious accidents, are usually tested using this method. Local governments offer guidelines regarding testing the alcohol consumption for particular groups (e.g. commercial drivers or aviation related jobs). These usually require employers to carry out random mandatory alcohol testing using breathalysers. A company could carry out its own voluntary alcohol testing, especially in circumstances where an employee is suspected of being under the influence but denies it. In this circumstance a test can be administered, with the employee's permission, and if intoxication is detected the company could use the results as a basis for disciplinary action or referral to their EAP for treatment programmes.

Figure 6.1: Use of the breathalyser in the workplace (Wikipedia Creative Commons, 2014).

The intervention technique

Intervention usually consists around scheduling a session with the employee plus a number of people significant in their life (with the consent of the employee). These people could include children, their spouse, a member of the clergy, a co-worker or other significant friend. The meeting and subsequent intervention session would be led by a trained professional, for example an EAP counsellor. It involves having everyone present directly tell the employee how their alcohol abuse or misuse has affected their lives and what the consequences of that employee's drinking have been. If the intervention is effective, this can be a very powerful tool to counter denial and may help the employee consider treatment. It is extremely important that such an intervention be led by a trained professional and not by a lay person, because it can be a very emotional and powerful event and, if not conducted properly, may very likely backfire. Supervisors should contact an agency EAP counsellor for more information about the intervention technique.

Treatment approaches

An alcohol abuser rarely stops consuming alcohol or stays sober for long periods without outside help and some kind of pressure. This pressure could come from friends, health care workers, family, judicial authorities, or their boss. Alcohol abusers do not initially want to get help or go into treatment, but they will normally consider taking treatment when faced with some kind of serious threat such as loss of their job or possible jail. Personal acceptance of the problem by the individual is crucial for the treatment to be successful, and this is where the employer is very powerful. When the employee is informed through the official channels, of disciplinary action and referral to the EAP for an appropriate treatment programme, the reality and gravity of their situation becomes apparent and they usually take responsibility for their treatment.

There are various kinds of treatment programmes for alcoholism, which include the following:

- **Detoxification:** a process which can last between two to seven days whereby the alcoholic undergoes a supervised withdrawal. The body can begin to recover from the toxic effects of alcohol (if supervised in a medical setting) and the patient can become sober.

- **Alcoholics Anonymous (AA):** the 12-Step programme involves a spiritual component (not affiliated with any particular religion) and a supportive group of fellow alcoholics to provide a network for total abstinence from alcohol. Some individuals find approaches other than AA to be more useful in their treatment (e.g. Rational Recovery group).

- **In-patient treatment:** this consists of a one to six week formal, residential programme sometimes connected to a local hospitality, which incorporates educational support and medical treatments, consisting of nutrition, group therapy sessions, drug and alcohol testing to ensure compliance with the programme. These programmes can be costly and will usually include day release elements for the patient.

- **Outpatient treatment:** this consists of counselling and treatment on a daily or weekly basis between one month to a year in an office or clinic setting. The treatment is often a follow-up to an in-patient or detox programme.

(adapted from OPM, 2014).

6.5   Policy development

Rationale for employees and employers

Alcohol misuse is the number one cause of fatalities among the 25 to 60 year olds (ICAP, 2014). This group accounts for most of the general working population and it is for this reason that the workplace has been identified as an ideal setting to promote health and well-being. For workers, these abuses can result in deteriorating health, family and relationship problems, injury, disciplinary action and other work related problems. For employers these abuses can lead to safety problems affecting the business, the workforce and the public at large (WHB, 2003), and reducing them will result in a reduction in sickness and occupational injuries, improved staff relations, a healthier workforce and an improved corporate image (Modell & Mountz, 1990). You should consult Chapter 10, *Policy Making for Alcohol: Towards a Combined Approach*, for more on the inter-related issues involved in this area.

Government policies

Governments across the world are charged with the responsibility of ensuring that the safety and productivity of their workforce is protected from the challenge of alcohol consumption in the workplace. In the United States, workplaces are specifically required to adopt alcohol polices, and legislation under the Occupational Safety and Health Administration (1970) sets out the official requirements for safe working environments and provides guidance to employers on how to maintain a workplace free of alcohol and substance abuse. This requirement is similar in the UK and France. Both countries do not prohibit alcohol consumption in the workplace but do contain specific provisions against intoxication (European Alcohol and Health Forum, 2011).

Employer policies

Zacharatos et al (2005) maintains that employer involvement makes perfect sense, due to the health and general problems created by alcohol abuse in the workplace. From an international context, general guidelines from the International Labour Office for employers to assist them in dealing with alcohol related problems have been in place since 1996. These encourage employers to address health issues by adopting preventative and support systems for employees with drink problems. Employers are normally allowed to formulate their own policies regarding alcohol consumption in the workplace. For this reason policies will differ, but the majority of policy guidelines will contain specific interventions for vulnerable professions (e.g. bartenders, night shift workers, heavy machinery workers). The vulnerable professions also include jobs with a high degree of repetitive tasks or, as Frone and Brown (2010) state, high levels of stress or boredom, and clearly need strong alcohol policies. Major industry employers will also have intervention systems which direct employees through EAPs to dedicated support providers. These interventions for drink problems can eventually lead to improved productivity and represented a cost savings to employers (Osilla et al, 2010).

Developing an alcohol policy for the workplace

The key elements of a policy should include a framework to address alcohol issues in a supportive way while complying with responsibilities in relation to health and safety. The policy should also clearly outline how the company intends to deal with drug and alcohol issues in the workplace. The wording of the policy is very important – it should be clear and easy to understand. It should be communicated in a supportive way, while clearly detailing procedures. It should apply to all employees and staff grades, and address confidentiality issues. Crucially the policy should be monitored and reviewed at intervals. When you are designing and drafting the policy, the process is very importance. Consultation and negotiation between all the stakeholders involved is vital, and this consultation should also include senior managers, the human resources and occupational departments, health and safety advisors, employee representatives, and the unions. You should consider involving external agencies who can directly support the development of the policy, and these include health and enterprise agencies, community groups, local drug and alcohol services and the police.

Drafting the policy – stages of development

The process for drafting the policy should take as long as is necessary to fully consult with all the stakeholders and should usually have the following stages:

1 **Set up a working group**. The group should be representative of the workplace and include management, union and employee representatives.

2 **What is currently in place?** Review the existing policies and local legislation; review the current practices and finally review the required staff training, supports and resources.

3 **Assess your needs**. Ask yourself what are the real needs regarding alcohol and drug use in your workplace? You can now establish your priorities, set a timescale and consider the resource implications.

4 **Draft the policy or amend the current policy**. The issues to be discussed include education, intervention, training and staff development; review other national and international work done in this area.

5 **Consultation**. Circulate the draft documents to all the stakeholders and encourage feedback.

6 **Finalise**. Make the appropriate amendments and produce the final policy document.

7 **Dissemination**. How you will communicate it throughout your workplace?

8 **Implementation**. The organisation as a whole needs to become familiar with the policy and begin to use it.

9 **Monitoring and evaluation**. Organisations should continuously monitor, evaluate and update their policies so that they can continue to be used most effectively.

10 **Review**. Review the policy on a timely basis or in the light of new developments.

(WHB, 2003).

Figure 6.2: Alcohol and drug policy – sample workplace poster (MMC, 2014)

6.6   Alcohol and drug policy – sample and best practices

To help you in getting started there are many resources available on the Internet which offer samples of alcohol and drug policy documents relevant to different regions and countries. Given below is an example of one which was designed as a worksheet to assist working groups in developing a policy to meet the needs of their organisation. Questions have been included to create discussion and to highlight areas that will need to be addressed. While the policy relates to drugs and alcohol it is not intended to focus on drug-related issues within the workplace. If your organisation has a drug-related concern you should contact the local services or government agency in your area.

Workplace drug and alcohol policy worksheet

(*) *This symbol highlights the sections in which the staff members may adapt elements of the policy or add their company name. Any changes to your drug and alcohol policy should ideally emerge from active discussion and mutual agreement by all the stakeholders involved.*

Introduction: (* *company name*) acknowledges that its employees are its most significant resource and is therefore dedicated to providing a safe and secure workplace for all its employees. The consumption of drugs and alcohol can alter the performance, concentration and the co-ordination of employees, resulting in sickness, serious accidents and reduced productivity.

Section A: Fundamentals and objectives of this policy

(*company name*) will encourage a healthy environment for all of its employees by:

- advancing the adoption of a healthy lifestyle, free of drug and alcohol related problems

- increasing awareness levels amongst its employees regarding the risks of drugs and alcohol

- early identification of employees at risk or experiencing alcohol and drug related problems

- reducing problems at work arising from the effects of drugs and alcohol

- providing access to professional advice and treatment services for staff members who are experiencing the detrimental effects of drug and alcohol misuse

- **(*)** *possible additions*

Policy Statement: This policy is aimed at minimising the effects of drugs and alcohol on employees.

*Companies should also consider the following factors and incorporate them into their policy statement as appropriate: the number of hours their employees should be free of the effects of alcohol and or drugs before duty, how the company deals with alcohol and or drugs use/misuse and finally of off-site work-related activities (i.e. social events, training days).

Section B: Intervention and assistance

Management and supervisors share a common responsibility to recognise colleagues experiencing drug and alcohol related problems. This can be problematic and challenging because of the complexities and difficulties involved. All managers, supervisors and charge hands will be given access to professional training and dedicated support to carry out their duties effectively. Staff members are therefore actively encouraged to seek assistance on a voluntary basis. In this regard (* *company name*) will:

1   Allocate access to professional services, including training for staff in this regard

2   (*) *possible additions*

Problem identification: Close observation by management and supervisors of colleagues' actions and behaviour can help with early identification of alcohol or drug related problems. These problems are challenging and can re-occur on a regular basis. When it is clear that a problem exists, management will inform the employee in question and offer access to the appropriate support services (i.e. counselling). The management team will not delve into the more private issues which surround the problem, but leave these to the counselling service. The management team will bear in mind the on-going safety of the employee experiencing the problem, and of their colleagues while carrying out their duties in the workplace. If appropriate, their duties and responsibilities will be varied accordingly.

Further actions to be followed by management: Management will ensure that these employee records are secured in a private area and that the documentation is kept anonymous until the problem is fully investigated and confirmed.

(* *It is also important to establish protocols and standards to govern the access and confidentiality which surrounds these employees*.)

The following statements will be entered into the employee handbook:

(* *Company name*) will endeavour to ensure that any employee who seeks help will be treated with discretion and in confidence. If work-related problems persist, the staff member may be referred to support services with their agreement. Employees may also seek help from other sources if they prefer.

(* *Company name*) advises all employee who feel that they have an alcohol or drug related problem that they may approach the appropriate treatment services for support and assistance. (* *Company name*) assures that the procedures as agreed and set out in employee and company manuals shall apply to such contacts.

* *If an employee decides to seek their own treatment privately, you might have to consider how as the business will ensure that it receives updates about their progress with the relevant treatment service. It is the employee's responsibility to source and accept the support of professional services and failure to seek the necessary support could result in disciplinary action by the company or limit the employee opportunity to gain promotion in the future. Leave arrangements to attend treatment support services and workplace rights (after submission of medical documentation) for employee suffering with alcohol and drug related problems should be treated in a similar fashion to the general ill-health issues experienced by all employees. Your company will need to decide if the employee's position can be covered internally and for what period, plus the arrangements for employee payment during the intended leave period. It is possible that after treatment, or lack of engagement, the employee's workplace actions and performance have not improved. If this scenario develops, the employee must be afforded the same due process and disciplinary actions offered to their colleagues.*

Management will monitor the employee's progress and in agreement with the individual/s in question refer them to the appropriate support and treatment services. Reoccurrences will be dealt with in a similar fashion to the process already highlighted above.

Section C: Promoting alcohol and drug awareness in the workplace

(* *Company name*) will actively promote a sensible and healthy approach to drugs and alcohol by providing training and educational opportunities to all its employees to promote awareness and to increase the knowledge of the risks linked to alcohol and drug misuse; to encourage the consumption of alcohol in a responsible fashion; and to increase awareness of the early signs of alcohol and drug dependency. This will be done through educational programmes for all staff members and especially new employees, providing access to appropriate documentation, and encouraging special awareness events which highlight these problems in your company.

* The management should also take the opportunity to add further additions to its awareness programmes and procedures and to take all other opportunities to promote the policy (i.e. during interviews or inclusions in future job descriptions).

Section D: Co-ordination of the alcohol and drug policy

Establishing and finally implementing a good and meaningful alcohol and drug policy is the collective responsibility of all employees of (** Company name*). The overall responsibility and co-ordination lies with (** add in the named person or post here*). To ensure that this policy works in an efficient manner, managers, representatives from the relevant trade unions, human resources and supervisory personnel will be afforded and allocated special responsibilities and duties with regard to the policy. Some of these duties will include dissemination of relevant up to date information to employees, providing employees with support throughout their treatment period, reviewing and updating the policy and maintaining a thorough knowledge of all elements of the policy.

* The management should also take the opportunity to add further additions to the co-ordination of the policy. The final issue to consider is to set the review and implementation dates.

6

The following text should be displayed within the policy:

The alcohol and drug policy for (*Company name*) will come into effect on (*fill in the appropriate date here*)

This policy will be subject to review commencing on   (*fill in the appropriate date here*).

(adapted from WHB, 2003)

The challenges and limitations of workplace policies and interventions

Numerous studies have highlighted the positive impacts of policies and strategic interventions aimed at reducing alcohol problems in the workplace, however some researchers maintain that the majority of these programmes have not been rigorously tested, and that further research is required to investigate how to make workplace programmes more effective (Cook et al 1996; Spicer & Miller, 2005; Sieck & Heirich, 2010). Companies that employ a large number of freelancers, casual or part-time workers, plus small and medium sized companies, may not have the resources to develop good policies which provide interventions and treatment for their employees (ILO, 2002).

Case example: Alcohol polices in the workplace

AKAN – Norway

The AKAN organisation has been in operation since 1963. It is a coalition of trade unions, business interests and government that aims to prevent workplace drug and alcohol problems in Norway. It also ensures that employees with problems get help. AKAN helps companies to devise alcohol policies and trains managers to handle employees with difficulties. It is involved in over 1,250 Norwegian companies.

6.7   Illegal drugs in the workplace

Maintaining a drug free workplace is not an easy task for establishments, when the majority of illegal drug taking occurs in the toilet cubicles which are typically the most private places in the premises. But clearly employers and their staff have a responsibility in this area and if they do not take the proper preventative measures, the business and its trading licence could be at risk (Murphy, 2011).

Assistance and advice

The local police appreciate it is a tough issue for establishments to deal with, and usually like a partnership approach to address the problem. One police officer stated to me that their aim was 'to inform the establishment about approaches to actively try and stop it.' He added they suggest putting oil on flat surfaces to make it more difficult to snort drugs off them. Apparently some hospitality managers have been known to use WD40 on the flat surfaces in their toilets to deter users – but this is not recommended because of the potential harm it could cause. Interestingly the majority of establishments never test their own premises for drug usage, though this may be readily done. You can, for example, buy swab cloths, to test for traces of cocaine on surfaces. If the cloth turns blue, it's a positive test.

Table 6.1: Most common illegal drugs to look for in the workplace. (Adapted from BBPA, 2011)

Most common illegal drugs used in the workplace				
Depressants: These drugs affect concentration and coordination, and slow down a person's ability to respond to unexpected situations. In small quantities depressants can cause a person to feel more relaxed. In larger quantities they can cause unconsciousness, vomiting and death. The major types include; alcohol, cannabis, barbiturates, GHB (Gamma-hydroxybutrate), opiates and opioids (heroin, morphine, codeine, methadone, pethidine) and some solvents and inhalants.				
Name	**Form and how it is taken**	**Effects**	**Signs to look for**	**Exposure to harm**
Cannabis also called blow, hash, pot, draw, ganja, bush, tac, tarry, grass, skunk, dope, spliff, weed and marijuana.	Resin or herbal forms. Smoked in hand rolled cigarettes known as joints, reefers, doobies and spiffs. Resin can be eaten	Produces a relaxed sense of wellbeing, making the individual more talkative and less inhibited.	Initial signs are a distinctive smoke odour which is aromatic, and sweet. Torn beer mats or foam upholstery used to make filters.	Some individuals will experience sickness known as a 'whitey'. Impaired co-ordination and judgment, affects short-term memory
Gamma-hydroxybutrate also referred to as GBH, Gabba and liquid gold.	GHB comes in small bottles or capsules and is both odourless and colourless.	Small doses cause increased friendliness; larger doses cause sleepiness, stiffness, loss of co-ordination & vision.	A sudden appearance of drunkenness despite minimal drinks consumed by the individual.	Convulsions and breathing problems. This drug is often associated with drug assisted sexual assault.
Heroin also referred to as gear, H, smack, horse, skag, junk, brown, dragon, china white, kit, toot, burn.	Powder, varies in colour from brown to white. Injected, sniffed or smoked through a 'tooter' on foil or in a tobacco-based joint	Causes euphoria, drowsiness, dehydration and lack of appetite. Users feel tremors, cramps and severe sweating when unable to obtain another 'fix'.	Burnt tin foil, burnt spoons. Users normally heat a spoon to turn the powder into liquid which is drawn up into a syringe.	When searching users, great care must be taken as used needles can spread diseases such as hepatitis or HIV/ AIDS.
Stimulants: these drugs speed up the brain's activity. As a result, a person who takes a stimulant may feel more awake, alert or confident. Stimulants increase heart rate, body temperature and blood pressure. Mild stimulants include caffeine, nicotine, and ephedrine (used in medicines for bronchitis, hay fever and asthma). Stronger stimulants include amphetamines (speed, crystal meth, ice), cocaine and ecstasy. Strong stimulants can mask some of the effects of depressant drugs such as alcohol.				
Name	Form and how it is taken	Effects	Signs to look for	Exposure to harm
Amphetamines Also referred to as speed, uppers, sulph, base or whiz.	Tablet, capsules or powder form or a as a wet putty-like substance known as base. Generally white or pale grey.	Increased alertness, an abundance of energy and confidence.	Confusion, rapid speech, enlarged pupils.	Effects increased by alcohol. Increased blood pressure.
Cocaine also referred to as coke, charlie, C, snow, dust or posh.	White powder which is grainy and can appear slightly shiny. Taken by snorting more rarely injected.	Exhilaration, strength, alertness, strong sense of self importance.	Traces on top of toilet cisterns or toilet roll holders. Payment with tightly rolled bank notes. Runny nose, sniffing.	Euphoria but sometimes causes anxiety; this drug numbs pain, fearless feeling even after injury and restraining.

6

Ecstasy also referred to E's, mitsubishi, 69's or ferrari.	Tablet, capsule or powder. Tablets have logos and are usually swallowed varying in shape, size and colour.	Abundance of energy and confidence, increased sociability, greater colour perception, loss of co-ordination and increased thirst	Dilated pupils. Excessive energy, dancing, euphoria, large demand for non-alcoholic beverages (dance venue drug).	Increased blood pressure and body temperature with risk of heart failure and liver damage. Hyperactivity, anxiety and paranoid behaviour.

Hallucinogens: these drugs affect the way people see, or imagine they see and because the effects of hallucinogens can vary a great deal it's impossible to predict how they will affect a particular person at a particular time. Types of hallucinogen drugs include (datura, ketamine, LSD (lysergic acid diethylamide), magic mushrooms, mescaline (peyote cactus), PCP, cannabis and ecstasy.

Name	Form and how it is taken	Effects	Signs to look for	Exposure to harm
Crack also referred to as stone, rock, base or crystal.	Quarter inch yellowish rocky lumps sold in medicine bottles or in paper and foil wraps, which are usually smoked on home-made pipes or heated on foil.	Produces a rush of euphoria, a loss of self-control and often increased aggression, followed by a rapid depression.	Users can be very aggressive and unpredictable making them difficult to deal with.	Hallucinations will result in feelings of super human strength.
Ketamine also referred to as K, special K or Ket.	A white powder that can also be sold as a tablet or as a liquid.	Increased sociability, larger doses cause sleepiness, muscle stiffness, loss of coordination and vision.	Individuals under the influence will suddenly appear drunk despite having only consumed 1-2 alcoholic drinks.	Can cause vision problems hallucinations, mixed with alcohol may cause heart failure.
LSD also referred to as acid, tabs.	Paper squares with various designs, gelatine, microdots, less commonly found in tablet form.	Incoherence.	Erratic and unpredictable behaviour.	Hallucinations.

Maintaining a drug free workplace – some best practice procedures for managers

- Clean and sanitise toilets and surroundings on a regular basis.
- Put up notices informing that checks are carried out regularly in your bar toilets and general bar area and there is zero tolerance of drug use.
- Regularly inspect toilets for illegal activity; use portable UV lights or swabs by staff members to carry out these checks.
- Remove toilet seat lids (within reason, as there are health and safety issues here).
- Treat surfaces (especially in your toilets) with non-toxic substance such as vaseline

- Consider using opaque glass doors to toilet cubicles to identify possible abuse.

- Encourage your staff to take a very proactive approach to preventing drug abuse in our premises, security staff could also conduct random searches.

- Consider designing your toilets with special lighting which inhibits the locating of veins to stop heroin users from injecting. This works up to a point, determined abusers have found ways around this by subtly marking themselves up before the go out in public and prior to going into the cubicle so they can still find a vein under the coloured light.

Always try to encourage your employees and managers to report all incidents of drug misuse in your establishment, including any suspicions they may have regarding drug misuse. Don't be tempted to ignore a small problem or an isolated incident, as failure to take decisive action may encourage further drug activity and highlight your premises as a soft target. Local trade industry bodies that organise training and identification schemes are an ideal way of promoting a joint, zero tolerance approach to illegal drug misuse. These schemes and the subsequent meetings also enable information on drug misuse to be shared amongst members from the hospitality, tourism and retail industries to help them to build up a picture of what is happening in their county or area.

6

Conclusion

Workplace policies designed and negotiated by all the organization's stakeholders (both internally and externally), which addresses alcohol issues in a supportive way while complying with responsibilities in relation to health and safety, can be beneficial for both employers and employees. Setting a clear policy on alcohol and drugs and offering EAP programmes for employees who are at particular risk of alcohol related harm or need treatment will help organizations to maintain more productive, safe and healthy workplaces for all their employees.

Alcoholism is a disease and employees who suffer from need it their organization's support. This support must be firm in order to remind the employee, that while their employer is happy to help to get them the appropriate assistance, they are principally responsible for their own rehabilitation, recovery, and performance.

Web resources

Alcohol and drugs in the workplace (South Australia)

www.safework.sa.gov.au/show_page.jsp?id=5914#.U_T4mntOPIU

Alcohol workplace policies (N. Ireland)

www.hseni.gov.uk/workplace_drugs_and_alcohol_policies_-_guidelines...

Intoxicants in the workplace (Ireland)

www.ibec.ie/IBEC/ES.nsf/vPages/Health_and_safety~Workplace_hazards_and_health_
issues~intoxicants#.U_mKe3tOPIU

Impact of alcohol & other drugs in the workplace (South Africa)

www.safework.sa.gov.au/uploaded_files/workplace_report.pdf

International Forum for Drug & Alcohol Testing (IFDAT)

www.ifdat.com

National Council on Alcoholism and Drug Dependence, Inc (US)

ncadd.org/learn-about-alcohol/workplace

The Health & Safety Executive (UK)

/www.hse.gov.uk/pubns/indg91.pdf

Work Safe (Victoria, Australia)

www.vwa.vic.gov.au/__data/assets/pdf_file/.../alcohol_workplace.pdf

7 Alcohol Related Crime and Disorder

Aims and learning outcomes

This chapter introduces the areas central to reducing alcohol related crime and disorder. After reading, you should be able to:

- Establish the interrelated factors which encourage some individuals to engage in disorderly behaviours around drinking venues.

- Identify appropriate interventions to improve public safety and to discourage alcohol related disorderly behaviours.

- Outline the challenges involved for policy makers and individual establishments in reducing alcohol related conflict and violence.

- Use the appropriate techniques and skills adopted by effective managers and door staff to prevent disorderly conduct and violence in drinking environments.

7.0 Introduction

Employers across the tourism, hospitality and retail industries have a duty to sell alcohol in a lawful and responsible manner. Millions of individuals enjoy consuming alcohol with few, if any, negative effects, but alcohol abuse by a small minority causes crime, anti-social behaviour and harm to the safety and security of employees, customers and society. Although the origins of these disruptive behaviours are complex, some of the interconnected factors can include the age of customers, their social class, and the environment and culture surrounding the establishment in question. In this chapter we will explore how in recent years businesses have adopted community partnerships, strategies and training schemes to enhance safety and discourage alcohol related disorderly behaviours. Policy makers and individual establishments can encounter specific challenges and cultural differences which drive the local drinking patterns, but governments, the police, local authorities and businesses have joined forces to enforce existing laws and to reduce alcohol related crime and disorder. The skills and style of managers and door staff are also crucial when dealing with alcohol related disorder. These skills include the use of appropriate aggression reduction techniques and control strategies to minimise the potential for conflict and crime arising.

7.1   Disorder and disruptive behaviour around drinking venues

Reynolds et al (1997) suggest that increased alcohol availability can lead to increased consumption, which in turn creates a greater risk that individuals will engage in public disorder behaviours. The more extreme and disruptive behaviours can include noise and disturbances, public vomiting and urination, damage and destruction of property, offensive behaviour, assaults and violence. Research studies conducted by Reid et al (2003) and Wechscler et al (2002) support this contention in linking alcohol sales and the number of premises to public disorder and negative outcomes. This association between alcohol and availability appears to be a simple challenge to overcome, but the relationship is much more complex and there are other inter-related factors which must be taken into account.

MCM Research Ltd discovered that in the United Kingdom very different levels of violence were found in pubs according to the social class of customers for which they cater. Fights among males and attacks on managers and staff are considerably higher in the working class pubs than in those which cater for a predominantly middle-class population. Those with a mixed social class customer profile experience intermediate levels of violence (MCM, 1990). Quigley et al (2003) point to drinking outcomes, which they believe are also related to the prevailing cultural norms and attitudes of particular establishments and areas, which attract individuals seeking to take part in heavy drinking patterns and anti-social behaviour. Tomsen (1997) adds that disruptive behaviours, which include vandalism and violence, in the drinking environment can also occur from individuals who have been ejected from bars which strictly enforce rules on behaviour. Individuals interested in anti-social and risky behaviours appear to tend to gather in establishments where heavy drinking patterns are tolerated as they believe that these behaviours will be accepted in there. Moore (1990) explored one of these environments and reported that after analysing skinhead drinking culture in Australia, that casual sexual activities, rowdy behaviour and heavy drinking were a natural expectation of a night out with fellow skinheads.

Some establishments target young people, and in some locations where the ratio of young males is very high there is a tendency for disruptive behaviour. Felson (1997) contends that young men who attend these venues and engage in nightlife activities are more likely to encounter violence. Drinking environments that cater predominantly for the 18-30 years age group have been reported to experience far higher numbers of fights than do those which are used mainly by older customers. The levels of attacks on managers and staff, however, are highest in those pubs which also cater for customers who are rather older – the 'mixed' age category. The frequency of both fights and attacks on managers is lowest in those pubs which attract very few young people. Campbell (2000) attributes this behaviour to the need of some men to demonstrate their masculinity in keeping up their end. In a research study from Australia, Tomsen (1997) reported that young men got real pleasure from engaging in aggressive behaviour while drinking. Females are not immune to these behaviours. Parks & Miller (1997) reported that half of all frequent females drinkers were affected by aggression and one third experienced a sexual assault linked to consuming alcohol in a bar.

The design and management of drinking establishments can impact on their vulnerability to disorderly behaviour (Quigley et al, 2003). These include over-crowding, improper ventilation or lighting or permitting illegal activities. A further consideration relates to aggressive or anti-social behaviour; Tomsen (1997) states that individuals may become involved if it appears to be the thing to do. It is reasonable to suggest that not all aggressive and anti-social behaviour is linked to intoxication, but research from hospitality establishments has shown that changes in the design of drinking environments and in management practices can help to decrease violence and other public offences.

7.2   Strategies to discourage alcohol related disorderly behaviours

Homel et al (2004), ICAP (2002) and Sloan et al (2000) report that most countries adopt a mixture of targeted interventions and regulations to improve the safety of the public and to discourage alcohol related disorderly behaviours. These strategies can range from restricting the concentration levels of large drinking establishments and training schemes for security and serving staff, to strict enforcement of alcohol licensing laws (Burns et al 2003; Graham et al, 2004). In this section we will explore some of these strategies.

Community interventions

Community interventions that include all the relevant stakeholders (i.e. community steering groups, local government, tourism, hospitality and retail establishments) which are aimed at creating codes of practice and responsible drinking practices at a local level can deliver impressive results. The research of Homel et al (1997) indicated that these initiatives can result in significant decreases in physical and non-physical altercations. Secure, reasonably priced and convenient private and public transport systems contribute to reducing drink driving and public disorderly behaviour. Stimson et al (2007) highlight one such scheme which operates in Brazil during their major festivals and carnivals, where they offer free taxis and public transport to get people home safely. Community approaches to limit or restrict the time periods for the sale and service of alcohol are also effective. Norstom (2000) talks about limiting the number of establishments (especially bars and nightclubs) within specific areas, and this approach has reduced alcohol-related violent crime. HMSO (2003) propose an alternative approach, suggesting that by extending the officially regulated hours of service (allowing staggered closing times for bars, etc.) can help to reduce the impact of closing time when mass crowds spill onto the streets and anti-social behaviour takes place. Community interventions which include local agreements can work. Carvolth (1983) points to these community efforts and offers the local accords which are used in Australia and New Zealand as an excellent example. These accords involve all the stakeholders who develop agreements to deliver secure drinking environments and good transport systems (New South Wales Department of Gaming and Racing, 2004).

Changing the consumption environment

Interventions adopted by many countries have been targeted at changing the consumption environment to create secure drinking experiences. Portman Group (2000) and Deeham (1999) give examples of these interventions, which include maintaining high levels of house-keeping, strategic space allocation to reduce over-crowding, providing keenly priced foods and non-alcoholic drinks and limiting drink promotions.

Clever design, with a strong emphasis on the colour schemes, and the layout of establishments can discourage alcohol related disorder.

Colour

The use of colour in both domestic and commercial environments has received a lot of attention in psychological literature; Carl Jung is the most prominently associated with the pioneering stages of colour psychology.

Jung was most interested in colours' properties and meanings (Jung, 1916). MCM (1990) argue that the development of appropriate designs for drinking environments, should involve a balance between colour and complexity which, on average, is perceived as neither over-stimulating nor psychologically 'flat'. Various colours have been shown to effect mood and behaviour in significantly different ways. Short wavelength colours, such as green and blue, are known to produce restful states while colours with long wavelengths (reds, etc.) have the opposite effect. Red can increase levels of arousal, but the effects of large areas of saturated red, for example, tend to wear off after a short period of time as subjects habituate to the stimuli. More importantly, other variables, such as the texture of the coloured surface, lighting conditions and the visual complexity of the environment all modify the impact of the colour. Visual complexity refers to the amount of variation present in a given setting. Different patterns and colours, changes in surface texture, reflectivity and lighting, the level of ornamentation, etc. all contribute to this. Such variance in complexity affects behaviour in a similar way to variance in colour, with highly complex environments producing effects similar to those of red, while visually simple ones evoke the restful states associated with green.

These initial design considerations have influenced establishment owners in recent years to move towards removing the more energetic colours and over-stimulating elements from drinking environments. But another danger can arise here which is under-stimulation, as patrons who frequent drinking environments expect a degree of psychological arousal and in establishments where their expectations are not met there is a risk of aggression arising directly, or indirectly as a result of frustration. Drinking environments must try to incorporate a balanced level of stimulation.

It is also necessary to consider the interactions between colour and complexity. The designers must be aware of the extent to which their customers' reactions are influenced by the texture and reflectivity of surfaces within their establishments. It has been reported that highly reflective interiors, in particular, can have distinctly energising effects.

Layout and monitoring

The interior layout of drinking environments requires designers to balance two of the most important, and unfortunately conflicting, challenges which are the need to ensure adequate levels of surveillance against the needs and expectations of their customers.

- **The open plan or single drinking environment design:** this offers ease of surveillance and monitoring of customers by the manager and staff, which is essential for conflict prevention and control. It also involves the removal of potential blind spots. This design has the additional benefit of increasing trading space. Open plan designs can lead to increased frequencies of fights among customers, due to a lack of appropriate separation leading to the contagion of conflict and aggression (MCM, 1990). Though managers may be able to prevent a number of violent incidents because of the increased ease of monitoring, this advantage is often outweighed by the fact that aggressive behaviour will tend to spread more widely in such settings.

■ **The sub-divided open space design:** some customers prefer a sense of enclosure and a degree of separation which can achieved by adopting distinct differences in the lighting, seating, table arrangements and the internal décor which includes elements of screening to create the illusion of separation. These design techniques help to create spaces and reduce the contagion element of conflict and aggression because patrons will usually pay little attention to the behaviour of fellow patrons on the opposite side of the screening area. Sub-divided areas which are clearly marked and strategically positioned can also control the movements of customers within drinking environments which helps to reduce areas of frustration.

Training

Rigorous training of all servers in the responsible serving and sale of alcohol is also a common strategy adopted by many businesses across the world. Graham et al (2004) maintain that if this training is strictly enforced through local laws, it can be crucial to the enjoyment of consumers and more importantly to their safety. They argue that training should not only be limited to servers, and suggest that responsible hospitality training should target all employees (i.e. security and restaurant staff). Please refer to also Chapter 9, *Responsible serving of alcohol* under section 9.4.

Case example: Strong community partnerships reduce alcohol related crime and disorder

Best Bar None (BBN) scheme

This is a recognised award scheme supported by the United Kingdom Home Office, aimed at promoting the responsible management and operation of alcohol-licensed premises. It has been adopted by over 95 towns and cities across the UK and is even now being taken up in other countries. The schemes provide an incentive for the operators of licensed premises to improve their standards of operation to the level of a commonly agreed national benchmark. It has proved to be an excellent vehicle for partnership working as: (a) it provides an incentive for operators to improve their standards, (b) it gives licensees the chance to show how well they manage their businesses, (c) it acts as a reference point for authorities to work with local pubs and clubs in tackling crime and disorder issues. It sets a minimum standard of operation and encourages the sharing of best practice by rewarding safe and well-managed licensed venues. An evaluation carried out in 2009 of 40 BBN schemes showed that BBN is one of the major contributors to reducing crime in their areas and substantially helps towards the solution of alcohol related crime in the night time economy. Early indications of statistics show a (15-35%) reduction in local area crime statistics (Home Office, 2010). Establishments can join the BBN scheme through the BBN website at: http://www.bbnuk.com

7.3   Alcohol related conflict and violence

Research studies in recent years have highlighted the link between particular patterns of alcohol consumption and some types of violent acts, however these studies are limited and do not categorically prove that alcohol consumption causes violence. White and Gorman (2000) suggest that violence originates from numerous causes which include cultural, psychosocial, community and individual elements. Lipsey et al (1997) inform us that because of these inter-related elements theorists are still struggling to develop a model to properly address the relationship between violence and alcohol.

Even though alcohol can be involved when crime and disorder offences are committed, evidence does not exist that alcohol is the cause of the offences (Pernanen, 1991). A huge amount of violence incidents do not involve alcohol consumption. Martin (1993) highlights the link between heavy drinking patterns and violent individuals and maintains that the figures for these individuals are much higher than the wider population. Abusive consumption patterns have also been linked with suicide and domestic violence; the Home Office (2004b) report that these patterns directly lead to nearly half of all sexual assault incidents. The implications of these research studies have presented many challenges for policy makers and potential victims, but if we can cultivate a deeper understanding of these challenges we can reduce the possibility of higher levels of alcohol related crime and violence.

The challenges for policy makers, potential victims and individual establishments

Cultural differences

Room & Rossow (2001) argue that countries which incorporate moderate alcohol consumption into their everyday life (e.g. Mediterranean countries) report much smaller levels of alcohol related crime and violent disorder when compared to other countries where there is significant opposition to alcohol (e.g. North America) or where alcohol's role and moderate use is not fully adopted (e.g. Nordic countries). Coid (1986) indicates that the relationship of alcohol to violence is the strongest in societies that condone violent behaviour. Although these studies and their conclusions are important, they do not fully incorporate every cultural and contextual variable and their impact on the individuals involved. Further research is required to explore these variables.

The consumption environment

Alcohol related crime and disorder which leads to violence is more likely to take place in drinking establishments like pubs, late night bars and nightclubs. Roncek and Maier (1991) state that these locations can offer the perfect opportunity for potential offenders and their victims to converge. This phenomenon occurs especially in venues that do not enforce strict behavioural and responsible drinking codes, Arnold and Laidler (1994) add that some of these locations also indirectly encourage alcohol related crime and disorder through overcrowding, aggressive employees, poor design and management practices. See also 'Changing the consumption environment' above and Chapter 9 for further discussion of this issue.

Challenges at the individual level

The link between alcohol and violence at the individual level has been widely reported. Boles and Miotto (2003) suggests that alcohol drives violent tendencies because it impairs the cognitive processes which control perceptions about behaviour, judgement and awareness of consequences. Abusive alcohol consumption patterns can also lead to aggressive behaviour originating from the lack of sleep, food and personality disorders (Badawy, 1986). Moncrieff and Farmer (1998) explored the more sinister elements of violent behaviour linked to alcohol abuse. They proposed that violent individuals choose environments and groups that promote heavy drinking, and that some of these individuals will also use alcohol to lessen the blame for their violent actions.

Some other research studies focused instead on the common risk factors in the relationship between harmful drinking patterns and violence. White and Gorman (2000) state that these risk factors include poor relations with parents, personality disorders, temperamental traits and copying their parent's aggression and harmful drinking patterns. Even though support for these conclusions is widespread it still does not consider the highly individual factors in the relationship between harmful drinking patterns and violence. The British Beer and Pub Association highlight further significant factors in the occurrence of violent incidents in drinking establishments and other late-night venues, they maintain that these elements include:

(a) social tension and rivalry (sporting, territorial),

(b) romantic rivalry (past and desired relationships),

(c) frustration – waiting to get served,

(d) over-crowding and discomfort – pushing to the bar and lavatories,

(e) intolerance – bumping on dance floor/busy area, spilled drinks,

(f) influence of drugs taken before entry,

(g) smoking restrictions,

(h) queues at the door and refused entry (ID checks),

(i) staff (lack of intervention or too aggressive),

(j) refusal to serve those underage or drunk,

(k) removal of glasses with drinks remaining and

(l) failure to clear tables

(BBPA, 2007).

Case examples: Intervention programmes aimed at reducing violence in night life settings

The Safer Bars programme (Toronto, Canada)

This programme was developed in consultation with police, lawyers, community health professionals, civic leaders, liquor licensing officials, bar owners and staff, and aimed to reduce aggression in bars. The programme provided: three hour training sessions for bar staff and management; a booklet for bar owners and managers to address environmental risk factors for aggression; and a pamphlet informing bar owners and staff of their legal responsibilities in preventing violence and injury in nightlife. The training focused on teamwork, communication and early intervention to prevent problems from escalating. Graham et al (2004) stated that findings from the project evaluation indicate the programme had a significant effect in reducing severe and moderate aggression in bars.

Burnley against Night Time Disorder (BAND) – (United Kingdom)

BAND is a multi-agency partnership developed to tackle violence and disorder in and around Burnley's nightlife area through banning perpetrators of nightlife violence from all licensed premises and establishing a Pubwatch scheme. This enables details of potentially violent incidents to be shared quickly and accurately and to help apprehend offenders. In addition, protocols are established between all licensed premises to prevent unruly customers from entering premises. Although levels of violence remained stable throughout the implementation of BAND, significant increases in the number of people visiting the town centre at night have been observed. BAND has been recognised as an example of best practice by the Home Office in the UK (Home Office, 2004).

7

7.4   Reducing conflict and violence through effective management practices

Preventing and handling aggressive or potentially violent situations in drinking establishments, especially in bars and nightclubs, is unfortunately a common area of concern. The most common origins of conflicts between managers, staff and customers occurs when dealing with disorderly customers, many of whom are deemed to be drunk, either individually or in groups. This accounts for nearly two thirds of all the violent encounters which managers and staff experience (MCM, 1990).

In this section we will examine the styles and skills of managers who deal effectively with aggression and violence in drinking establishments and highlight some of the unique characteristics distinguishing them from their peers in the industry. It should be remembered at this point that the most effective managers view physical confrontation or restraint as being the last resort when dealing with alcohol related violence. Murphy (2013) identifies the significant features which effective managers employ within drinking establishments; he suggests that they should demonstrate elements of the following.

Firmness and fairness

Managers who are able to deal effectively with potentially belligerent and aggressive customers emphasise the need for firmness, of an assertive rather than aggressive nature, but also insist that this will only be effective if applied fairly. Fairness is developed gradually in dealings with customers and is part of the more general process of winning respect.

Involvement and detachment

While the essentially sociable nature of management requires a degree of involvement with customers, effective managers stress that this needs to be coupled with an appropriate sense of detachment. Being one of the lads, in their view, can lead to distinct problems when a manager needs to act in a more formal role and constrain the behaviour of certain customers. Managers of drinking establishments must therefore always: (a) set clear and consistent standards, (b) create a sociable atmosphere, (c) combine firmness with fairness, (d) be friendly, but professional.

Monitoring and surveillance

Very few aggressive incidents arise spontaneously or erupt 'out of thin air'. They have a distinct pattern of development which, if detected at an early stage, can often be curtailed. The diligence of the manager and his staff in detecting these antecedents is directly related to the number of aggressive and violent incidents which a drinking establishment experiences. It is characteristic of effective managers that they rarely stay in one place in their establishment for more than a few minutes. During busy sessions in particular they will be seen engaged in apparently trivial activities such as collecting glasses or emptying ash trays. In this way they are able to see and to listen to the conversations of various groups of customers without being too obtrusive and without appearing to spy. Managers must therefore always: (a) know the danger signals, e.g. changing behaviours, rowdiness, drunken behaviour and anti-social antics, large groups forming with opposing opinions, (b) use low profile monitoring techniques, e.g. covert CCTV cameras, undercover security personnel, management and senior staff members collecting glasses and cleaning tables, (c) combine monitoring with sociability, talking and engaging with your guests relating small stories of current affairs, sport and family events coming up. Intervene early but tactfully.

Calming strategies

In addition to the need for the manager to remain calm when faced with aggression, there is an equal need to reduce the level of aggression in the customer before attempting to apply control measures. A highly emotional individual is unlikely to respond to direct instructions or demands. Only when the aggression has been reduced through the use of calming strategies can controls be effectively enforced. Managers must therefore always: (a) get the offending individual away from an audience, (b) stay calm, and not respond to provocation, (c) use relaxed non-aggressive body language, (d) be assertive and not aggressive. Managers should consider what they are trying to achieve when faced with an aggressive situation and what they want the outcome to be. The answer, of course, is always a non-violent resolution, a win-win situation where nobody gets hurt.

Control

Successful establishment owners and their managers emphasise the need to stay calm and use phrases such as 'not adding fuel to the fire'. By taking such an approach they are more able to reduce the anger and emotion in the customer/s with whom they are interacting. Once calming procedures have been employed, the application of control strategies is likely to be much more effective. At this stage there is a need for managers to make clear what they require of the offender. Where ambiguities exist, there is the potential for further conflict so effective managers typically use phrases which allow the offender to accept easily the need for control measures. When refusing service, entry, asking people to leave or removing offenders from the premises, effective managers emphasize their legal or professional obligations, to make it less personnel.

Reducing frustration

Our ability to think clearly and logically is impaired through intoxication. This, in turn, reduces our ability to employ coping strategies when in situations which are frustrating or aggressive. So managers should try to: (a) look at the drinking establishment from the customer's point of view and (b) identify and remove potential sources of frustration through good housekeeping and good customer service. Asking the staff or customers about the frustration points of an establishment can be revealing. The most common frustration points include; slow or inefficient service, no acknowledgement from bar staff, poor seating layouts spills, no locks on toilet doors, faulty furniture, poor ventilation (hot/cold), last orders or poor signage. The two paths between alcohol and violence interact with each other. Because we can't think so clearly, we come to depend much more on cues in the situation to help us understand what is going on. A heated argument among a group of people, for example, can trigger aggression in others who have been drinking and witness it. Hostility from managers or staff becomes magnified in the eyes of people who are intoxicated. Levels of frustration can become far more significant.

Closing time

Effective managers maintain a regular routine that everyone understands. They give a clear and consistent message, for example, at last orders, flashing the lights and calling 'last orders', followed by a gradual wind down. They are always firm but polite when dealing with the end of the evening session.

Self-audit systems

Effective managers will also usually have in operation a system for self-audit, which assists them in identifying areas of the establishment, where potential risks could occur. This system could cover, for example, areas associated with the signage compliance, transport options, RSA or door staff training or house policies. Table 7.1 is a sample self-audit system which can be adapted for your establishment. You must also ensure that your self-audit system incorporates an understanding of all the local legislation which governs the sale, service and responsible consumption of alcohol in your area or region.

Table 7.1: Self-audit system for managing alcohol consumption through responsible service (adapted from Murphy 2005, 2008).

Self audit item	Y	N	ACTION
Signage Compliance Proof of age signs at all entry points, no sale or supply of alcohol to minors. Stop entry signs to restricted areas. Intoxicated sign. Fail to leave sign. Signs in well-lighted areas and not obstructed, easily read by staff and customers. Under 18 – Responsible adult to authorised areas. Guest register – (if your venue is a registered club). House policy. Harm minimisation signage. Breath testing equipment – (if applicable).			
Evidence of Age ID Checking guide available for all staff, Staff fully trained to check ID. Staff trained in house policies on dealing with customers.			
Refusal of service Staff have working knowledge of house policy. Staff trained in identifying and preventing intoxication on premises. Staff trained in dealing with intoxicated customers.			
Transport options Regular advertising of courtesy bus (if applicable). Taxi (phone, rank), Bus, train.			
RSA register Is your register up to date, and available for inspection. Have all staff received RSA training; is all in-house training up to date and recorded			
House policy Is the house policy known and understood by all staff. Readily available for customers and staff.			
Incident register Do you have one. Location easily accessible. Staff trained in completing it.			
Security staff (door staff) Security staff know the standard operating procedures for your establishment. Security staff completed RSA training. All door staff competent in checking ID. Door and interior staff hold the appropriate licence required. All security staff holds a current valid licence.			

A drinking establishment which encourages a friendly and non-aggressive atmosphere is likely to provide an environment in which alcohol leads to increased sociability and well-being among drinkers. Many acts of violence among serious drinkers can be avoided if steps are taken to ensure that their mood is not negatively influenced by perceived aggressive cues, especially at closing time or through the actions of door staff which we will explore next.

The police or local law enforcement agencies advise bar staff: (a) know your limits, no heroics, (b) establish and maintain good relations for advice and information, and (c) don't expect the police to run your pub for you.

7.5 The role of door staff in preventing disorderly conduct and violence

The Centre for Public Health at Liverpool's John Moore's University conducted a study, supported by the WHO, on the role of door hosts, door supervisors, bouncers or other door staff in preventing violence. This argued that door staff have a key role in preventing violence in nightlife settings (Anderson et al, 2007). 'Door staff' means people who, as part of their duties, perform any of the following functions at or in the vicinity of the drinking establishment where a public or private event is taking place or is about to take place. They can be required to (a) intervene in acts of customer aggression and violence, (b) escort unruly individuals from the premises, (c) remove customers at closing time, and (d) refuse access to known troublemakers or underage individuals. In addition to these duties, Monaghan (2002) notes that they are also required to manage entry to venues to prevent overcrowding; conduct age verification to prevent access to underage individuals; patrol the establishment to deter and detect disorder; manage acts of misconduct among customers; conduct searches to prevent drugs or weapons entering the premises; and manage the movement of customers out of the establishment back into the night time environment. The use of door staff in drinking establishments has increased in recent years; this demand has been brought about by the anti-social, violent and drunken behaviour of some customers.

These challenges mean that door staff can frequently be placed in aggressive situations where they will be expected to prevent alcohol related disorders and violence taking place, or to control its impact on patrons. In this section we will explore the role of door staff in violence prevention and outline a small selection of the measures being adopted to enhance their role.

Disorderly conduct and crowd control

Disorderly conduct in drinking establishments and its effects on the guests is an emotive area. In most countries, establishment owners must not permit disorderly conduct and any individual engaging in this behaviour must leave the drinking establishment upon being requested to do so by the owner, his nominee or a police officer. Murphy (2008) reminds us that establishments should introduce a system of crowd control which is focused on active monitoring, prevention and intervention at the earliest possible moment. This leads to greater guest security, comfort and enjoyment (as noted under Management style and skills above). These measures should not be used in isolation; they should form an active integrated approach, which will help create a sociable atmosphere, and happy satisfied customers.

Table 7.2: Aggression reduction techniques   (adapted from MCM, 1990).

1. Remove the audience effect	

2. Employ calming strategies:		
a. Language skills:	Allow the aggressor to talk and express (release) anger Use a role-appropriate style of language.
	Avoid using hostile phrases and questions.
	Respond indirectly to hostile questions, accusations etc.
	Express your understanding of the reasons for aggressor's emotional state.
b. Non-verbal skills:	Increase the distance between yourself and the aggressor.
	Avoid sustained and potentially threatening eye contact.
	Adopt a relaxed, non-aggressive posture.
	Move slowly and avoid sudden changes of posture.

3. Employ control strategies:	
	Clearly establish your requirements.
	Depersonalize the encounter.
	Emphasise the role requirements.
	Encourage the offender's own decision making.
	Offer possibilities for face-saving to the offender.

The link between door staff and violence

International research studies have consistently demonstrated that door staff are placed at high levels of risk of being involved in violence. Graham et al (2005) state that three quarters of all the staff members involved in incidents of aggression in the night time environment were door staff, Rigakos (2004) adds that door staffs were significantly more likely to experience physical violence than police working in the same locality. Interestingly in England the ability to fight has been identified by Hobbs et al (2002) as a key characteristic upon which door staff's commercial value rests. This prerequisite, Anderson (2005) suggests, has contributed to the fact that 15% of all patients presenting at a UK Accident and Emergency department with an assault injury sustained in a pub or nightclub had been injured by door staff. Maguire and Nettleton (2003) agree and state that in Wales, door staff were three times more likely to be accused of assaulting a member of the public, than a member of the public was of being accused of assaulting a door man or women.

Lister and Hobbs (2000) add that in England door staff were less likely to be convicted for an alleged assault against a member of the public (2%), than vice versa (57%). A study conducted in Australia concluded that night-life violence was more likely to occur in drinking environments employing aggressive door staff (Homel and Tomsen, 1992). See also Appendix V – *Ten golden rules for door staff.*

Case example: The link between door staff and violence

A member of the door staff working in a gay bar stuck his thumb in a customer's eye socket and twisted around. He then carried the customer to the door of the bar, tossing him in the air where he landed on his head, side and leg. It was reported that this sudden and without warning vicious and brutal assault ended in the Circuit Civil Court were damages of €15,000 was awarded to the victim (Irish Independent, 2004).

Training schemes and regulation requirements for door staff

Faced with these challenges, and acknowledging the vital role which door staff play in enhancing nightlife safety, most countries have developed their own training programmes to provide door staff with the necessary skills to perform their role. These programmes were developed to raise awareness levels in relation to their own actions' impact on customer behaviour and to help them develop skills in customer relations and management techniques. Hobbs et al (2003) outlined the major topics explored in these programmes which included: civil and criminal law, health and safety at work, drug and alcohol awareness, conflict management, appropriate searching methods and emergency evacuation management. The high levels of involvement by door staff in violence, as discussed above, prompted many local authorities and governments to adopt regulation which required door staff to complete compulsory registration and training schemes. Monaghan (2002), reports that since 2004 door staff working in England and Wales must hold a licence issued by the National Security Industry Authority. He states that individuals with previous convictions for offences such as violence and drug dealing are excluded, and all licence holders must have undertaken training.

Applicants will be usually vetted by the local police before any license is issued and the majority of authorities will also usually maintain a register of both contractor and individual license holders on their websites. These registers are useful tools for drinking establishments and the public, who can ensure that their door staff or private security provider is licensed by checking the details on the register. Fines can be imposed on establishment owners who engage unlicensed door staff or private security providers (Murphy, 2013). Some other countries have established voluntary codes of conduct and training programmes to promote best practice in the security industry across the world, especially in regions or areas where national training schemes and appropriate legislation do not exist or are not actively enforced (New Zealand Security Association, 2006). Community partnership approaches have also been used to reduce violence in nightlife. One programme based in Sweden, incorporates door staff training into wider community measures to create a safer nightlife environment in Stockholm.

Case example: The STAD project (Stockholm, Sweden)

The STAD project is a ten-year multi-component programme designed to tackle alcohol-related violence in Stockholm, Sweden. It focuses on community mobilisation, training in responsible beverage service for servers and stricter enforcement of licensing laws.

The two-day training programme is targeted at servers, door staff and bar owners and covers alcohol law, medical effects of alcohol, alcohol-related crimes, other drugs and conflict management. It concludes with a written assessment, with successful candidates receiving a diploma. Wallin et al (2002) reports that an evaluation of the programme highlighted a (29%) reduction in violent crime in the intervention area.

The road ahead

Door and security staff numbers will continue to increase in line with the changing late night drinking environment, and their responsibilities in relation to preventing alcohol related violence will also increase. Training schemes can empower door staff to carry out their duties in this sometimes aggressive environment, but without them staff cannot be expected to effective at reducing violence (Wells et al, 1998). Government regulation, strictly enforced, which requires all door and security staff members to register and complete appropriate training is also crucial towards creating the right atmosphere.

Conclusion

A series of targeted strategies, which includes intervention programmes at community and individual levels aimed at reducing alcohol related crime and disorder, can help to reduce the potential for violent behaviour. These interventions must consider the cultural, environmental, contextual and consumption differences of the local areas. Changes in the design and management of drinking establishments can have a direct impact on their susceptibility to encourage disorderly behaviour. The use of door staff has increased in recent years, in response to the anti-social, violent and drunken behaviour of some customers. Door staff can frequently be placed in aggressive situations where they will be expected to prevent alcohol related disorder and violence from taking place, or to control its impact on patrons. The research highlights that the most effective managers view physical confrontation or restraint as being the last resort when dealing with alcohol related violence. Confrontations can be reduced if the customers' mood is not negatively influenced by aggressive cues especially at closing time or through the actions of door staff.

These progressive approaches can only be successful if they have broad participation and include various segments of the wider society which surrounds the drinking establishments.

Web resources

British Beer & Pub Association (BBPA)

   www.beerandpub.com

Bar Entertainment and Dance Association (BEDA)

   www.beda.org.uk

BII (British Institute of Innkeeping)

   www.bii.org

The Pub Design Doctor

   /www.pubdesigndoctor.com/

The 'Safer Bars' Intervention for reducing bar violence

   www.drugtext.org/Education-and-Prevention/the-safer-bars-intervention-for-reducing-bar-violence.html

WHO – Alcohol and Violence

   www.who.int/violence_injury_prevention

   www.who.int/gender/violence/en/

8 Selling and Marketing Alcohol Responsibly

Aims and learning outcomes

This aim of this chapter is to examine the marketing of alcohol and explore the ways in which national governments, major industries and individual establishments have collaborated to create agreed national standards for the marketing and selling of alcoholic products in a responsible manner. After reading this chapter you should be able to:

■ Explain the challenges involved within the marketing environment for the advertising, promotion and merchandising of alcohol products.

■ Describe how the partnership, self-regulation and social norm approaches towards developing alcohol policies operate individually.

■ Demonstrate a knowledge of the impact of alcohol sponsorship and of the labelling requirements which warn consumers about the health risks from alcohol products.

■ Apply good business practices for the sale of alcohol across the whole sector which includes retail and mixed trading premises.

8.0   Introduction

We must accept that there are many influences on the relationship between alcohol and consumers, and although many of these interact, there is no single factor that can be said to be dominant in the development of poor drinking patterns. For that reason, it is clear that no single prescription can be offered to any society regarding the harms associated with alcohol abuse. Similarly, no single sector can effectively tackle these issues alone. It is for this reason that the drinks industry, retail establishments and the relevant stakeholders need strategic partnership approaches which incorporate their moral and legal duties to sell and market alcohol products in a responsible manner.

These partnerships can be advanced through education, training, dialogue and joint action, but this collective work requires all stakeholders to respect one another's positions and to act in good faith. This chapter will examine these challenges and highlight how governments and industries across the hospitality, tourism and retail sectors have worked together to deliver training programmes and policies aimed at selling and marketing alcohol in a responsible manner.

8.1   Marketing alcohol

It is important to remember that marketing encompasses advertising, promotion and merchandising, sponsorship, labelling and point-of-sale materials.

The marketing campaigns for alcoholic beverages are constantly changing. In recent years some companies have targeted specific groups with enticing brands or have organised campaigns which influence drinkers to consume that brand. One group which has been targeted is that of young people, and the impact of this marketing has received special attention. For some drinks companies their marketing approach has revolved around the development of 'alcopops' (sweet-tasting, brightly coloured beverages with appealing names). With catchy slogans, the idea that drinking is trendy, and no mention of the negative side of the abuse of alcohol in most marketing and advertising campaigns, this can be dangerous. Research studies have indicated that underage consumption of alcohol is directly correlated with exposure to alcohol advertisements. This has brought some governments to ban alcohol ads on public transport. Nelson (2006) states that it is difficult to prove allegations regarding the response of young people to exposure to these types of advertisements, but believes that it is necessary to find ways in which the impact may be limited. Kuo et al (2000) suggest that alcohol advertising on college campuses has been shown to increase binge drinking among students, but they note that if these promotions are organised in a consistent and responsible fashion, they can actually help reduce harmful drinking patterns. Stacey et al, cited in Nelson (2010), speak about the effect of television ads on young people's feelings about alcohol and report that they have more positive feelings about drinking after viewing these ads.

The WHO adopted a 'Framework for Alcohol Policy for the Europe', which states five ethical principles including that 'all children and adolescents have the right to grow up in an environment protected from the negative consequences of alcohol consumption and, to the extent possible, from the promotion of alcoholic beverages' (WHO, 2006). These countries have moved towards a complete ban of alcohol advertising on billboard and television: France, Norway, Russia, (BBC News Europe, 2012) and Ukraine,(KyiPost,

2010). India, Myanmar, Sri Lanka, (Asian Tribune, 2006) and Kenya have banned all alcohol advertising on television and billboard (BBC News, 2005). The majority of drink companies, however, host websites which carry huge amounts of information about their brands. They nominally require an age of 21 to enter, but the security levels of these sites are poor and in most circumstances there are no restrictions besides simply entering a birth date. Parents, peers and the media have a large impact on young people's decisions to drink (Federal Trade Commission, 2003).

These challenges and the potential for abuse and misuse surrounding alcohol beverage products places a direct onus on private and public organisations to set rigorous standards around the responsible marketing and sale of beverages. These standards can be set through a series of approaches which include government regulation, self-regulatory, partnership and social norms approaches which are reviewed in the next sections.

8.2 Media reviews, advertising and celebrity endorsements of alcoholic drinks

Consumers can be influenced by media reviews and advertising which promote a brand's image. Research studies conducted in Australia concluded that individuals are exposed to alcohol promotions through a range of media channels, both directly, e.g. television and print media, official brand websites and alcohol sponsorship of sports and cultural events, (Jones and Gordon, 2013) and indirectly, e.g. product placement in films, music videos and television programmes, social media and in-store promotions (Smith and Folcroft, 2009; Roche et al 2007). The Australian Medical Association (2012) maintain that this exposure was increasing due to the expansion of alcohol advertising into digital media, and via globalised platforms, and is likely to have a cumulative effect (Roche et al, 2007). Sargent et al (2006) add that alcohol use in movies is also found to be a predictor of the prevalence and initiation of alcohol use. Additional longitudinal studies, mainly conducted in New Zealand (Casswell and Zhang, 1998) and the US (Stacy et al, 2004; Collins et al., 2007), consistently suggest that exposure to media review and alcohol advertisements which drive brand image is associated with the likelihood of adolescents starting to drink alcohol (Sargent et al, 2006; Fisher et al, 2007), and with increased drinking amongst baseline drinkers (Snyder et al, 2006). These studies possibly underestimate the true size of the effects since as Hastings et al (2005) maintain that in reality alcohol advertisers use a combination of different marketing strategies to promote brand image.

8

Celebrity endorsements

Celebrity endorsements of alcoholic drinks can be a very effective marketing tool. McCracken (1987) define a celebrity endorser as 'any individual who uses his or her public recognition on behalf of consumer goods by appearing in an advertisement'. The suggestion is that 'celebrities are successful spokespersons for a company's brand or product in that they deliver a company's advertising message and persuade consumers to purchase the sponsored brand' (Amoateng and Poku, 2003). Hsu and McDonald (2002) reported that celebrities used in advertisements have considerable influence on consumers' attitudes and purchase intentions. Celebrity endorsement is not a new phenomenon. The following list is just a small collection of the film, sports and musical celebrities who have endorsed certain alcoholic brands: Woody Allen – Smirnoff Vodka; Ed McMahon and Frank Sinatra – Budweiser; Ice Cube – Coors Light; Leonardo di Caprio – Jim Beam; P Diddy (Sean Combs) – Cîroc Vodka; Will Ferrell – Bud Light; Dan Aykroyd – Crystal Head Vodka; Roger Federer – Moet Chandon; and Dita Von Teese – Cointreau. The list is endless. Till et al (1998) point to the risks involved with celebrity endorsement, arguing that a celebrity's image may have a negative impact on the alcohol brand that they endorse as a result of negative news or publicity. Amoateng and Poku (2013) reported that respondents overwhelmingly endorsed musicians as the personalities that attract them the most, with film makers and television presenters next and sports personalities last, in adverts of alcoholic beverages. They found that people are enticed to consume more alcoholic beverages if musicians are portrayed in advertisements singing their favourite songs.

Individuals are also likely to be attracted to an alcoholic beverage advertisement if it exposes the functions or performances of the product. The suggestion here is that, when an advertising message presents detailed information about the functions of the alcoholic beverages, many individuals are likely to be attracted to consume more. O'Guinn et al (2003) related this attraction to consumers determining the meaning of these messages based on the pre-existing values, attitudes, motivations, and beliefs they bring to the message.

8.3   The partnership approach

One of the most popular approaches to dealing with the challenge of marketing alcohol responsibly is the partnership approach, which involves regular dialogue and cooperation between the drinks industry, the public health community, and others interested in alcohol policy. This approach starts with setting the case for partnership alliances, then highlights the partners and their individual responsibilities and finally identifies the areas of common ground and the issues surrounding strategy specification, implementation, evaluation and feedback. ICAP carried out a comprehensive review of the partnership approach and they suggest in their Guide to Building Partnerships that we should consider these headings in the following manner.

1 **A case for partnership**: Strategic alliances between business, government and civil society are a growing feature of social and policy development internationally. It is increasingly clear that no one sector in society can address the complexities surrounding these issues on its own. Collaborations involve voluntarily sharing the risks and pooling resources and talents in order to optimize the delivery of outcomes, which are viewed as mutually beneficial.

2 **Partners**: A critical feature of effective partnership is the inclusion of all relevant sectors of society on an equal basis. The key stakeholders include:

■ *Governments* who are responsible for formulating, implementing, and enforcing legislation and regulations about alcohol;

■ *Intergovernmental organizations* who provide a vehicle for communication between governments at the global (e.g., the United Nations) or regional (e.g., the European Union) level;

■ *Nongovernmental organizations-NGOS* who can be particularly important at the community level, with local expertise and networks;

■ *The public health and research communities* providing the best possible scientific evidence, free from ideological or political influences;

■ *The private sector* which includes those in the drinks industry, who have social responsibilities to their customers, employees, suppliers, and to the wider communities in which they operate. The beverage alcohol industry is quite active in supporting harm reduction organizations and programmes around the world.

3 **Building partnership:** This relies on mutual respect among all the relevant parties; working together with transparency and third party support to overcome obstacles. A prerequisite for partnership is the recognition that benefits need not always be identical for all parties. The implementation of partnerships in the area of policy development relies on a series of steps that can help increase the probability of success these include:

1 Identify relevant stakeholders and build partnerships;

2 Identify issues of interest and areas of common ground;

3 Strategy specification and implementation; and

4 Evaluation and feedback.

(adapted from ICAP, 2008).

Case example: Community alcohol partnerships (CAPs) to reduce underage drinking

Community Alcohol Partnerships were developed in the UK by the Retail of Alcohol Standards Group and local partners to address underage drinking. CAPs were aimed at tackling the problems caused by underage access to alcohol, through co-operation between retailers and local stakeholders, such as Trading Standards, police, local authority licensing teams, schools and health networks. The largest CAP so far, run with Kent County Council, was independently evaluated by Kent University, and reported that the six out of seven pilot areas witnessed a substantial reduction in criminal damage and levels of anti-social behaviour. CAP officers manage these approaches and with local authorities develop new partnerships in their areas (Home Office, 2010). You can get more information about CAP schemes at: www.communityalcoholpartnerships.co.uk.

8.4   The self-regulation approach

Self-regulation is a system by which the major stakeholders of the advertising industry (advertisers, agencies and the media) actively police themselves. They agree on best practices and contribute to promoting high standards for all advertisers and advertisements. Although this approach is different from legislation, it can complement the laws of the land and it may go beyond the regulatory requirements set in some countries. Major international industries have come together in recent years to set up these self-regulatory systems and to publish information offering guidance for companies to market their products in responsible and ethical fashion. *The International Guide to Developing a Self-regulatory Organisation* published by the European Advertising Standards Alliance, in collaboration with ICAP, the World Federation of Advertisers and the International Advertising Association, is one such guide for those individuals or companies who are interested in formulating a self-regulatory system or improving an existing one. The guide is endorsed by International Chamber of Commerce (ICC) and is principally aimed at countries where there are no proper self-regulatory systems in place. (ICAP, 2014).

Self-regulation in the drinks industry

Self-regulation systems will differ according to the local market or region, but do reflect the traditions of the country in which they are. All marketing communications are subject to the International Chamber of Commerce (ICC) Consolidated Code of Advertising and Marketing Communication Practice which guides the wider principles related to marketing, irrespective of the media type adopted. The code requires marketers and practitioners to make sure that their advertising and marketing communications are fair, decent, honest, truthful, suitable for children, socially responsible, clearly distinguishable and carry honest product endorsements (EASA, 2009). Marketing alcohol products involves quite specific requirements which traditional codes of practice cannot cover, and for this reason the drinks industry have designed codes of practice to cover alcoholic beverages. This self-regulation can take numerous forms but it will normally incorporate the self-regulatory organisation's guidelines for the sector and follow the company's internal guidelines. The majority of drinks companies will have in place their own codes of practice for marketing activities, and these codes would also cover those companies who do business with them. For more information, please refer to EASA International Guide to Developing a Self-regulatory Organisation which was published in 2009.

Self-regulatory code – standards, pre-vetting and monitoring

These codes must be reviewed and updated on a continuous basis. They must reflect the evolving challenges in the wider society incorporating any technological advances. The self-regulatory code of practice should be disseminated around the industry and the public; crucially it should contain the following best practice guidelines for advertisements for alcoholic drinks:

- **General principles**: The advertisements should be legal, decent, honest and truthful. They should conform to accepted principles of fair competition and good business practice. They should be prepared with a due sense of social responsibility and based on principles of fairness and good faith, including when using testimonials. They should not show anti-social behaviour or portray dangerous or distressing situations; they should not be unethical, offend against generally prevailing standards of taste and decency or otherwise offend human dignity and integrity in the country where they are appearing.

- **Misuse**: the advertisements should not encourage, condone nor portray excessive or irresponsible consumption, present abstinence or moderation in a negative way, or suggest any link with violent, aggressive, dangerous or anti-social behaviour.

- **Dangerous activities:** advertisements should not associate drinking with dangerous or daring activities (e.g., driving).

- **Alcohol content:** they should avoid any confusion about the nature and strength of alcoholic drinks. They may present information for consumers on alcoholic strength but should not emphasise high alcoholic strength in itself as a positive quality. Equally, messages may not imply that consuming beverages of low alcohol content will avoid alcohol misuse.

■ **Medical aspects**: advertisements must not suggest that alcoholic drinks can prevent, treat or cure a human disease, or refer to such properties.

■ **Performance**: they should not create the impression that consumption of alcoholic drinks enhances mental ability or physical performance (e.g. when engaging in sports).

■ **Minors (i.e. persons below the legal age for drinking under national law**): advertisements should not be specifically aimed at minors or show minors consuming alcoholic beverages. Advertisers should avoid media or events where a majority of the audience is known to be underage.

■ **Social success**: they should not create the impression that the consumption of alcohol is a requirement for social success and should not imply that the successful outcome of a social occasion is dependent on the consumption of alcohol.

■ **Sexual aspects**: advertisements should not create the impression that consumption of alcohol is a requirement for sexual success.

(adapted from ICC, 2014).

Pre-vetting tools are used by self-regulatory organisations (including drinks companies) to prevent the appearance of advertising which does comply with the codes. SROs also actively monitor advertisements within their sectors to enable them to spot issues which could lead to further complaints. The drinks industry benefits from this type of proactive work, especially in countries or regions without SROs. EASA (2014) maintains that organisations use these proactive self-regulation tools for the following reasons:

1 **Copy advice:** This is the provision by an SRO of an opinion as to whether or not an advertisement complies with national advertising rules. It is provided on a confidential basis, usually accompanied by advice on the amendments necessary to bring a non-compliant advertisement in line with the rules. Copy advice is provided upon request to advertisers, agencies or the media.

2 **Pre-clearance:** This is required by legislators or industry bodies in some countries. The advertisement is submitted and it is not allowed to be run until it is cleared, which helps to reduce the risk of complaints.

3 **Monitoring advertisements and compliance:** This aims to provide data and evidence demonstrating the levels of compliance with the codes and laws of a specific sector. This activity helps to identify trends and to provide feedback to the industries in question.

International case examples: self-regulation structures and codes for alcohol advertising

Europe: The European Spirits Organisation (CEPS) acts as the representative body for producers of spirit drinks. With members from across Europe, CEPS ensures that no form of commercial communication about their products encourages or condones excessive consumption or misuse of spirits, or specifically targets underage drinkers. All members adhere to the principles enshrined in the European Forum for Responsible Drinking (EFRD) Common Standards for Commercial Communications.

North America: The Distilled Spirits Council of the United States (DISCUS) represents America's leading distillers and nearly 80% of all distilled spirits brands sold in the US. The DISCUS Code of Responsible Practices for Beverage Alcohol Advertising and Marketing provides for a Code Review Board comprised of senior company representatives charged with reviewing complaints about advertising and marketing materials.

Latin America: Latin American Brewers (Cerveceros Latino Americanos) is a non-profit association created in 1959 in Peru. The association is committed to social responsibility and promotes healthy lifestyles. It believes in applying self-regulatory rules to industry marketing communications (including advertising and promotion materials) in addition to laws applicable in Latin American countries.

Details regarding additional international self-regulation organisations can be found in the *Web resources* listing below.

8.5   The social norms approach

Social norms marketing is an approach to alcohol education which is targeted at young people. It attempts to provide them, through mass media and other communication techniques, with accurate information about the reality of alcohol consumption amongst their peers, to help reduce misconceptions about drinking to excess. The social norms approach in marketing is evidence based, balanced and one that encourages harm-reduction measures by using techniques to help modify beliefs about behaviour which takes place around and within drinking environments. Perkins (2002) argues that this approach to date has been targeted at young people, particularly in US college campuses. He added that most students on college campuses tend to overestimate their peers' drinking, both in quantity and frequency (Perkins, 1997; Perkins et al, 1999). This misconception by young people generally leads them to increase their personal consumption (Fabiano, 2003) Dejong et al (2006) maintain that if we can correct these types of misconceptions, it will lead to reductions in alcohol abuse and harmful outcomes. However, Perkins (1997) reminds us that these misconceptions are often accepted as typical behaviour, which implies that some people perceive excessive drinking as normal rather than exceptional. This marketing has been used, as Haines and Barker (2003) report, by many college campuses to target many young people and encourage them to drink responsibly and in a safe environment. Haines et al (2004) report that the configuration and design of social norms marketing programmes and their eventual implementation takes place over four stages, which should include:

1 **Data collection**: data is collected regarding the drinking patterns of the target group; this should include the quantity and frequency measures, outcomes, and the prevailing perceptions. The data should also identify protective, healthy behaviours already prevalent in the target group.

2 **Development of intervention strategy:** carry out market research to identify the target group's most popular media and what they perceive as credible and memorable. Select the most appropriate medium to deliver the message and plan. Develop a prototype message that is simple, positive, truthful, and consistent; refine the approach following the test run.

3 **Implementation:** implement a marketing campaign that delivers messages frequently and consistently.

4 **Evaluation:** assess the extent to which messages reach the target audience, collect and analyse outcome data to assess te effectiveness and impact on drinking behaviours and outcomes.

Haines and Barker (2003) add that other approaches which have been applied on university campuses in the US with great success, include intensive campaigns through newspaper advertisements, posters, leaflets, editorials and articles which address the misunderstanding and correct misperceptions.

Pros and cons of social norms marketing

Turner et al (2008) and Moreira et al (2009) report that social norm marketing approaches have delivered good results among young people on college campuses, with decreases in alcohol abuse and misuse and harm related injuries. Haines et al (2003) state that these programmes and similar approaches have been used at secondary level to clarify misconceptions. Perkins et al (2010) add that the programmes have also been adopted to address numerous risky behaviours (i.e. drugs, smoking, sexual violence and drink driving). Although social norms marketing programmes have gathered many supporters, Dejong et al (2009) suggest that this approach is difficult to replicate because each programme is tailored to a particular target group. Environmental elements can also play a critical role in the effectiveness of social norms marketing (Scribner et al, 2011) and their subsequent success.

Case example: Nightclub's promotion breached national code on responsible promotion of alcohol

A drinks promotion by a nightclub breached the National Code of Practice on the Naming, Packaging and Promotion of Alcoholic Drinks. A member of the public complained that the following advertisement on the nightclub's Facebook page encouraged illegal or irresponsible drinking it stated:

"Mexican Party, Free Tequila for Everyone all night long!!!, Sombrero Hat Giveaway with DJ Tom!, Free Admission before 12.30 am", "Gona be messy madness – who's up for some?", The Independent Complaints Panel noted that under the National Code: "a drink, its packaging and any promotional material or activity must not in any direct or indirect way... encourage illegal, irresponsible or immoderate consumption, such as binge-drinking, drunkenness or drink-driving". It also noted that in the Code Guidance Notes, it states that promotions offering "entry fees that are linked with unlimited free drinks" should not be run as they "entail a disproportionate risk that they will lead directly to alcohol misuse and anti-social behaviour". The Independent Complaints Panel concluded that the promotion advertising free admission before 12:30am (and an admission charge after 12:30am), together with "Free Tequila all night long", contravened the National Code Guidance Notes and was therefore in breach of the Code (MEAS, 2011).

8.6   Alcohol sponsorship

The relationship between alcohol sponsorship and festivals, sports events and significant celebrations has been long established, for example the association between the champagne shower and the conclusion of Formula One motor racing events is well known. In recent times however this relationship has come under the microscope. Arthur's Day, for example, was a marketing ploy by the drinks company Diageo dressed up as a cultural contribution, aimed to encourage people to raise a glass to the memory of the Guinness founder. Devlin (2014) argued that this event, which was established as a faux holiday in 2009, highlighted a range of social problems arising from alcohol promotion. The Royal College of Physicians in Ireland reporting that there was a 30% increase in ambulance callouts on this day and subsequently the event was discontinued in 2014. The Centre for Alcohol Marketing and Youth (2004) argue that sport is still one of the major areas for the promotion and consumption of alcohol. Drinks companies spend huge amounts of money annually advertising and placing their brands in sport (i.e. Heineken European Rugby Cup, whiskey companies and golf, up to recently Busch Series in NASCAR,

FA Carling Football Premiership). O'Brien and Kypri (2008) and O'Brien et al (2011) maintain that these types of associations and sponsorship of sports participants or athletes are directly associated with more hazardous drinking.

Dr Kerry O'Brien from the Monash and Manchester Universities conducted a research study in the United Kingdom which consisted of 2,048 university-based sports people. The main conclusion highlighted that being in receipt of alcohol sponsorship was associated with higher levels of alcohol consumption, and a higher likelihood of both hazardous and dependent drinking amongst students (O'Brien, 2014).This excess consumption, which leads to health problems for individuals and lost productivity for employers, has driven some countries to ban alcohol industry sponsorship and advertising in sport completely (e.g. France). Devlin (2014) notes however that some countries like Ireland will adopt a phasing out of alcohol sponsorship up to 2020 to allow new sponsors to get involved.

Figure 8.1: The Heineken cup (European rugby cup), known as the H cup in France due to strict legislation (Photo: Wikimedia Commons).

8.7   Labelling of alcoholic beverages

Labelling of alcoholic beverages can serve a number of purposes, which include providing information about the beverage, enticing the consumer to buy the beverage and warning of dangers and health risks from the product. Listing the ingredients contained in a particular product can also help to alert the consumer to the presence of any potentially harmful or problematic substances. Providing the nutritional information such as calorie content can allow consumers to monitor their diets better and maintain a healthier lifestyle. Graves and Kaskutas (2002) maintain that standard drinks labelling is limited to those beverages whose strengths are known, or ones which are served in standard containers. Consequently standard drinks labelling is most useful for commercially produced alcoholic beverages or home produced alcoholic beverages whose strength is well defined. Labelling in the European Union is a contentious issue. Currently under the Food Information to Consumers legislation alcoholic beverages (which covers those containing more than 1-2% alcohol by volume) are exempt from the obligation to list their ingredients and to provide nutrition information; consumers are still unable to know exactly what is in wine, beer or spirits or how many calories they are consuming.

Banwell (1999) insists that we must also consider the fact that the majority of alcoholic beverages are consumed in the home or alternate venues ,where the sizes of glasses may vary and the alcoholic drinks served are not quantified. In contrast Gill and Donaghy (2004) argue that the ability to understand the relationship between drinks sizes, strengths, and drinking patterns can still help individuals gauge their intake even under these circumstances. The European Commission however state that by the 13th December 2014 they will produce a report concerning the application of the current regulation and address whether alcoholic beverages should in future be more rigidly covered. This could also consider the need to propose a definition of alcopops (Euro Care, 2014). Ahead of this report some countries in the European Union are already leading the way in alcohol labelling, for example the Portman Group (2014) reported that in the United Kingdom alcohol companies have pledged to implement an innovative health labelling scheme to provide more information about responsible drinking on alcohol labels and containers. This voluntary scheme is the first of its kind in Europe and has been developed in conjunction with the UK Department of Health. Drinks companies have pledged to display the number of units, the Chief Medical Officers' guidelines and a pregnancy warning on 80% of drinks containers on shelves in the UK off-trade by the end of December 2013.

For more detailed information which is directly relevant to your region in relation to the labelling of alcoholic beverages see 'Beverage alcohol labelling requirements by country' (www.icap.org/table/alcoholbeveragelabeling). At the time of writing, this table held the general information and legislative requirements for on-product labelling in 43 nations and the European Union.

8

Case example: Alcoholic beverage labelling in the U.S

The Alcoholic Beverage Labelling Act (ABLA)

This legislation was enacted in 1988 and its main provisions mandate that a government warning statement appear on all alcohol beverages. It is unlawful for any person to manufacture, import, or bottle for sale or distribution in the U.S. any alcoholic beverage unless the container of such beverage bears the following statement:

"GOVERNMENT WARNING: (1) According to the Surgeon General, women should not drink alcoholic beverages during pregnancy because of the risk of birth defects. (2) Consumption of alcoholic beverages impairs your ability to drive a car or operate machinery, and may cause health problems" (adapted from US Legal, 2014).

Figure 8.2 and 8.3: Alcohol label samples (Sources: Wikimedia Commons).

8.8   The sale of alcohol in retail establishments

The sale of alcohol in retail premises and mixed trading premises brings plenty of business opportunities and added responsibilities. The best practice guidelines highlighted in this section address the main areas which retailers and their staff members should follow. They are: staff training, underage purchases, promotions and advertising, and the siting of alcohol in their store. This review covers good business practices across the whole retail sector, but note that no one system will cover all types of operations because of their size, scale, cultural influences and the local environment.

Mixed trading premises are those which sell alcohol (including wine, beer and spirits) in addition to other goods, for example supermarket, convenience store or petrol filling station, which may also sell hot and cold food, newspapers, petrol, etc. to the public (RRAI, 2010).

Who can sell alcohol? In most countries, only persons over 18 may sell alcohol otherwise a criminal offence will be committed. Persons employed in retail and mixed trading premises who are under 18 cannot sell alcohol and must therefore seek the assistance of their manager or an assistant who is over 18 to complete any alcohol transactions.

When and where can alcohol be sold? In most countries, the sale of alcohol products is only permitted during the licensing hours (check with your local laws to ensure that you are not selling alcohol outside of these times). Alcohol products should be only sold at clearly designated checkout points. Alcohol should not be sold at unsupervised self-service checkouts .

These guidelines are prepared for the benefit of retailers who are responsible for all the sales of alcohol in their premises. They should also check the laws which apply to their area to ensure that they are completely aware of their legal obligations. Changes to the legislation in most countries have brought about closer examination of retailing activities and promotions surrounding alcohol. The main areas to focus on are covered below.

Figure 8.4: Alcohol display in a retail establishment.

The incident book

Retail establishments, like licensed premises, should keep an incident book in which staff can record anything out of the ordinary which may occur during their shift, for example underage or drunken persons trying to buy alcohol, a visit from the local police (when the reason should be stated) or similar incidents. The details should be noted clearly, and the incident brought to the attention of the manager or employer at the earliest opportunity. Entries in the incident book may be important for court evidence. The details should include the date and time, the reason service was refused, the names of any other staff members or witnesses who were present in the shop at the time of the incident, a description of the person who tried to buy alcohol and a note of the conversation with the person when the sale was refused (RRAI, 2010).

Customer complaints

Under most codes of practice for responsible retailing of alcohol, customers are permitted to lodge complaints if it appears that the agreed Code of Practice is not being followed within the store. For anyone receiving a complaint, the procedure should be:

1   Acknowledge the complaint, call the store manager so that they may deal with the complaint and try to resolve the issue at store level.

2   If no manager is available, take the customer details and the details of the complaint and pass the information to the manager when they return.

3   Record the details of the complaint and the customer's details in the incident book.

Customers can take the complaint further, for example, to the representative body. A copy of the code should be displayed prominently with the name of the license holder and the correct contact details for the representative body (e.g. British Retail Consortium).

Preventing underage purchases, responsible retailing

Young people are getting access to alcohol and consuming it at very early ages. Selling alcohol to persons under the age of 18 is against the law in most countries; even liqueur chocolates cannot be sold to those under the legally agreed age (e.g. 16 in the U.K). Retailers and their staff have a responsibility to play by preventing young people from obtaining alcohol from their store. Identifying someone's age can be challenging, and factors which can make this even more challenging include their dress code, deception tactics, a busy store, an intimidating attitude, large groups or threatening behaviour. The 'No Proof No Sale' policy coupled with a strategy which incorporates a cautious, consistent, courteous, clear and careful techniques can be most effective.

■ **Proof of age point of sale signage**: For example 'No ID No Sale' with the relevant legislation displayed in prominent positions inside and outside.

■ **Proof of age cards**: Today there are a number of legitimate sources of ID that young people can access to prove their age. These includes a photo driving licence, a passport, and proof of age cards (with photos) agreed by the local police or industry bodies – see the case example below. There are people willing to make, supply and use fake proof of age. The most likely form of fake ID will be a card with which you are not familiar. They can sometimes be identified by running your thumb and forefinger over the photo. If it is raised from the face of the card, then the card is less likely to be genuine (see also Appendix VI, *Best practice procedures for ID checking*).

■ **Youths congregating outside retail premises**: these meeting places are often considered to be a flash point for anti-social behaviour. It is clear that retailers suffer from this problem, with young people causing litter, deterring customers and possibly intimidating staff. To counteract these problems, a store can make its frontage less attractive as a place to congregate, by removing any low level walls and any directly adjoining canopies that provide shelter. Really well-lit areas usually deter youths from congregating.

- **Siting of alcohol in store**: alcohol in some premises is only sold from an agreed controlled area. The siting is important (alcohol theft is huge, especially in shops where it is placed near the exits). Staff should regularly check alcohol displays, making themselves visible, and customers loitering should be offered help in the usual way to deter thefts or underage purchasing. Security tags will protect those items that are most targeted (i.e. strong spirits). If the alcohol is sold in a mixed trading shop, CCTV must cover the whole area.

- **Promotions of alcohol**: There is a significant growth in alcohol-related problems. Retailers form part of the alcohol industry and have a part to play in ensuring that the way alcohol is promoted is done responsibly.

- **Awareness**: Point of sale or promotional activities should be in line with the local codes.

- **Retailer alert bulletins**: These are issued by industry groups to give up-to-date information about products whose naming, packaging or presentation have been held to infringe the local code of practice on the sale of alcoholic drinks.

- **Sensible drinking levels**: it is a good idea to display information at the point of sale on sensible drinking levels and sensible drinking messages.

- **In-store tastings**: Free tastings are permitted under the law in most countries, but the following guidelines should be followed: the sample size must be appropriate (e.g. 5ml) and amounts should be closely monitored; there should be point of sale material stating the law; alcohol must not be provided to anyone underage or who is drunk. Alcohol should not be left unattended in the demonstration area.

- **Staff training**: Staff must know about the law and the responsibilities of alcohol retailing, before they are allowed to serve alcohol. They should be given a course, or at least the company's training manual on the retailing of alcohol, and their knowledge checked before they are authorised to sell alcohol. Getting formal qualifications can be of benefit to the staff and the company. Staff training records must be kept up-to-date.

    adapted from (BRC, 2004; RRAI, 2010).

Aiding and abetting

Employees who sell alcohol to underage drinkers can themselves be prosecuted in most countries for 'aiding and abetting'. While the prime responsibility for such matter lies with the license holder (the employer), responsibility also lies with the person involved in the transaction. In some countries the police are now prosecuting employees and employers who have been involved in the sale of alcohol to under age persons.

Drunken persons

It is against the law in most countries to sell alcohol to someone who is drunk. A conviction can result in a temporary closure of the premises and loss of business. Staff members should therefore be always on the lookout for customers who display signs of drunkenness (i.e. slurred speech, swaying, staggering, rowdy behaviour) and inform the manager immediately. If the manager is not available then the employee should politely take the customer aside, explain that they are unable to sell alcohol to them and ask them to leave the premises. If the customer refuses to leave, the police should be called immediately.

For advice regarding further areas of concern including disorderly conduct, consumption of alcohol within certain parameters of the shop, refusal of service and sale – reasonable belief and the powers of the police to enter premises, for retail and mixed trading establishments, you should the seek advice and assistance of your local retail trade associations.

Case examples

PASS - Proof of age card scheme

The Proof of Age Standards Scheme (PASS) is operated in the UK. It carries the PASS hologram which has been adopted by nearly all legitimate schemes, including Citizencard, Connexions, Portman Group, Young Scot, Validate, and many local authority schemes. PASS is a voluntary industry initiative supplied by the retail and hospitality industries and endorsed by the UK Government.

The Trading Standards Institute advises retailers only to accept cards from the issuers who are signed up to PASS, or a passport or photo driving licence. All retail staff should be trained to look for the PASS hologram (BRC, 2004).

Figure 8.5: In support of 'No ID no Sale' cards (Blomfield, 2014).

Teens test rogue bar and retail establishments

Legislation in Ireland now allows the police to send young people under 18 (with the consent of their parents) into licensed premises to make test purchases of alcohol. The results can then be used in evidence in court (Brady, 2008).

Conclusion

Individuals, private and public organizations, and retail establishments have a collective duty to market and sell their alcohol products in a responsible manner. Retail industries and establishments involved in the sale of alcohol can pursue legitimate profits and promote the public good through the responsible retailing, and by encouraging their customers to drink sensibly, which is both ethical and in the long-term economic interest of the businesses. Industry efforts directed at promoting more responsible marketing of alcohol products will go a long way to demonstrating to everyone, most notably those concerned about public health, that they are serious about contributing to the effort to reduce alcohol misuse and harm.

Web resources

Alcohol Research UK
   www.alcoholresearchuk.org

Association of Canadian Distillers (ACD)
   www.acd.ca/

Comité Européen des Enterprises Vins (CEEV)
   www.wineinmoderation.eu.

Drink Aware (UK), (Ireland)
   www.drinkaware.co.uk and www.drinkaware.ie

Distilled Spirits Industry Council of Australia (DSICA)
   www.dsica.com.au

Distilled Spirits Association of New Zealand
   www.asa.co.nz

Latin American Brewers (Cerveceros Latino Americanos)
   www.cerveceroslatinoamericanos.com

The Beer Institute - USA
   www.beerinstitute.org

The Brewers Association of Canada
   www.brewers.ca/

The Brewers of Europe
   www.brewersofeurope.org

The Distilled Spirits Council of the United States (DISCUS)
   www.discus.org/about/

The European Spirits Organisation (CEPS)
   www.europeanspirits.org.

The European Forum for Responsible Drinking (EFRD)
   www.efrd.org

8

9 Responsible Service of Alcohol

Aims and learning outcomes

This chapter aims to provide the knowledge necessary to understand the context and commercial environment in which alcohol is consumed. It also looks at best practice procedures and strategies which can be adopted to help individual establishments and large commercial operations to meet their obligations to serve alcohol in a responsible manner. After reading this chapter you should be able to:

- Explain how the context and environment where alcohol is consumed influences consumers' expectation and eventual outcomes.

- Establish the approaches and strategies used by businesses to make their premises safe and to reduce alcohol related problems.

- Identify the current structural and systematic approaches to training in the field of responsible service of alcohol (RSA).

- Apply RSA strategies and training for all staff members and management to prevent guest intoxication, to identify over-consumption and to practice responsible serving techniques.

- Conduct responsible service of alcohol audits to highlight areas you need to address with further training and new procedures.

9.0 Introduction

Tourism and hospitality companies run hotels, restaurants, bars, nightclubs, cruise liners, guest houses, visitor centres and other licensed establishments where people can relax and socialise with alcohol beverages. These also provide food and non-alcohol beverages, entertainment, a place for family and friends to get together, jobs for hospitality staff including bartenders, chefs, waiters, etc. and vital tax revenues. The well-being of customers is crucial to the success of these industries, and this consideration in the modern era extends to the responsible serving of alcoholic beverages. The priority of real hospitality is to make sure that customers have a memorable experience, but when they consume alcohol they relax and lower their inhibitions and sometimes get a little intoxicated. This reality places a firm responsibility on hospitality staff members to refuse service to intoxicated individuals because they might injure themselves or others. In recent years the licensed establishments across these industries, along with the co-operation of industry bodies and health officials have developed training programmes to help managers and servers to recognise the symptoms of intoxication and to serve alcohol beverages responsibly.

9.1 Towards a context and venue to enjoy alcohol

The famous American sociologist Ray Oldenburg, in his book *The Great Good Place: Cafes, Coffee Shops, Bookstores, Bars, Hair Salons, and Other Hangouts at The Heart of a Community*, maintains that where people choose to drink is one of the numerous facets of drinking behaviour (Oldenburg, 1999). He also added that drinking is an integral component of social interaction in many cultures. Heath (2000) agrees and states that the majority of alcohol consumption takes place in public settings and commercial venues. The venue chosen is often closely related to expectations and eventual outcomes. Quigley et al (2003) propose the link between certain drink venues and the risk of violence as an example of this. Haworth & Simpson (2004) adds that the quality of alcoholic beverages, especially in developing countries where traditional beverages are consumed, can cause potential harm for patrons at some venues.

Nightclubs, pubs, bars and restaurant venues have focused on increasing their business in recent years through entertainment which is usually offered to patrons as late-night activities. Single (1997) maintains that although these venues are popular in the majority of cities, the activities are also the origin of numerous social problems. These arise because most late night entertainment activities are targeted at young people and are closely linked with alcohol consumption. The consequence of this association leads Room et al (2003) to conclude that some of the most undesirable features of late night entertainment include crime, violence, anti-social behaviour and littering. Rossow and Hauge (2004) maintain that these activities are more closely associated with intoxicated or binge drinking individuals. The impact of this behaviour on the local community is huge. Chisholm et al (2004) argue that these effects place a particular strain on local public services, for example public transportation, policing, emergency services and street cleaning. Late night entertainment venues are concentrated in urban or central city locations in

9

most countries, and for many individuals who do live in the city this entails transportation, and this requirement can lead to drink driving, road crashes, and traffic injuries (Wagenaar and Holden, 1991). Dealing with under age persons who will try to gain entry and service of alcohol at licensed premises is another concern, especially in countries and regions where there is a defined legal purchase age in operation (Toomey et al, 1998). To meet these particular challenges Wallin et al (2003) inform us that several strategies have been developed which include:

- Policies to control the availability of alcohol through zoning and hours of sale
- Incentives for businesses to modify marketing and other practices
- Social education efforts to redefine norms on individual behaviour (see Chapter 8)
- Policies which address the service of alcohol.

Quigley et al (2003) contends that adopting policies which address in particular the responsible service of alcohol, including harm minimization techniques, can help to create safe and comfortable venues for drinking alcohol, which in turn will also help to improve communities. Responsible service and consumption of alcohol needs the active co-operation and engagement of all the stakeholders, which includes hospitality establishments, the community and the legislators (Smith et al, 2001).

Figure 9.1: Bartender prepares pre-dinner cocktails for his guests.

9.2   Developing policies and procedures to reduce alcohol related problems

Daly et al (2002) and Graham et al (2004) report that a wide variety of policies and procedures have been developed to target the service of alcohol in licensed premises, offering approaches and strategies to assist them in making their premises safe and to reduce harm. In this section we will review some of these strategies.

Management and design practices

Customers' safety and overall enjoyment can be increased by:

- the proper control of the ventilation, lighting and noise level,
- good crowd control and security measures,
- a mix of patrons by age and gender,
- discouraging intoxicated customers,
- offering a good supply of food and non-alcoholic beverage choices,
- a clean and well maintained establishment, proper seating,
- limiting the size of individual parties and drink specials,
- displaying clearly the conditions of entry, e.g. dress codes

(Arnold & Laidler, 1994).

Safety concerns

To reduce the possibility for harm you should remove broken glasses immediately and consider (if appropriate) replacing them with more durable safety glass or with plastic containers; and use clever methods to advise customers of safety issues, e.g. on drip mats, or signs in the toilets (Graham & Homel, 1997).

Licensing hours

Heavy drinking around closing time can be a problem and reminders regarding customers that you are serving last drinks can encourage this activity. Duffy (1992) reports that extended licensing hours adopted in some areas have helped to reduce intoxication and its associated harmful behaviours. Graham & Homel (1997) advise staggered closing times.

Personnel training

Taking care of intoxicated customers is difficult. Johnsson and Berglund (2003) and Sloan et al (2000) maintain that in recent years training to help server judgement has proved effective. Intervention techniques adopted by

9

server staff like providing access to alternate means of transportation or designated driver schemes (Dresser & Giksman, 1998) can help reduce incidents such as alcohol-impaired driving. Toomey et al (1998) add that servers must be trained to identify under age persons by requesting official identification cards and refusing entry and service where appropriate.

Product quality

The quality and safety of alcohol products is paramount. Establishments must only sell products of good quality from reputable suppliers.

Policy development additional factors to consider

The desire to provide venues for socializing must be balanced against the need to ensure a safe environment, clean streets, and low rates of crime and public disturbance. This balance of commercial and social freedoms on the one hand, and safety and wellbeing on the other, presents a challenge to policy-makers. The development and eventual implementation of policies and practices to reduce alcohol related harm must be considered in social and cultural surrounds rather than just economic terms. The success of any policies will be based on their flexibility to react to the local environments in which they operate. Wiggers et al (2004) agree and state that policies and laws can be effectively enforced if they are easy to understand and implement. In many countries intervention programmes which involves partnerships between all stakeholders in the drinks industry, especially the service areas, have shown great success (Felson et al; 1997; Wallin et al, 2003). Two of the most important elements which these programmes focused on were education and modification of the environment for drinking. The following successful approaches can be adopted by serving establishments, retailers, community leaders and government supported agencies to meet these two elements:

- Recognizing the role of alcohol in entertainment and within social settings
- Close relationships with law enforcement agencies, especially in problematic areas
- Linking licensing requirements to responsible alcohol service practice
- Provision and access to public and private transportation
- Implementing server training schemes
- Educating all alcohol sale and service establishments and their employees about social and community issues
- Dialogue with the community and responsiveness to their needs.
  (Gehan et al, 1999; Toomey et al., 1998; Single, 1990)

See also 7.2 *Strategies to discourage alcohol related disorderly behaviours*

9.3   Structural and systematic approaches of delivery

Currently there is a range of terminology used to cover training in the responsible service of alcohol. The literature shows these phrases used on programmes across the world: 'Responsible Beverage Service (RBS)'; 'Responsible Serving of Alcohol (RSA)'; 'Server Intervention' and 'Server Training'. Saltz (1987) and Gliksman et al (1993) inform us that RBS began in North America with the first published evaluations concerning programmes initiated in California and Ontario. They contend that these early programmes had a predominant focus on the prevention of drink-driving, and in training managers and their staff to identify intoxication in customers. This early RBS programme was primarily developed to counteract the huge increase from the 1980s in civil actions taken against US licensees in establishments where patrons had been allowed to get intoxicated before driving and then injuring a third party (Solomon and Prout, 1996). These cases involved settlements amounting to millions of dollars for the injured individuals, based on the principle that the establishment had broken the law. Stockwell (2001) highlights that these civil cases also established a legal principle of negligence and vicarious liability for the actions of customers even after they have left the premises.

These challenges brought about the Dram Shop laws in the U.S. which were developed to bring clarity regarding liability; they were also a great motivator in the spread and uptake of RBS programmes. Defence lawyers were able to use the documentation from successful completion of RBS programmes by staff and management as acceptable evidence to successful defend establishments against legal action (Moscher, 1984).

RBS through community approaches

A comparison of RBS research studies conducted in America and Australia concluded that when RBS training was carried out at a community wide level, the impact and value was diluted. Although all the factors that contributed to the poor impact are not apparent, it was clear that some of the dilution was associated with a failure to really support the principles of RBS. These programmes appear to be effective when there is strong support from management, which is not supplied on a voluntary basis (Stockwell, 2001).

RBS through legal approaches

Rydon and Stockwell (1997) suggests that the low priority and difficulties involved in defining intoxication leads to a lack of enforcement by many police authorities. RBS and its association with the duties of the police has received

9

some scholarly attention in the past. McKnight & Streff (1994) reported on one particular initiative which involved plain clothes police officers visiting licensed premises un-announced for the purpose of identifying intoxicated patrons and observing alcohol service practices. Licensees of these locations were given prior training and support literature. The findings highlighted praise for good practice, suggestions for improvements, warnings, and fines for serious breaches of the laws. It was also discovered that refusal figures rose to over 50% from a very low initial base after RBS training (McKnight, 1988). Figures for alcohol associated road accidents dropped significantly after the start of this initiative. Grube's (1997) research examined access to alcohol in 479 liquor stores by under-age persons, in six communities in California which were equally split between intervention (police enforcement programme) and control (no police enforcement programme). The research concluded that intervention did deliver positive results. RBS programmes which contain or are supported by a concentrated enforcement approach with penalties actively applied for establishments who break the law will have a better impact and chance of success than RBS programmes not linked to enforcement programmes at community wide level.

The pioneering work of Homel et al (1992) in Australia during the 1990s lead to a new model for regulating licensed premises which became known as the Accord. This approach involved a partnership between the police, community representatives, licensees and council officers to create a secure environment and to build a better reputation for the area involved. Codes were developed and signed by licensees who agreed to reduce risky alcohol serving practices (i.e. discounting, happy hours), discourage under-age, intoxicated and anti-social customers. If an establishment broke the code they were reported and fined. The findings highlighted significant improvements, but Rumbold et al (1998) discovered after two years that these improvements diminished or differed in areas where the police did not have the time or resources to actively monitor the agreement.

The Accord approach can be useful if it is supported by the whole community and closely monitored by law enforcement agencies.

9.4   Responsible serving of alcohol (RSA) - techniques for managers and servers

The wider hospitality, tourism and retail industries encompasses pubs, restaurants, clubs, hotels, off-licenses, cruise liners, airports, theatres, train stations etc. and in all these businesses management and staff have the task of serving and dealing with all types of people from all walks of life and status of society. There are however many occasions when servers and their management teams have to deal with people who may well have for various reasons consumed too much alcohol. This situation requires considerable patience, tact, firmness and above all experience. Anderson and Bauberg (2006) define responsible serving of alcohol as 'an education programme that trains managers of alcohol outlets and alcohol servers or sellers how to avoid illegally selling alcohol to intoxicated or underage patrons'. Alcohol awareness and responsible service can ultimately lead to informed and wise decision making by staff in these circumstances (Murphy, 2013). Graham (2000) reports that the training of servers and managers should focus on attitudes, knowledge, skills and practices relating to serving patrons and adds that such courses generally include efforts to address the following issues:

- **Attitudes**: that preventing intoxication is beneficial, that servers and managers have a responsibility to prevent intoxication.

- **Knowledge**: the effects, the physiology of alcohol, blood alcohol concentration, problems associated with intoxication, signs of intoxication, laws and regulations relating to serving alcohol, legal liability, strategies for dealing with intoxicated patrons and strategies for refusing service.

- **Skills:** ability to recognise intoxication, ability to refuse service and avoid problems in dealing with an intoxicated person.

- **Practice**: checking of IDs of young patrons, preventing intoxication, refusing service to someone who is intoxicated or on the way to becoming intoxicated, arranging safe transport for intoxicated patrons, one programme (Carvolth, 1988) also includes referring patrons for help with drinking problems (Graham, 2000).

The following sections will address these issues in further detail, suggesting strategies and techniques which can be implemented by licensed establishments to assist them in serving alcohol responsibly.

Alcohol service and the law / better business practices

The laws relating to the provision of alcohol differ from country to country and sometimes even by region, state or village. Servers may be held responsible for injury to others that are caused by an intoxicated customer who has been served unlawfully. It is therefore crucial that the bar owner (license holder), management and staff members develop ways to monitor the service of alcohol and learn the laws which apply to their country or area. Once someone has consumed alcohol to a level that they are showing signs of drunkenness, their normal judgment is impaired. Therefore, it is up to the server, not the customer, to decide whether they should be served or not.

Failure to act responsibly in the service of alcohol can result in accidents or even death. If negligence is proven against the employer or employee, the court may allow substantial damages to cover loss, medical fees, and loss of income, pain and suffering. If more than one party is involved, the compensation will be assessed as to what degree each member of the party has contributed towards the loss, and the damages will be allocated accordingly. Responsible alcohol service practices can also lead to better business practices, which contribute to improving the atmosphere of the bar, and ultimately to achieving greater profits.

In summary, bar owners should improve their responsible service of alcohol practices and training to:

- maintain a good reputation,
- increase customer satisfaction,
- decrease damage done to the bar,
- avoid potential legal cases,
- reduce police attendance,
- improve morale, boosting productivity and reducing staff turnover (Failte Ireland, 2003).

Note: Servers should also consult the corresponding chapters in this book which deal with the following areas; recommended safe levels of consumption, facts about alcohol and its effects on the body, distribution and removal of alcohol, BAC levels and tolerance to alcohol and proof of age identity cards, to develop their wider understanding of the issues surrounding responsible serving of alcohol.

Management responsibilities in server training

Management must clearly state their expectation of servers and give them the authority to make decisions, and they must consider how to support the decisions made by their servers. This can be achieved by having a written house policy, serving both alcoholic and non-alcoholic beverages, holding staff meetings, and keeping an incident log book for recording and subsequently reviewing particular incidents. Servers need to be sure that they have the backing of their managers, as with this support they will be more comfortable with the responsible serving of alcohol programme for your establishment. Managers should also note the strategies for reducing alcohol related problems outlined in Chapter 7 and Section 9.2 above.

Case example: Girls night out

Read this case study and discuss the questions below.

It's Thursday evening, and it's Caroline's birthday. She is out with a group of friends she has known since her college days. They are in a lively music bar in the city centre and there is a special offer on spirits, if the patron orders double measures of the chosen spirit. Caroline and her friends quickly calculate that the special offer will give them a second drink at one third of the full price, so they decide to take the offer and double up their drink. As the night progresses, they start to show the signs of drunkenness and they all appear to be having a great laugh together. Sarah, Caroline's friend asks her if she wants another drink, Caroline declines, saying she wants to take it easy and feels quite drunk already. When Caroline visits the toilet, her friends take her drink to the bar, where they ask the server to add another vodka to the drink. The server does so, and this happens several times throughout the evening. Just before closing, a staff member notices Caroline slumped against a wall, a man who is not from her original group of friends is kissing her and supporting her. Caroline's friends are now getting ready to leave; one of them makes a comment about Caroline 'getting lucky' on her birthday.

- Have any of your local laws been broken?

- What are the dangers of the above situation?

- What policies could the bar have in place to prevent this situation from arising?

Adapted from ICAP (2008).

Preventing guest intoxication and identifying over-consumption

Stepping in to stop someone from becoming intoxicated stems from a concern for their safety and the safety of others. The following actions should be taken by staff to avoid guest intoxication:

- First and foremost, notify management of potential problems (i.e. guests drinking fast), keep track of how much is being consumed and how fast.

- Engage guests in conversations; ask details that would be a good test of mental alertness (i.e. recent news, sports events).

- Suggest selling food (especially high protein food such as fried cheese, potato skins.

- Promote healthy non and low alcoholic drinks/events.

- Use attractive signage and price incentives and remember that servers can influence customers' decisions regarding drinks so avoid unacceptable serving practices. (Murphy, 2005).

Identifying guest intoxication

Some people are very clever at hiding intoxication, so how do we identify over-consumption? Here are some of the signs to help servers decide. These must not considered in isolation because rash decisions can cause major problems, for example a person with a disability might display some of them.

■ A noticeable change in the customer's behaviour, becoming loud, erratic, animated, boisterous, using bad language, annoying others, slurred speech, argumentative, obnoxious, over-friendly to strangers, sudden quietness.

■ A lack of judgment, careless with money, making silly, irrational or repeated statements, boasts about their financial situation, 'conquests', physical or mental strength, drinking faster, complaining about drink prices.

■ Clumsiness, losing muscular control, becoming clumsy, spilling drinks and difficulty in picking up their change. The loss of co-ordination, swaying and staggering, difficulty in walking straight, bumping into furniture.

■ Decreased alertness, becoming drowsy (heavy eyelids), delays in responding to questions and paying attention, hearing, concentration and focus 'glazed eyes', or becomes detached, brooding.

■ The smell of alcohol (an important indication).

Case example: Two bar staff charged after the death of a customer

in 2008 a 26 year old father of two children who died after a drinking session where he had been drinking beer for a while before one shot of vodka was put in his beer which he drank in one go, two shots were put in another which he drank, this drinking competition continued with the deceased claiming he could down 10 shots in a pint glass before his colleagues could down their beer. The deceased's friends carried him to a conference room and left him until he was discovered next morning dead. In 2011 after a 5 day trial in the criminal courts the two bartenders were acquitted. Despite a finding of gross negligence in the discharge of their duties the Court directed the jury to an acquittal on the basis of 'supervening event' – the fact that the deceased had made a personal decision to consume the alcohol.

The two men were charged with common law manslaughter. A civil case for damages was subsequently taken by the deceased family against the licence holder (The Guardian, 2004; Stack, 2011).

Delaying or suspending service

When a customer has reached their maximum number of drinks, service can be delayed; if the customer is showing signs of intoxication, service of alcohol may be stopped for the duration of the evening. The server should alert management of any potential problems before a decision is made, and if a problem arises, it should be left to security or management to handle. Servers and management should be prepared to call the police if necessary.

Refusal of service technique (T.A.K.E C.A.R.E): Advice to servers

If you believe that the guest is intoxicated, you are morally and legally bound to take appropriate action, but you must always take care of your personal security and the security of your other customers. You should also follow the guidelines listed below:

- **T**ell them early. Have a quiet discrete word or use other members of a group to warm the offending person.

- **A**void put-downs. Don't be judgmental, or say, "you're drunk", or scold the customer, or appear to be blaming them.

- **K**eep yourself calm. Your tone of voice is very important. You need to be firm without being aggressive. Do not raise your voice. Behaviour breeds behaviour. You can calm them down if you remain calm yourself.

- **E**ver courteous, respect breeds respect. You might say, "I'm sorry, if I served you another drink I'd be breaking the law"; or "I'd lose my job"; or "I'm concerned about your safety".

- **C**larify your refusal. Explain why service is being refused, and focus on the behaviour, not the individual. Explain that they are welcome back tomorrow if they behave. Offer alternatives. Offer to call a taxi, offer low or non-alcoholic drinks,

- **A**llow them to save face in front of friends.

- **R**eport the incident. Make all staff aware of what happened. Keep an incident logbook near the bar and write what has occurred. If the customer injures a third party, after leaving the premises, the record will be important.

- **E**cho. If the customer is a regular, staff can quietly reinforce the message when they return. Some other good tips are: never touch the customer, speak to them away from others (the audience) this is useful as a face-saving measure for the customer and don't be afraid to involve the management (Murphy, 2002).

9

Responsible service of alcohol: role-play scenarios

Scenario A: It's early morning, when a small group of guys and girls arrive at the bar to order drinks. The server observes that the group are exhibiting different conditions of behaviour (laughing, joking, loud, quite, singing and sleepy). What information could you supply to the servers to assist them with their decision?

Scenario B: A group of six young business people arrive at the bar and request service of a bottle of tequila and 6 shot glasses, what information could you supply to the server to assist them with the decision to be made?

9.5 Responsible serving of alcohol (RSA) audits

If you own or rent a licensed establishment, you must inspect your premises and consider the areas listed below. The report from the audit checks should highlight the areas which you need to address with further training and new procedures.

■ **Towards policy formulation**: (a) is your house policy in place and updated, (b) are drinks related incidents documentation reviewed regularly, (c) what partnerships do you have with community groups, government and law enforcement agencies, hospitality organisations and (d) is your insurance cover risk assessed for RSA training?

■ **Towards server training**: are your managers and servers trained in (a) the local laws, (b) effect of alcohol on the body, (c) signs of intoxication, (d) recognition of false IDs, (e) handling an intoxicated patron, (f) strengths of different alcohol beverages. Employers must check that their servers have read and understand the house policy and have signed and follow the policies. Servers should not be encouraged to promote harmful alcohol consumption (e.g. by incentives to sell more spirits). Are your servers supported to take decisions on refusals of alcohol service? Finally is your training system for RSA updated regularly?

■ **Towards controlling the serving of alcohol beverages**: (a) do you have standardised recipes and portion sizes for all your beverages, (b) is your measuring equipment (spirit/wine measures etc.) in good working order, (c) do you use standard glassware, (d) do you allow drinks to be served in extra-large sizes (jugs of cocktails), (e) are free or special promotion drinks strictly monitored, (f) are customers risk assessed for intoxication, (g) do you sell high protein foods and or provide free complimentary salt free snacks, (h) do your servers upsell strong drinks, (i) are RSA signs in use?

- **Towards closing time**: (a) are notices for last drinks circulated in good time (30-45 minutes before closing), (b) do you offer high protein food and reduced priced non-alcoholic beverages at last call?

- **Towards the entrance**: (a) are crowd numbers limited, (b) are patrons IDs checked every time on entry, (c) do you have enough of door staff employed?

- **Towards under-age patrons**: (a) are the correct procedures for checking IDs in place and understood, (b) do you confiscate fake IDs, (c) do you restrict alcohol service to adults who give alcohol drinks to under-age persons?

- **Towards intoxication**: (a) are your systems set up to prevent intoxication, (b) is service reduced or stopped when a customer shows sign of intoxication, (c) are intoxicated patrons treated with discretion, (d) are care provisions in place for intoxicated customers, (e) do you have transport – taxi numbers etc. available, (f) do you have a designated driver programme (i.e. identifying the driver and recording his name in the log book, ensuring that they don't consume alcohol but free or low-priced non-alcohol drinks). (adapted from NRA, 1996; Murphy, 2005)

Conclusion

Ensuring that the environment for alcohol consumption remains safe and conducive to enjoyment and positive social interaction is crucial for those responsible for selling and serving alcohol, especially licensed establishments. Targeted interventions like the RSA courses and strategic approaches around responsible serving of alcohol require a mix of incentives, enforcement, regulation and education, involving all the stakeholders in a partnership approach. These partnerships should be cognizant of local needs and resources which will differ between areas and regions. There are clear benefits to servers and establishment owners from responsible practices. There are advantages in increased safety not only within and around establishments, but also in the urban areas where these venues are located. A number of effective harm reduction approaches have been implemented in countries around the world to ensure the safety of establishments where alcohol is served. This work is on-going and it will require the continued support of individuals working in prevention, licensed premise owners, managers and staff, suppliers, urban planners, residents, and regulatory and enforcement officials to succeed. Finally it should also be remembered that everyone involved in the sale and service of alcohol products can make a difference in ensuring that they are served and enjoyed in a responsible manner.

9

Web resources

APSAD (Australia)

www.apsad.org.au

European Forum for Responsible drinking

efrd.org

Responsible service of alcohol – a servers guide

www.dartmouth.edu/~orl/greek-soc/docs/servers_guide_final_2008.pdf

Responsible service of alcohol – a servers guide (UK)

www.dartmouth.edu/~orl/greek-soc/docs/servers_guide_final_2008.pdf

Responsible service of alcohol (Australia)

www.youtube.com/watch?v=ya-d8VEFkao

Serve-safe (USA)

www.servsafe.com

Serving it right (British Columbia)

www.servingitright.com/

TIPS (U.S.A) Training for Intervention ProcedureS

www.tipsalcohol.com/

10 Policy Making for Alcohol: Towards a Combined Approach

Aims and learning outcomes

This aim of this chapter is to explore the efforts of policy makers in creating alcohol policies through regulatory and legislative structures which contribute towards increasing understanding of the benefits of moderate alcohol consumption at the individual and societal levels. After reading this chapter you should be able to:

- Explain the reasons behind the need to increase the understanding of moderate alcohol consumption at individual and societal levels.

- Outline the policies currently used to control alcohol consumption and define alcohol consumption patterns around the world

- Identify the regulatory and legislative structures, and direct and indirect regulatory measures used towards effective alcohol policies globally.

- Outline the steps and outputs involved in creating sustainable alcohol policies and describe examples of targeted educational programmes aimed at changing the harmful behaviour which surrounds alcohol consumption.

10.0 Introduction

This chapter addresses the key areas which underline international and local approaches towards developing and implementing alcohol policies, based on drinking patterns, targeted interventions and the building of partnerships. The amount of alcohol which individuals consume largely determines the outcomes they are going to experience. Harmful patterns of alcohol consumption have had a detrimental effect on society and national healthcare providers; we have witnessed increased levels of public order offences and violent acts, all related to the misuse of alcohol. It is for this reason that consumption patterns are a key consideration in policy development. In recent years research studies have indicated that individuals across the world consume alcohol differently, some abstain completely due to health reasons or religious beliefs. This limits the value of examinations of drinking patterns based on average measures of consumption of whole populations, when the majority of consumers enjoy alcohol on an occasional basis at special events, within the meal experience or for relaxation purposes. Effective prevention requires an understanding of how people actually drink. It is therefore crucial to know consumption styles at an individual or group level. These challenges have influenced governments, industry bodies and community groups in recent years to move towards a combined approach towards policy making for the sale, service and consumption of alcohol.

10.1 A rationale for alcohol policy making

The primary rationale of any policy for alcohol is to aim to reduce its harmful effects and to increase the knowledge base and understanding of the benefit of moderate consumption. Polices for alcohol are also intended to balance the rights and responsibilities of every person against those of society. Heath (2000) and Marshall (1979) state that the majority of people drink alcohol moderately because it gives them pleasure and it acts as a social lubricant, which is important in life. Although people usually consume their alcohol in a responsible manner, the abuse of these products can bring about harmful societal and health consequences for some individuals. A combined approach towards policy making for alcohol which incorporates policies at the individual and societal levels is required. The policies must include the following.

- **Individual level**: to safeguard wellbeing and health, offer protection from harm, increase the understanding of harms and benefits, and promote a change in behaviour. It should encourage positive and discourage negative drinking patterns, improve the ability of individuals to make informed decisions and ensure personal choice and freedom, without unduly impinging upon the freedoms of others.
- **Societal level**: to reduce the burden of harm due to alcohol misuse, decrease the overall cost to society, provide treatment and support services for those who are harming themselves or have been harmed by others' abuse of alcohol, ensure public safety and to create an informed society.

ICAP (2014e) propose that particular attention in the development of policy approaches is required especially in areas where the potential for positive and for negative outcomes exist. They suggest that these include:

- responsiveness to changes in the role of alcohol in society, especially under conditions of social and economic transformation;

- unencumbered availability while protecting those at risk of harm;

- responsible practice around advertising and promotion;

- education for the public;

- provision of health care for those who need it;

- responsible service of alcohol;

- product quality and integrity.

The challenge in developing policies that can address these areas is to create an approach broad enough in scope and emphasis to involve and satisfy the concerns of all sectors, public and private, governmental and nongovernmental (ICAP, 2014e).

Setting a context for adopting alcohol policies

If you are going to adopt a combined approach towards your policy making for alcohol, which incorporates the individual and societal levels, then you must consider the potential benefits to be increased and the potential harms to be reduced.

- **Potential benefits**: the economic, societal and health contributions of alcohol, which includes employment and revenue from the distribution, sales, manufacturing fields, plus the tourism, hospitality and retail industries. Production in some regions or countries may be vital to their economic sustainability especially in rural areas. Please refer also to Section 5.4 for a wider discussion of the benefits of moderate alcohol consumption.

- **Potential harms**: Stockwell et al (1996) highlight that these harms are traditionally associated with abusive or excessive drinking patterns, which cost society in the workplace (see Chapter 6); through the medical costs associated with accidents and injury at home, other venues or on the road (Chochinov, 1998; Nelson and Wechsler, 2003), through violence and aggression, sexual activities including pregnancy, disease, unwanted sex (Singh et al 2001; Ferrins-Brown et al, 1999). Please also refer to sections 5.2 and section 5.3 for more on the risks of alcohol consumption.

Prior to any policy being implemented you must also consider if (a) the benefits of implementation exceed the costs, or the other way round and (b) if all the variables (including the less obvious) have been fully assessed (Gmel et al 2003; Single and Easton, 2001). These considerations should assist you in deciding on the best policy approach which increases the benefits and reduces the harms of the policy to society.

10.2 Policies to control alcohol consumption

Reduce alcohol consumption

Alcohol policies were usually based on the association between a country's average level of consumption per person and their incidences of medical and social problems in the overall population (Babor and Del Boca, 2003; Ledermann and Tabah, 1951; Saunders and DeBurgh, 1999). This approach, which is used by many countries today, is aimed at reducing overall consumption, which should lead to reductions in alcohol related incidences.

Restrict its access and availability

This control traditionally covers entire countries, regions or areas depending on the legislation in place. It will also contain measures which control some of the following elements: restriction of licensing hours, banning the sale on certain days, pricing, taxation and duties, limiting the number of alcohol sale and service retail premises, setting minimum age limits for consumption, operating state-run monopolies to control sales, or in some circumstances total prohibition.

These control measures can also include cover restrictions on the marketing and advertising of alcohol. Grant and Litvak (1998) and Stockwell et al (1993) maintain that these types of measures are flawed because of their inability to distinguish between the moderate and the abusive consumer. Norstrom (2001) and Rehm and Gmel (1999) agree and add that these measures lack flexibility and fail to react to the individual or group needs at which they are aimed, especially harmful consumers.

Adopt a standardized approach for every country

Heath (2000) highlights a major flaw of this policy, arguing that drinking has been around since the dawn of time and the practices and traditions which follow its use in many cultures are tightly ingrained. For this reason, alcohol control policies which don't suit the local culture will not work. Ramstedt (2001) adds that because every country across the world contains their individual rituals, attitudes and beliefs in relation to alcohol, if you try to create a standardised approach for every country and every setting, the results are likely to differ in their intended outcomes.

Structuring alcohol policies – areas to consider

To structure policies which will deliver sustainable and effective results, you must recognise the role of alcohol in society and the potential risks and benefits associated with its consumption. Policies need to be relevant, practical and strategically targeted at the intended groups, in an appropriate manner and within a variety of cultural environments. The areas listed below came from the *Geneva Partnership on Alcohol: Towards a Global Charter*, and are just some of those which you should consider when structuring alcohol policies. These are not prioritised because their short or long term adoption will depend on the country or region in question.

- Comprehensive information and education
- Responsible service of beverage alcohol
- Ensuring product quality and integrity
- The role of alcohol in society
- Freedom of access and availability
- Responsible practices around advertising and promotion
- Healthcare and education of healthcare providers
  (ICAP, 2000c)

10.3 Regulation and legislation – the essential supports for effective alcohol policies

Alcohol policy must operate within a clearly defined regulatory structure. This structure must directly link the needs of society in terms of education, health and well-being, and some areas of consumption must be strictly controlled through enforcement measures (e.g. drink driving, under-age drinking). Countries will adopt a variety of regulatory structures to control consumption; these will be based on each country's culture and past experiences with alcohol. Pedlow (1998) proposes that there is room for balance with alternative approaches, even within a clearly defined regulatory structure. Nelson (1997) suggests self-regulation by drinks companies as an alternative to the regulatory control measures. Please refer to section 8.4 for more on the self-regulation approach. Some organizations have argued that government regulation and self-regulation should not be mutually exclusive, proposing that both should exist side by side; and when self-regulation is not working, regulation through legislation might be necessary (ICAP, 2002b). Every system, no matter how comprehensive it is structured, will have its limitations because of the decisions taken by humans during every drinking occasion. If you accept this argument, then you must ensure when regulations are introduced through alcohol policy structures that they are strategically aimed and strictly enforced. Listed below are some guidelines for ensuring the success and sustainability of any regulatory structure for alcohol policies. Policy makers should consider the following:

10

- **The objective of the proposed regulation**: this should be based on the available evidence which supports the best possible and available approach; it could involve a mixture of approaches.

- **The alternatives available to regulation**: other approaches might be more appropriate and could also be more cost effective (e.g. social responsibility through self-regulation or group partnerships)

- **Support from the public towards regulation**: the policy will need community support, which can be achieved through active participation and communication of the issues in hand. A rash or ill prepared approach which also does not respect cultural sensitive issues or the local expectation on the role of alcohol will not work in the long term.

- **Enforcement and resource issues**: when the proposed regulations are implemented, can they be effectively enforced? Are there enough resources available for the active enforcement of policies? If the answer to this question is 'no' then the impact of their implementation will be poor.

When governments factor these considerations into their regulatory structure for alcohol policies, they will usually explore all the indirect and direct regulatory measures that exist within structures currently in operation.

Indirect measures

Grant and O'Connor (2005) state that **self-regulation**'s main purpose is to adhere to high standards of conduct, which reduces the requirement for government restrictions. A balanced approach to the challenges can be ideally achieved by a partnership between government and industry. ICAP can assist in setting up and implementing self-regulatory practices, and they have developed a toolkit for emerging markets and the developing world.

Marketing and advertising measures agreed either on a local or international basis have tried to ensure that traditional or new approaches to product marketing is consistently legal, decent, truthful and does not mislead or confer harm (ICC, 2004), and that measures are operated in the best interest of producers, retailers, consumers and governments. Marketing and advertising approaches must be culturally sensitive –what could be seen to be amusing in one culture may be offensive in another.

Direct measures

Legal drinking age measures differ because countries base their age limits on past experience. ICAP (2002d) contend that these legal thresholds provide a vital understanding about the position of alcohol as an adult product, and they can be especially useful in areas of high under-age consumption.

Access and availability measures include regulating the number of establishments allowed to serve or sell alcohol, restricting the hours of trading or implementing government monopolies to strictly regulate every aspect. The success of these measures varies – in some circumstances they can create additional problems (Makela et al, 2002; Raistrick, 1999), in others they can produce good practices (Norstrom and Skog, 2003; Smart and& Mann, 1995).

Holder and Wagenaar (1994) and Saitz (1987) highlight that measures which required all hospitality, tourism and retail staff members involved in the **service and sale of alcohol** to undergo training have delivered positive impacts on customer satisfaction and reduced the levels of accidents. These have also contributed towards increased safety levels (Graham et al, 2004); however their effect is reduced if they are not backed up with enforcement (McKnight and Streff, 1994).

Legal limits for blood alcohol concentration (BAC) level were introduced to reduce the levels of drink related accidents, especially amongst motor vehicle drivers (Shults et al, 2001). The measures have now been extended to cover all forms of transportation in some countries. The combined support of the drinks industry, the public and community groups, operating in a strictly controlled legislation structure with heavy enforcement has contributed to the success of this measure.

Taxation generates revenue, contributes towards public services, including prevention and responsible consumption schemes, and can be geared to encourage sales of local over foreign products (Farrell et al, 2003; Manning et al, 1995; Chaloupka et al, 2002). The aim here is not to place unreasonable demands on consumers or producers. Although effective, Heyman (2000) argues that these measures do not affect abusers who tend to not respond to price changes. Research conducted in Scandinavia and eastern Europe, where taxation is extremely high, indicated that abuse patterns remain high, and there is a growth in smuggling and counterfeit alcohol, and increased levels of poor quality and illegal products (Harstedt, 2004; Lyall, 2003).

10.4 Alcohol consumption patterns

Grant and Litvak (1998) maintain that drinking experiences are closely linked with a wide range of good and bad experiences, which cover the various social and health elements of consumption. These experiences which are encountered are a direct outcome of alcohol consumption patterns and these patterns are an excellent indicator of the intended or unintended outcomes. In essence how individuals consume alcohol is just as important as the quantity consumed. Understanding these patterns is crucial for (a) the purposes of the policy; various groups consume alcohol in numerous ways so exploring large national samples of individuals will not give you the true consumption behaviours, (b) to identify at risk groups and (c) to provide further and more recent research.

Defining alcohol consumption patterns

Single and Leino (1998) state that the patterns of consumption describe the various ways in which people consume their alcohol. Plant and Plant (1997) add that further detail is required to predict the probable outcomes of its effect and to reduce the likelihood of accidents. The review below outlines a small selection of the alcohol consumption patterns:

- **Worldly variations**: incorporates the amount and speed of consumption over a set time period, included in these are harmful patterns, for example binge drinking, which leads to speed intoxication, and abusive drinking (Midanik, 1994; Stockwell et al, 1993)

- **Drinking environment and associated activities**: although the location of consumption and the related event can vary, they are very important. In some cultures alcohol consumption takes place within daily meals and get-togethers with family, friends and colleagues. In some consumption is restricted to special occasions only. Heath (2000) reports that excessive drinking can be linked with the types of events. Some drinking environments will involve transportation, which can lead to drink driving, or have a higher possibility of conflict.

- **Individual characteristics of the drinker**: these include their gender, religious beliefs, health status, ethnic background and age, which are factors that have a direct impact on the effects of alcohol and the vulnerability on the drinker.

- **Types of drink**: individuals across the world will consume various types of alcohol at different strengths and in some circumstances, as Haworth and Simpson (2004) suggest, purely for financial reasons. Sometimes these types of drinks will differ in product quality from illegal to high street, which presents health issues for some societies.

- **Cultural influence**: the expected behaviour and conduct of individuals across some cultures has a direct impact on their consumption pattern, Heath (2000) proposes that these differences have a major impact on the intended outcome.

For a more comprehensive discussion of the association between alcohol consumption patterns and their potential outcomes, please see Chapter 5 *Alcohol and Health*.

Case example: Anti-drink driving programme

Guinness (Nigeria) - Some things don't mix

The campaign was operated by Guinness Nigeria PLC from December 2010 to February 2011, and aimed to raise awareness about the dangers of drinking and driving, and to promote attitudinal and behavioural changes about responsible drinking. The campaign served as a pilot programme to test the research being conducted by Consumer Planning and Research team. The materials used include TVC, billboards and posters. Pre and post research were conducted for the pilot programme. Prior to the programme, research was commissioned to institute a tracking mechanism which would monitor public comments on alcohol misuse. Post research surveys found that there was an increase in awareness about the risks of drinking and driving. There was also an increase in those that totally disagreed with drinking and driving.

Figure 10.1: Some things just don't mix campaign (Diageo, 2014a)

10.5 Building comprehensive and sustainable policies

Successful structures for alcohol policies are based on solid steps which are individually and equally evaluated prior to implementation. These steps are not suited to every situation and their eventual adoption is primarily based on the policy structures which have already been adopted. In Table 10.1 below we highlight the suggested sequence which could be applied by the private sector, nongovernmental agencies, local governments and of course industry specific groups interested in alcohol policy development.

Table 10.1: Steps towards building comprehensive and sustainable alcohol policies (adapted from ICAP, 2001b).

1. Cultural context: this sets the scene, assessing the cultural context where the policy development is intended. Attention is paid to the drinking culture, the role of alcohol in society and the societal norms.	Output: A review of the drinking patterns, which identifies important historical, societal, and cultural trends which shape contemporary drinking behaviour.
2. Existing policy stocktake: the focus is on the existing policies and on the formal and informal mechanisms that influence them. The legal structure is considered, as are the roles of NGOs, intergovernmental organizations, the beverage alcohol industry, and other groups in developing, implementing, and enforcing policies.	Output: A detailed audit of the country's current policy profile, with analysis of the main directions; this will also cover any inconsistencies in policy components, and any proposals for policy change.
3. Issues identification: this hinges upon a thorough review of the key issues that are of relevance and concern to the primary stakeholders in policy building. The identification of key issues affords those ultimately responsible for shaping policies an opportunity for input.	Output: A prioritized list of key issues which , reflects the views of the major stakeholders.
4. Partnership: good working partnerships are essential to the success of this model. Partners should include representatives from the public and private sectors, and special attention should be given to maintaining dialogue and cooperation between them.	Output: A functioning partnership, with an agreed agenda for action.
5. Community participation: public input and participation are crucial if policies are to be effective and sustainable. It is necessary to ensure that measures are in keeping with community norms and practices and that the rights of all are respected, while at the same time ensuring their safety.	Output: Effective mechanism for facilitating the flow of community views into the partnership process, with effective feedback given to the community.
6. Goal and outcome clarification: policy goals and objectives should be agreed, resulting from a careful review of the issues identified. More detailed outcomes need to be specified; these should be quantifiable, measurable, and achievable within a realistic timeframe.	Output: Clear statement of the overall policy goals with specific outcomes and a method for assessing whether they are being achieved.
7. Strategy specification: strategies need to be selected that will lead to the desired outcomes. These should be consistent with the expectations of the public and should be supported by evidence.	Output: Consolidated action plan which specifies the strategies, timelines, resources, and target audiences.
8. Implementation: the actions needed to implement the agreed policy options should be described. Specifically, timelines need to be agreed upon from the outset, with well-defined milestones and reporting mechanisms put in place. Agreement is needed among the stakeholders regarding specific responsibilities.	Output: Experience in implementing agreed strategies, reflected in reports on progress.

9. **Evaluation**: evaluation of the outcomes that have been achieved is a critical component of building policies. Particular attention is needed to the way in which the outcomes fit with the overall goals established for the policy and individual objectives identified through the partnership approach. Any unanticipated outcomes that may arise from the implementation process should also be taken into account.	Output: Series of monitoring reports covering all phases of the implementation of each strategy from inputs to outcomes.
10. **Feedback**: the final step allows for feedback and review, focusing on the utility of the model implemented. The impact of partnership needs to be reviewed, as well as its capacity to persist over time as an instrument for designing and implementing policy.	Output: A sustainable mechanism that will ensure the continuing life of the partnership and its involvement in alcohol policy development.

10.6 Changing behaviour through alcohol education policies

ICAP (2014) maintain that a significant amount of our knowledge, drinking patterns and personal drinking influences are primarily shaped by our culture and our environment. A policy aimed at preventing the harmful effects of alcohol consumption through education can form one of the components required to reduce the risk of abuse and to encourage responsible consumption. Education structured in an appropriate fashion is a crucial factor in helping to offer preventative measures, solutions and balanced policies which can be used to disseminate information and ultimately to change behaviour. If we accept the ICAP's proposition regarding our views, attitudes, and behaviours around drinking, then we can move to the types of targeted educational measures which are highly specific and are more likely to be effective than broad based approaches, as highlighted by Turrisi and Ray (2010). Mares et al (2011) remind us that direct parental involvement is essential in this regard because parents, peers and others play a vital role in the lives of young people and they can be very effective in teaching youths about alcohol.

Any educational approach would need to (a) to help individuals who consume alcohol in harmful ways which can damage the health and well-being of themselves, friends, family, colleagues and others and (b) to raise awareness and to disseminate the knowledge and skills which can help consumers to make informed and healthy decisions in relation to their alcohol consumption.

Education around alcohol has been organised and disseminated over the years in many forms. The success and sustainability of these approaches has been reviewed in the literature under the following areas:

- Babor et al (2003) and Weschsler et al (2003) investigated *information campaigns and mass media approaches* and concluded that when implemented in isolation they are generally viewed as ineffective in changing behaviour. By contrast, Elder et al (2004) suggest that their research showed evidence which indicates that these campaigns may be helpful in raising awareness about certain issues.

- Milford and McBride (2001) explored *school based alcohol education programmes* and questioned their effectiveness in changing behaviour. However Foxcroft and Tsertvadze (2011b) state that some educational approaches at this level show more promise than others.

- *Programmes which target* specific individuals and groups are quite common. Vermeulen et al (2012) highlight that these efforts contain specific courses for problem drinkers, young people, or other at-risk groups. These types of interventions have also been adopted to deal with the extremely harmful drinking patterns, such as drink driving and more recently binge drinking.

- Weintraub et al (2003) propose that education on alcohol can be integrated into *general health education* and provided through social workers, nurses, physicians and other health care personal.

- In most countries, *warning labels* are placed on alcohol products, aimed at addressing possible health outcomes, drinking and driving, or drinking during pregnancy. These labels do raise some awareness, but when adopted without media etc. support, they have been largely ineffective in changing behaviour (Greenfield et al 1999).

Case example: Partnership approach to education

Bacardi Limited – A Guide to Social Responsibility

The International Bartenders Association (IBA) is a federation of the bartending trade associations of over 59 countries, with more than 40,000 members working across all five continents. In 2008 Bacardi Limited and the International Bartenders Association (IBA) joined together in a partnership approach to launch a worldwide training manual which highlighted the importance of social responsibility as an integral part of bartending skills. Andreas Gembler, President & Chief Executive Officer Bacardi Limited stated that he was delighted to welcome the new book as part of their ambition to demonstrate leadership in the field of social responsibility. He also applauded the IBA for showing educational leadership in this important area of their profession (IBA, 2008).

Figure 10.2: Pernod Ricard partnership approach   (Pernod-ricard.com, 2014).

Conclusion

A new combined approach towards policy making is required to ensure that consumers are informed about the potential risks and benefits associated with alcohol consumption. If alcohol policies are to be successful and effective they must recognize the role which the consumption of alcohol plays in the everyday life and culture of every individual. Alcohol policies need to be practical and relevant at the micro and macro levels, they must also be supported by regulation and legislation measures which are strictly followed. Sustainable policies can be developed if they are based on structures which recognise individual alcohol consumption patterns and incorporate active education policies which are culturally sensitive and supported by everyone involved in the marketing, selling, service and consumption of alcohol.

Web resources

AMPHORA (EU)
 www.amphoraproject.net

APN: Alcohol Policy Network (EU)
 www.alcoholpolicynetwork.eu

Alcohol Harm Reduction Strategy for England
 www.newcastle-staffs.gov.uk/.../caboffce%20alcoholhar%20pdf.pdf

Alcohol in Australia: Issues and Strategies
 www.health.gov.au/internet/drugstrategy/.../alcohol_strategy_back.pdf

Alcohol: no ordinary commodity
 www.oxfordscholarship.com/view/10.1093/acprof:oso/9780199551149.001.0001/
 acprof-9780199551149

Bureau of Alcohol, Tobacco, Firearms and Explosives (US)
www.atf.gov/

Eurobarometer Special Surveys (EU)
ec.europa.eu

Eurocare: European Alcohol Policy Alliance (EU)
www.eurocare.org/

Government in markets
www.gov.uk/government/uploads/system/...data/.../OFT1113.pdf

Liberalising Nordic alcohol policies
www.nordicwelfare.org/.../Nordic%20alcohol%20policies%20and%20th...

Office of Drug & Alcohol Policy & Compliance (US)
www.dot.gov/odapc

The Institute of Alcohol Studies   (UK)
www.ias.org.uk/

STAP Dutch Institute for Alcohol Policy (The Netherlands)
www.stap.nl/en

A Appendices

I: Family of alcohols

Chemical Formula	IUPAC Name	Common Name
Monohydric alcohols		
CH_3OH	Methanol	Wood alcohol
C_2H_5OH	Ethanol	Alcohol
C_3H_7OH	Isopropyl alcohol	Rubbing alcohol
C_4H_9OH	Butyl alcohol	Butanol
$C_5H_{11}OH$	Pentanol	Amyl alcohol
$C_{16}H_{33}OH$	Hexadecan-1-ol	Cetyl alcohol
Polyhydric alcohols		
$C_2H_4(OH)_2$	Ethane-1,2-diol	Ethylene glycol
$C_3H_6(OH)_2$	Propane-1,2-diol	Propylene Glycol
$C_3H_5(OH)_3$	Propane-1,2,3-triol	Glycerol
$C_4H_6(OH)_4$	Butane-1,2,3,4-tetraol	Erythritol, Threitol
$C_5H_7(OH)_5$	Pentane-1,2,3,4,5-pentol	Xylitol
$C_6H_8(OH)_6$	Hexane-1,2,3,4,5,6-hexol	Mannitol, Sorbitol
$C_7H_9(OH)_7$	Heptane-1,2,3,4,5,6,7-heptol	Volemitol
Unsaturated aliphatic alcohols		
C_3H_5OH	Prop-2-ene-1-ol	Allyl alcohol
$C_{10}H_{17}OH$	3,7-Dimethylocta-2,6-dien-1-ol	Geraniol
C_3H_3OH	Prop-2-in-1-ol	Propargyl alcohol
Alicyclic alcohols		
$C_6H_6(OH)_6$	Cyclohexane-1,2,3,4,5,6-hexol	Inositol
$C_{10}H_{19}OH$	2 - (2-propyl)-5-methyl-cyclohexane-1-ol	Menthol

(adapted from IUPAC, 1997).

II: International standard alcohol units

Standard drink / unit size (gms of ethanol)	Country
8	United Kingdom
9.9	Netherlands
10	Australia, Austria, France, Ireland, New Zealand, Poland, Spain
11	Finland

12	Denmark, Italy, South Africa
13.6	Canada
14	Portugal, United States

(adapted from ICAP, 2003).

III: Strength of alcohol chart

Formula to calculate units of alcohol:

Amount of liquid in ml (millilitres) × % ABV × 0.001 = units of alcohol contained.

Standard drinks	Units of alcohol
One pint (568 ml) of beer at 4% abv (568 × 4 × 0.001 = 2.27)	2.27 (2.3)
One can (440 ml) of premium lager at 9% abv (440 × 9 × 0.001 = 3.96)	3.96 (4)
One bottle (275 ml) of flavoured alcoholic beverage at 5% abv (275 × 5 × 0.001 = 1.375)	1.375 (1.4)
One bottle (330 ml) of premium lager at 6% abv (330 × 6 × 0.001 = 1.98)	1.98 (2)
One 35 ml measure of whisky at 40% abv (35 × 40 × 0.001 = 1.4)	1.4 (1.4)
One 25ml measure of vodka or gin at 37.5% abv (25 × 37.5 × 0.001 = 0.9375)	0.9375 (1.0)
One 175 ml glass of wine at 12% abv (175 × 12 × 0.001 = 2.1)	2.1 (2.1)
One vermouth (50 ml measure) at 15% abv (50 × 15 × 0.001 = 0.75)	0.75
Dry Martini cocktail: *Large gin* (75 ml) at 40% abv (75 × 40 × 0.001 = 3.0). *Two dashes dry vermouth* (10 ml) at 18% (10 × 18 × 0.001 = 0.18)	3.0 (3) 0.18 **3.18** total amount
Margarita: *Silver Tequila* (25 ml) at 40% abv (25 × 40 × 0.001 = 1.0) *Fresh Lime Juice* (25 ml) = 0 unit. *Cointreau liqueur* (20 ml) at 40% abv (20 × 40 × 0.001 = 0.8)	1.0 0 0.8 **1.8** total amount

(adapted from BIIAB, 2005).

IV: Hangover remedies

Some time-tested antidotes (potentially beneficial remedies)

- *Eat a hearty meal beforehand,* as this slows down your absorption of alcohol
- *Drink a glass of water* for every alcoholic drink you consume, as alcohol is a diuretic and dehydrates you.
- *Avoid dark spirits* (i.e. brandy, cheap red wine and dark rum) as these products have high levels of congeners and cause heavy hangovers.
- *Before bedtime drink water* and put a little salt on the tip of your tongue to speed up rehydration (Wiese et al, 2000).
- *Opuntia ficus-indica,* an extract of a species of cactus, may reduce some effects of hangover, especially in individuals who consume drinks with high levels of congeners (Verster & Penning, 2010).
- *Zetox:* these tablets were developed by a British firm, made from volcanic ash, and launched in the middle 2000s. They are supposed to soak up alcohol's toxins and prevent hangovers from happening.
- *Lifeline capsules:* these contain calcium, activated carbon and vitamins. Two capsules taken before or with the first drink should prevent a hangover. These are based on the technology that created RU21, developed by the USSR in the 1980s, to stop its agents becoming drunk while attempting to win the confidence of informants over a crate of vodka.

(Murphy, 2006).

V: Ten golden rules for door staff

- Dress immaculately and remember the importance of good grooming.
- Make sure to make eye contact with everybody who walks up to the door and offer them a polite greeting.
- Never chew gum, eat or use mobile phones when on duty.
- If trouble arises, always try to ease the problem with words.
- When physically removing someone, use minimum force.
- Watch out for signs of excessive drinking, drug taking and be aware of spiked drinks.
- Bring hazards like broken glass to the attention of bar staff.
- Always hold the door open for people on the way out and thank them for their custom.
- Never socialize at the venue and ask partners and friends not to either.
- Don't rise to provocation. People's thoughts become impaired when they have consumed alcohol.

(adapted from Murphy, 2008).

A

VI: Best practice for checking ID

Acceptable forms of identification can include:

- current valid passport
- current motor vehicle driver's license, or licensed permits officially issued by the local government or interstate equivalent
- current proof of age card or the interstate equivalent.

Proof of age cards are constantly upgraded to include increased security measures to counteract counterfeit cards. The following are usually present:

1 A hologram outline of the local police of government agency

2 A magnetic strip on the reverse side of the card

3 An additional ghosted photo image under the personal details on the front of the card

4 A clear and distinct logo or emblem (based on the local agency or government) to differentiate the card

Checklist for identification

All forms of identification must be checked for validity and using the following steps will help you to ensure that all points of the ID have been checked to satisfy staff of the authenticity of the card supplied by the customer.

1 Examine the ID throughout, especially the edges, where any alterations will be easier to see.

2 Always ask the patron to take their identification from their wallet or purse. Never inspect any form of identification inside a pocket of a wallet.

3 Check the photograph; ensure the photograph matches the person who gave you the ID.

4 Check the issuing and date of birth dates, is the patron over 18? Are there any alterations?

5 Check the lamination and hologram. Are there any anomalies with the lamination and is the hologram complete?

(BRC, 2004).

# Bibliography.

Aaron P, Musto D (1981). Temperance and prohibition in America: an historical overview. In Moore MH, Gerstein D, (Eds). *Alcohol and Public Policy: Beyond the Shadow of Prohibition* Washington (DC): National Academy Press: 127–81.

Abbey, A, Mcauslan, P & Ross, L T (1998). Sexual assault perpetration by college men: The role of alcohol misperception of sexual intent and sexual beliefs and experiences, *Journal of Social and Clinical Psychology*, **17**, 167-195.

Abel, E L (1998). *Foetal Alcohol Syndrome: Foetal Alcohol Effects*, Plenum Press: New York.

ACCR (2008). Red wine may lower lung cancer risk, *American Association for Cancer Research*, 1st October: USA.

Ahola K, Honkonen T, Pirkola S, Isometsa E, Kalimo R, Nykyri E (2006). Alcohol dependence in relation to burnout among the Finnish working population, *Addiction*: **101**(10), 1438-1443.

Alcohol Edu (2008-2009). *College National Survey Database, Outside the Classroom*: USA.

Ames G M, Grube J W & Moore R S (2000). Social control and workplace drinking norms: a comparison of two organizational cultures, *Journal of Studies on Alcohol*: **61**(2),203-219.

Amoaten G F, Poku K (2013). The impact of advertisement on alcohol consumption: a case study of consumers in Bantama Sub-Metro, *International Review of Management and Marketing*, **3** (1), 28-36.

Anderson P & Baumberg B (2006). *Alcohol in Europe*, Institute of Alcohol Studies: London.

Anderson Z (2005). Data from Trauma and Injury Intelligence Group, Centre for Public Health, Liverpool John Moores University: Liverpool.

Anderson Z, Hughes K, Bellis MA (2007). *The Role of Door Staff in Violence Prevention - Violence Prevention Alliance Working Group on Youth Violence, Alcohol and Nightlife*, World Health Organisation: Geneva.

Arnett JJ (2005). The developmental context of substance use in emerging adulthood, *Journal of Drug Issues*: **35**, 235-254.

Arnold JP (2005). *Origin and History of Beer and Brewing: From Prehistoric Times to the Beginning of Brewing Science and Technology*, Cleveland, Ohio: Beer Books.

Arnold M J & Laidler T (1994). *Alcohol Misuse and Violence: Situational and Environmental Factors in Alcohol-Related Violence*, Commonwealth of Australia: Canberra, Australia.

Aronson K (2003). Alcohol: A recently identified risk factor for breast cancer, *Canadian Medical Association Journal*: **168**, 1147-1148.

Ashley M J, Ferrence R, Room R, Bondy S, Rehm J & Single E (1997). Moderate drinking and health: Implications of recent evidence, *Canadian Family Physician*: **43**, 687-694.

Ashley M, Rehm J, Bondy S, Single E & Rankin J (2000). Beyond ischemic heart disease: Are there other health benefits from drinking alcohol?, *Contemporary Drug Problems*: **27**, 735-777.

Asian Tribune (2006). Sri Lanka bans public smoking, alcohol, tobacco advertising, available http://www.asiantribune.com/node/944 accessed 14/7/14.

Austin GA (1985). *Alcohol in Western Society from Antiquity to 1800: A Chronological History*, ABC Clio: Santa Barbara, CA.

Australian Medical Association, (2012) *Alcohol Marketing and Young People: Time for a New Policy Agenda*, Australia.

Axelsson L (1998). Lactic acid bacteria: Classification and physiology, in: *Lactic Acid Bacteria, Microbiology and Functional Aspects*, Ed. S Salminen and A Von Wright, Marcel Decker Inc: New York, USA.

Babor, T (1986). *Alcohol: Customs and Rituals*, Chelsea House: New York.

Babor T F & Del Boca F K (Eds.) (2003). *Treatment Matching in Alcoholism*, Cambridge University Press: Cambridge, UK.

Babor T F, Caetano R, Caswell S, Edwards G, Giesbrecht N, Graham K (2003). *Alcohol: No Ordinary Commodity—Research and Public Policy*, Oxford University Press: Oxford, UK.

Badawy A A (1986). Alcohol as a psychopharmacological agent, in P F Brain (Ed.), *Alcohol and Aggression*, 55–83, Croom Helm: London.

Baer D J, Judd J T, Clevidence B A, Muesing R A, Campbell W S, Brown E D (2002). Moderate alcohol consumption lowers risk factors for cardiovascular disease in postmenopausal women fed a controlled diet, *American Journal of Clinical Nutrition*: **75**, 593-599.

Bainbridge K E, Sowers M, Lin X & Harlow S D (2004). Risk factors for low bone mineral density and the 6-year rate of bone loss among premenopausal and premenopausal women, *Osteoporosis International*: **15**, 439-446.

Bakalkin, G (2008). Alcoholism-associated molecular adaptations in brain neurocognitive circuits, available www.eurekalert.org, accessed 6/6/14.

Baliunas D, Rehm J, Irving H & Shuper P (2010). Alcohol consumption and risk of incident human immunodeficiency virus infection: A meta-analysis, *International Journal of Public Health*: **55**(3), 159-166.

Banwell, C (1999). How many standard drinks are there in a glass of wine? *Drug and Alcohol Review*, **18**, 99–101.

BBC News (2005). Kenya to outlaw alcohol adverts, available news.bbc.co.uk/2/hi/africa/4080074.stm accessed 18/7/14.

BBC News Europe (2012). Russia slaps ban on alcohol advertising in media, available www.bbc.com/news/world-europe-18960770 accessed 13/8/13.

BBC News (2000). Alcohol linked to thousands of deaths, 14th July, available news.bbc.co.uk/2/hi/health/833483.stm accessed 3/5/14.

BBPA (2007). Managing safety in bars, clubs and pubs, British Beer Pub Association, available www.beerandpub.com accessed 17/7/14.

Becker U, Deis, A, Sorensen T I A, Grønbæk M, Borch-Johnsen K, Muller C F (1996). Prediction of risk of liver disease by alcohol intake, sex, and age: A prospective population study, *Hepatology*: **23**, 1025-1029.

Beckman LJ, Ackerman KT (1995). Women, alcohol, and sexuality, *Recent Developments in Alcoholism*: **12**, 267-285.

Begleiter H & Porjesz B (1995). Neurophysiological phenotypic factors in the development of alcoholism. In H Begleiter & B Kissin (Eds.), *Genetics of Alcoholism*, 269-293, Oxford University Press: New York.

Beilin L J (1995). Alcohol, hypertension and cardiovascular disease, *Journal of Hypertension*: **13**, 939-942.

Benjamin G M A (1991). *A History of the Anti-Suffrage Movement in The United States from 1895 To 1920: Women Against Equality*, Edwin Mellen Press: Lewiston.

Berg K M, Kunins H V, Jackson J L, Nahvi S, Chaudhry A, Harris K A, Malik R & Arnsten J H (2008). Association between alcohol consumption and both osteoporotic fracture and bone density, *The American Journal of Medicine*, **121**(5), 406-418.

BIIAB (2005). *Handbook for the BIIAB Level 2 - National Certificate for Personal License Holders*, BIIAB: Surrey, England.

Bing L L, Solomon DH, Costenbader K H & Karlson E H (2014). Alcohol consumption and risk of incident rheumatoid arthritis in women: a prospective study, *Arthritis & Rheumatology*: **66** (8), 1998-2005.

Birmingham Beverage Company (2014). Beer the Brewing Process, available at http://alabev.com/resources/beer-101/ accessed 9/10/14.

Blas E & Kurup AS (2010). Equity, social determinants and public health programmes. Geneva: World Health Organization, available http://whqlibdoc.wh.int/publications/2010/9789241563970_eng.pdf accessed 7 April 2014.

Bloomfield K, Grittner U, Kramer S & Gmel G (2006). Social inequalities in alcohol consumption and alcohol-related problems in the study countries of the EU concerted action, Gender, culture and alcohol problems: A multi-national study, *Alcohol and Alcoholism*: **41**, 26-36.

Blow F C & Barry K L (2002). Use and misuse of alcohol among older women, *Alcohol Research and Health*: **26**, 308-315.

Blomfield P (2011). Supporting 'No ID, No Sale' to stop under age sales, available http://www.paulblomfield.co.uk/news/news-story/article/supporting-no-id-no-sale-to-stop-under-age-sales.html accessed 10/7/14.

Blomberg, R D (1992). *Lower BAC limits for youth, Evaluation of the Maryland.02 law*, National Highway Traffic Safety Administration: Washington, DC.

Boffetta P, Hashibe M, La Vecchia C, Zatonski W & Rehm J (2006). The burden of cancer attributable to alcohol drinking, *International Journal of Cancer*: **119**, 884-887.

Boles S M & Miotto K (2003). Substance abuse and violence: A review of the literature, *Aggression and Violent Behaviour*: **8**, 155-174.

Bond G E, Burr R L, McCurry, S M, Rice, M M, Borenstein, A R & Larson, E B (2005). Alcohol and cognitive performance: A longitudinal study of older Japanese Americans. The Kame Project, *International Psychogeriatric*: **17**, 653-668.

Booyse FM, Pan W, Grenett HE (2007). Mechanism by which alcohol and wine polyphenols affect coronary heart disease risk, *Ann Epidemiol*: **17**, s24-31.

Borsari B, and Carey KB (2003). Descriptive and injunctive norms in college drinking: A meta-analytic integration, *Journal of Studies on Alcohol*: **64**, 331-341.

B

Borynski M L (2003). Factors related to reductions in alcohol consumption among college students: The role of religious involvement, *Current Psychology*: 22, 138-148.

Brady, T (2008). Tackling alcohol abuse - teens to test rogue publicans, 24 April, p.19, *Irish Independent*: Dublin.

BRC (2004). *Responsible Retailing of Alcohol: Guidance for the off-trade*, British Retail Consortium: UK.

Braudel F (1974). *Capitalism and Material Life, 1400-1800*. Translated by Miriam Kochan, Harper and Row: New York, NY.

Brewery Workers (2000). October issue, available http://www.shapingsf.org/ezine/labor/brewery/main.html accessed 12/6/14.

Bright, M (2005) The Story of Beer, *Licensing World*, Jemma Publications Ltd: Dublin.

Briscoe S & Donnelly, N (2001). *Temporal and Regional Aspects of Alcohol-Related Violence and Disorder*, No 1, Bureau of Crime Statistics and Research : Australia.

Brotherton, B (2008). *International Hospitality Industry: Structure, Characteristics and Issues*, Elsevier: Oxford.

Brownlee, N (2002) *This is Alcohol*, Sanctuary Publishing, MPG Books: UK.

Brown, F W (1932). Prohibition and Mental Hygiene, *Annals of the American Academy of Political and Social Life*, **163**, 61-88.

Bullers S, Cooper ML and Russell M (2001). Social networks drinking and adult alcohol involvement: A longitudinal exploration of the direction of influence, *Addictive Behaviours*: **26**, 181-199.

Burns E D, Nusbaumer M R & Reiling D M (2003). Think they're drunk? Alcohol servers and the identification of intoxication, *Journal of Drug Education*: **33**, 177-186.

Byrne, S (2010) *Costs to Society of Problem Alcohol Use in Ireland*, Health Service Executive: Dublin.

Cahalan D (1970). *Problem Drinkers: A National Survey*, Jossey-Bass: San Francisco.

Campbell, H (2000). The glass phallus: Public masculinity and drinking in rural New Zealand, *Rural Sociology*: **65**, 562-581.

Campbell NR, Ashley MJ, Carruthers SG, Lacourciere Y & McKay DW (1999). Recommendation on alcohol consumption, *Canadian Medical Association Journal*: **160**, 13-20.

Campbell N & Reece J (2005). *Biology*, 7th ed. Benjamin Cummings.

Carey, KB, Correia, CJ (1997). Drinking motives predict alcohol-related problems in college students, *Journal of Studies on Alcohol*: **58**, 100-105.

Carey, T (2010) Why a glass a day will keep the doctor away, *Mail on Line*, available http://www.dailymail.co.uk/health/article-1256471/Why-glass-day-WILL-doctor-away-.html#ixzz3j.ueemh.ps accessed 10/6/14.

Carvolth C (1988). Patron Care: Initial process evaluation of hospitality industry, *Drug and Alcohol Review*: **7** (2), 157-161.

Carvolth R J (Ed.) (1983). National Drug Institute innovations: Proceedings of the National Drug Institute, Canberra, Australian Foundation on Alcoholism and Drug Dependence: Brisbane, Australia.

Casarett & Doull (1986). *Toxico - the basic science of poisons*, 3rd Ed, pp. 648-653, Macmillan Publishing Company: New York.

Casswell, S & Zhang J F, (1998). Impact of liking for advertising and brand allegiance on drinking and alcohol-related aggression: a longitudinal study, *Addiction*: **93**(8), 1209-17.

Cavalieri D, McGovern PE, Hartl DL, Mortimer R, Polsinelli M (2003). Evidence for S cerevisiae fermentation in ancient wine, *Journal of Molecular Evolution*, **57**(1), 226–32.

Centre on Alcohol Marketing and Youth (2004). Alcohol Advertising on Sports Television 2001 to 2003, available http://www.camy.org/bin/s/a/Alcohol_Advertising_on_Sports_Television.pdf accessed 11/7/14.

Ceyana A & Jen S (2013). *Prohibition and the Speakeasies, History of the Roaring Twenties*, http://theroaringtwentieshistory.blogspot.co.uk.

Chaloupka F J, Grossman M & Saffer H (2002). The effects of price on alcohol consumption and alcohol-related problems, *Alcohol Research and Health*: **26**, 22-34.

Chander G & McCaul M E (2003). Co-occurring psychiatric disorders in women with addictions, *Obstetrics and Gynaecology Clinic of North America*: **30**, 469-481.

Charnley S B, Kress M E, Tielens A G G M & Millar T J (1995). Interstellar Alcohols, *Astrophysical Journal*: **448**, 232.

Chartier KG, Vaeth PAC & Caetano R (2013). Ethnicity and the social and health harms from drinking. *Alcohol Research: Current Reviews*: **35**(2), 229-237.

Chassin L, Pitts S C & Prost J (2002). Binge drinking trajectories from adolescence to emerging adulthood in a high-risk sample: predictors and substance abuse outcomes, *Journal of Consulting and Clinical Psychology*: **70**(1), 67-78.

Cheney S (1889). Speak-easies, Sep 13th, *Washington Post*: Washington DC.

Cherrington, E H (1920). *The evolution of prohibition in the United States of America*, American Issue Press: Westerville, Ohio.

Chisholm D, Rehm J, Van Ommeren M & Monteiro M (2004). Reducing the global burden of hazardous alcohol use: A comparative cost-effectiveness study, *Journal of Studies on Alcohol*: **65**, 782-793.

Chochinov, A (1998). Alcohol on board, man overboard: boat fatalities in Canada, *Canadian Medical Association Journal*: **159**, 259-260.

Coffey TG (1966). Beer Street: Gin Lane – some views of 18th-century drinking, *Quarterly Journal of Studies on Alcohol*: **27**, 669-671.

Cohen S, Tyrrell DA, Russell MA, Jarvis MJ, Smith AP (1993). Smoking, alcohol consumption, and susceptibility to the common cold, *American Journal of Public Health*: **83** (9), 1277-83.

Coid, J (1986). Socio-cultural factors in alcohol-related aggression. In P F Brain (Ed.), *Alcohol and aggression*, 184-211, Croom Helm: Dover MH.

Collins RL, Ellickson PL, McCaffrey D & Hambarsoomians K (2007). Early adolescent exposure to alcohol advertising and its relationship to underage drinking. *Journal of Adolescent Health*: **40**, 527-534.

Colson E, Scudder T (1988). *For Prayer and afor Profit: The Ritual, Economic and Social Importance of Beer in Gwembe District, Zambia, 1950-1982*, Stanford University Press: Stanford, CA.

Cook C C (1997). Alcohol policy and aviation safety, *Addiction*: **92**(7), 793-804.

B

Cook R F, Back A S & Trudeau J (1996). Preventing alcohol use problems among blue-collar workers: a field test of the Working People program, *Substance Use & Misuse*: **31**(3), 255-275.

Cooper ML, Agocha VB and Sheldon MS (2000). A motivational perspective on risky behaviours: The role of personality and affect regulatory processe, *Journal of Personality*: **68**, 1059-1088.

Corvallis O (2014). Moderate alcohol consumption may help prevent bone loss, Oregon State University, http://oregonstate.edu/ua/ncs/archives/2012/jul/new-study-suggests-moderate-alcohol-consumption-may-help-prevent-bone-loss   accessed 20/11/14.

Cousins J, Lillicrap D & Weekes S (2014). *Food and Beverage Service*, 9th Ed, Hodder Education: London.

Crowe LC & George WH (1989). Alcohol and human sexuality: Review and integration, *Psychological Bulletin*: **105** (3), 374-386.

Cunningham R, Walton M, Maio, R, Blow F, Weber J & Mirel L (2003). Violence and substance use among an injured emergency department population, *Academic Emergency Medicine*: **10**, 764-775.

Currie C, Zanotti C, Morgan A, Currie D, de Looze M and Roberts C, (Eds). (2012). *Social determinants of health and well-being among young people: Health behaviour in school-aged children (HBSC) study: International report from the 2009/2010 survey*, WHO: Copenhagen.

Currier G W, Trenton A J & Walsh P G (2006). Innovations: Emergency psychiatry, Relative accuracy of breath and serum alcohol readings in the psychiatric emergency service, *Psychiatric Service*: **57**(1), 34-36.

Daglia M, Papetti A, Grisoli P, Aceti C, Dacarro C & Gazzani G (2007). Antibacterial activity of red and white wine against oral streptococci, *Journal of Agricultural and Food Chemistry*: **55** (13), 5038-5042.

Daily Mail (2009). Medical miscellany: Why hangovers get worse with age, 11th November, Daily Mail Newspapers Ltd: London.

Dale C E & Livingston M J (2010). The burden of alcohol drinking on co-workers in the Australian workplace, *Medical Journal Australia*: **193**(3), 138-140.

Daly J B, Campbell E M, Wiggers J H & Considine R J (2002). Prevalence of responsible hospitality policies in licensed premises that are associated with alcohol-related harm, *Drug and Alcohol Review*: **21**, 113-120.

Dasgupta, A (2011). *The Science of Drinking: How Alcohol Affects Your Body and Mind*, Rowman & Littlefield Publishing Inc: Plymouth, UK.

De Araujo Burgos M G, Bion F M & Campos F (2004). Lactation and alcohol: Clinical and nutritional effects, *Archivos Latinoamericanos de Nutricion*: **54**, 25-35.

Deehan A (1999). *Alcohol and Crime: Taking Stock*. Crime Reduction Research Series Paper 3. Research, Development and Statistics Directorate, Home Office: London.

DeJong W, Schneider S K, Towvim L G, Murphy M J, Doerr E E & Simonsen N R (2006). A multisite randomized trial of social norms marketing campaigns to reduce college student drinking, *Journal of Studies on Alcohol*: **67**, 868-879.

DeJong W, Schneider S K, Towvim L G, Murphy M J, Doerr E E & Simonsen N R (2009). A multisite randomized trial of social norms marketing campaigns to reduce college student drinking: A replication failure, *Substance Abuse*: **30**, 127-140.

Denke MA (2000). Nutritional and health benefits of beer, *American Journal of Medical Science*: **320**(5), 320-326.

De Vegt F, Dekker J M, Groeneveld W J, Nijpels G, Stehouwer C D & Bouter L M (2002). Moderate alcohol consumption is associated with lower risk for incident diabetes and mortality: The Hoorn Study, *Diabetes Research Clinical Practice*: **57**, 53-60.

Devlin, M (2014). Why restricting alcohol sponsorship in sport makes sense, *Irish Independent Newspaper*, available http://www.independenTie/opinion/columnists/martina-devlin/why-restricting-alcohol-sponsorship-in-sport-makes-sense-30385751.html accessed 11/7/14.

Diamond I (2012). Jazz age comes to London, available at www.culturecompass.co.uk /2012/01/12/the-jazz-age-comes-to-london/ accessed 15/1/14.

Diaz N M, O'Neill T W, Silman A J & European Vertebral Osteoporosis Study Group (1997). Influence of alcohol consumption on the risk of vertebral deformity, *Osteoporosis International*: **7**, 65-71.

Dirar H (1993). *The Indigenous Fermented Foods of the Sudan: a Study in African Food and Nutrition*, CAB International: UK.

Disney E R, Lacono W, McGue M, Tully E & Legrand L (2008). Strengthening the case: Prenatal alcohol exposure is associated with increased risk for conduct disorder, *Paediatrics*: **122**, 1125-1230.

Djousse L & Gaziano J M (2007). Alcohol consumption and risk of heart failure in the Physicians Health Study, *Circulation*: **115**, 34-39.

Djousse L, Biggs M L, Mukamal K J & Siscovick D S (2007). Alcohol consumption and type 2 diabetes among older adults: The cardiovascular health study, *Obesity*: **15**, 1758-1765.

Dobyns F (1940). *The Amazing Story of Repeal*, , Willett, Clark & Co: Chicago.

Donnellan E (2002). Sharp rise in murder rate could be linked to increase drinking, *Irish Times*, 29 Oct: Dublin.

Donnellan E (2003). Calling time on office drinkers, *Irish Times*, 24 Nov, p. 23: Dublin.

Dowden A (2002). The good tipple guide, *Ireland on Sunday – Body & Soul*, 10 Nov: Dublin.

Dresser J & Gliksman L (1998). Comparing state-wide alcohol server training systems. *Pharmacology, Biochemistry and Behaviour*: **61**, 150.

Drugs.ie (2014). How drink can affect families, available http://www.drugs.ie accessed 4/5/14.

Dudley R (2004). Ethanol, fruit ripening and the historical origins of human alcoholism in primate frugivary, *Integrative and Comparative Biology*: **44** (4), 315-323.

Duffy J C (1992). Scottish licensing reforms. In M A Plant, E B Ritson & R J Robertson (Eds.), *Alcohol and Drugs: The Scottish Experience*, Edinburgh University Press: Edinburgh, UK.

Dufour, M C (1999). What is moderate drinking? Defining drinks and drinking levels, *Alcohol Research and Health*: **23**, 5-14.

EASA (2009). *Alcohol Module - Looking at advertising self-regulatory standards related to alcoholic beverages, International edition*, available www.easa-alliance.org accessed 13/6/14.

B

EASA (2014). *International Guide to Developing a Self-regulatory Organisation*, available www.easa-alliance.org accessed 30/6/14.

Eccles J S & Barber B L (1999). Student council, volunteering, basketball, or marching band: What kind of extracurricular involvement matters?, *Journal of Youth and Adolescence*: **6**, 281-294.

Edwards T (2013). *The Good News about Booze*, Premium Book: London.

Eggert J, Theobald H & Engfeldt P (2004). Effects of alcohol consumption on female fertility during an 18-year period, *Fertility and Sterility*: **81**, 379-383.

Elder R W, Shults R A, Sleet D A, Nichols J L, Thompson R S & Rajab W (2004). Effectiveness of mass media campaigns for reducing drinking and driving and alcohol-involved crashes, *American Journal of Preventive Medicine*: **27**, 57-65.

Ellingboe J (1987). Acute effects of ethanol on sex hormones in non-alcoholic men and women, *Alcohol and Alcoholism,* Supplement **1**, 109-116.

Ellis N (2005). Letting it all hang over, p. 18, 26th November, *Weekend Herald*: Dublin.

Emmanuelle N V, Swade T F & Emmanuelle M, A (1998). Consequences of alcohol use in diabetics, *Alcohol Health and Research World*: **22**, 211-219.

Eng MY, Luczak SE & Wall TL (2007). ALDH2, ADH1B, and ADH1C genotypes in Asians: a literature review, *Alcohol Research and Health*: **30** (1), 22-27.

Engs RC, Diebold BA & Hanson DJ (1996). The drinking patterns and problems of a national sample of college students. *Journal of Alcohol and Drug Education*, **41**(3), 13-33.

Euro Care (2014). Labelling, European Alcohol Policy Alliance, available www.eurocare. org/resources/policy_issues/labelling accessed 14/6/14.

Euro Care (2014). Alcohol related diseases, European Alcohol Policy Alliance, available www.eurocare.org/ accessed 3/5/14.

European Alcohol and Health Forum (2011). *Alcohol, Work and Productivity: Scientific Opinion of the Science Group of the European Alcohol and Health Forum*, European Alcohol and Health Forum: Brussels.

Fabiano P (2003). Applying the social norms model to universal and indicated alcohol interventions at Western Washington University. In H W Perkins (Ed.), *The social Norms Approach to Preventing School and College Age Substance Abuse: A Handbook for Educators, Counsellors and Clinicians*, pp. 83–99, Jossey-Bass: San Francisco, CA.

Failte Ireland (2003). The responsible service of alcohol programme, Failte Ireland: Dublin.

Falgreen Eriksen H L, Mortensen E, Kilburn T, Underbjerg M, Bertrand J & Stovring H (2012). The effects of low to moderate prenatal alcohol exposure in early pregnancy on IQ in 5-year-old children, *Bjog*: **119**(10), 1191-1200.

Farrell S, Manning W G & Finch M D (2003). Alcohol dependence and the price of alcoholic beverages, *Journal of Health Economics*: **22**, 117-147.

Federal Trade Commission (2003). *Alcohol Marketing and Advertising: A Report to Congress*: Washington, DC.

Felson M, Berends R, Richardson B & Veno A (1997). Reducing pub hopping and related crime. In R Homel (Ed.), *Policing for Prevention: Reducing Crime, Public Intoxication, and Injury*, pp. 115–132, Crime Prevention Studies, No 7. Monsey, Criminal Justice Press: NY.

Felson RB (1997). Routine activities and involvement in violence as actor, witness, and target, *Violence and Victims*: **12**, 209-221.

Ferrara J S (2014). The World of Retail: Hardlines vs. Soft lines, Value Line, available http://www.valueline.com/Tools/Educational_Articles/Stocks/The_World_of_Retail__ Hardlines_vs__Softlines.aspx#.U8PjCntOPIU, accessed 15/6/14.

Ferrins-Brown M, Dalton S, Maslin J, Hartney E, Kerr C & Orford, J (1999). Have a sip of this: The impact of family on the drinking patterns of untreated heavy drinkers living in the West Midlands, *UK Contemporary Drug Problems*: **26**, 413-437.

Fink A, Morton S C, Beck J C, Hays R D, Spritzer K & Oishi, S (2002). The alcohol-related problems survey: Identifying hazardous and harmful drinking in older primary care patients, *Journal of The American Geriatrics Society*: **50**, 1717-1722.

Fisher LB, Williams I, Austin B, Camargo CA & Colditz GA (2007). Predictors of initiation of alcohol use among US Adolescents, Findings from a Prospective Cohort Study, *Archives of Pedriatric & Adolescent Medicine*: **161**, 959-966.

Forbes R J (1970). *A Short History of the Art of Distillation: From the Beginning up to the Death of Cullier Blumenthal*, Brill: Leiden, Netherlands.

Foxcroft D R & Tsertsvadze, A (2011b). Universal school-based prevention programs for alcohol misuse in young people, *Cochrane Database of Systematic Reviews*: 5.

Freiberg M S, Cabral H J, Heeren T C, Vasan R S & Ellison C R (2004). Alcohol consumption and the prevalence of the Metabolic Syndrome in the US: A cross-sectional analysis of data from the Third National Health and Nutrition Examination Survey, *Diabetes Care*: **27**, 2954-2959.

Frias J, Torres JM, Miranda MT, Ruiz E & Ortega E (2002). Effects of acute alcohol intoxication on pituitary-gonadal axis hormones, pituitary-adrenal axis hormones, beta-endorphin and prolactin in human adults of both sexes, *Alcohol and Alcoholism*: **37** (2), 169-173.

Fromme K, Katz E & D'Amico E (1997). Effects of alcohol intoxication on the perceived consequences of risk taking, *Experimental and Clinical Psychopharmacology*: 5, 14-23.

Frone, M R (2008). Are work stressors related to employee substance use? The importance of temporal context assessments of alcohol and illicit drug use, *Journal of Applied Psychology*: **93**(1), 199-206.

Frone M R (2009). Does a permissive workplace substance use climate affect employees who do not use alcohol and drugs at work? A US national study, *Psychological Addiction Behaviour*: **23**(2), 386-390.

Frone M R & Brown A L (2010). Workplace substance-use norms as predictors of employee substance use and impairment: a survey of US workers, *Journal of Studies in Alcohol Drugs*: 71(4), 526-534.

Furnas, J C (1965). *The Life and Times of the Late Demon Rum*, Putnam: New York City.

Galanis D J, Joseph C, Masaki K H, Petrovitch H, Ross G W & White L A (2000). Longitudinal study of drinking and cognitive performance in elderly Japanese American men: The Honolulu-Asia Aging Study, *American Journal of Public Health*: **90**, 1254-1259.

Gamella JF (1995). Spain. In DB Heath (Ed.), *International Handbook on Alcohol and Culture*, pp. 245-269, Greenwood: Westport, CT.

B

GEC (2014). Non-alcoholic Malt Beverages, GEC Liquid Processing, available at http:// www.gea-liquid.com/gealiquid/cmsdoc.nsf/webdoc/webb85db6v accessed 10/10/14.   .

Gehan J P, Toomey R L, Jones-Webb R, Rothstein C & Wagenaar A C (1999). Alcohol outlet workers and managers: Focus groups on responsible service practices1, *Journal of Alcohol and Drug Education*: **44**, 60-7.

Gifford M (2009). *Alcoholism - Biographies of Disease*, Greenwood Press: US.

Giglia R C & Binns C W (2008). Alcohol, pregnancy and breastfeeding, a comparison of the 1995 and 2001 National Health Survey data, *Breastfeeding Review*: **16**(1), 17-24.

Gill J S & Donaghy M (2004). Variation in the alcohol content of a 'drink' of wine and spirit poured by a sample of the Scottish population, *Health Education and Behaviour*: **19**, 485-491.

Gliksman L, McKenzie D, Single E, Douglas R, Brunet S & Moffatt K (1993). The role of alcohol providers in prevention: an evaluation of a server intervention programme, *Addiction*: **88**, 1189-97.

Gmel G, Rehm J & Kuntsche E (2003). Binge-trinken in Europa: Definitionen, epidemiologie und folgen Binge drinking in Europe: Definitions, epidemiology, and consequences, SUCHT: *Zeitschrift für Wissenschaft und Praxis*: **49**, 105-116.

Gmel G, Gutjahr E & Rehm J (2003). How stable is the risk curve between alcohol and all-cause mortality and what factors influence the shape? A precision-weighted hierarchical meta-analysis, *European Journal of Epidemiology*: **18**, 631-642.

Goetzel R Z, Long S R, Ozminkowski R J, Hawkins K, Wang S & Lynch W (2004). Health, absence, disability, and presenteeism cost estimates of certain physical and mental health conditions affecting US employers, *Journal of Occupational and Environmental Medicine*: **46**(4), 398-412.

Goldberg JH, Halpern-Felsher BL & Millstein SG (2002). Beyond invulnerability: The importance of benefits in adolescents' decision to drink alcohol, *Health Psychology*: **21**, 477-484.

Graham K (2000). Preventive interventions for on premise drinking: a promising but under researched area for prevention, *Contemporary Drug Problems*: **27**, 593-667.

Graham K, Osgood D W, Zibrowski E, Purcell J, Gliksman L, Leonard K (2004). The effect of the Safer Bars programme on physical aggression in bars: results of a randomized controlled trial, *Drug and Alcohol Review*: **23**, 31-41.

Graham K & Homel R (1997). Creating safer bars. In M Plant, E Single & T Stockwell (eds.), *Alcohol: Minimising the harm: What works?* 171–192, Free Association Books: New York.

Graham K, Bernards S & Osgood DW (2005). Guardians and handlers: the role of bar staff in preventing and managing aggression, *Addiction*: **100**, 755-766.

Graham K, Jelley J & Purcell J (2005). Training bar staff in preventing and managing aggression in licensed premises, *Journal of Substance Use*: **10**, 48-61.

Grant M & Litvak J (Eds.) (1998). *Drinking Patterns and their Consequences*, Taylor & Francis: Washington, DC.

Grant M & O'Connor J (Eds.) (2005). *Corporate Social Responsibility and Alcohol: The Need and Potential for Partnership*, Brunner-Routledge: New York.

Grant M (Ed.) (1998). *Alcohol and Emerging Markets: Patterns, Problems and Responses*, Brunner/Mazel: Philadelphia, PA.

Grant S A, Millar K & Kenny G N (2000). Blood alcohol concentration and psychomotor effects, *British Journal of Anaesthesia*: **85**, 402-406.

Graves K & Kaskutas L A (2002). Beverage choice among native American and African American urban women, *Alcoholism: Clinical and Experimental Research*: **26**, 218-222.

Greenfield T K, Graves K L & Kaskutas L A (1999). Long-term effects of alcohol warning labels: Findings from a comparison of the United States and Ontario, Canada, *Psychology and Marketing*: **16**, 261-282.

Grimes A B (2009). Bar, what bar? 2 June, *New York Times*: USA.

Grobbee D E, Rimm E B, Keil U & Renaud S (1999). Alcohol and the cardiovascular system. In I Macdonald (Ed.), *Health Issues Related to Alcohol Consumption*. 2nd Ed, 125–179, Blackwell Science: Oxford, UK.

Grube JW (1997). Preventing sales of alcohol to minors: results from a community trial. *Addiction*: **92**, 251-60.

Gustield J R (1963). *The Symbolic Crusade*, University of Illinois Press: Urbana.

Häggström M (2009). Possible long term effects of ethanol, Medical gallery of Mikael Häggström, *Wikiversity Journal of Medicine*: **1** (2).

Haines M P & Barker G (2003). The NIU experiment: A case study of the social norms approach. In H W Perkins (Ed.), *The Social Norms Approach to Preventing School and College Age Substance Abuse: A Handbook for Educators, Counsellors, and Clinicians*, 21–34, Jossey-Bass: San Francisco, CA.

Haines M P, Perkins H W, Rice R M & Barker G (2004). *A guide to Marketing Social Norms for Health Promotion in Schools and Communities*, National Social Norms Resource Centre: DeKalb, IL.

Hall W, Flaherty B, Homel, P (1992). The public perception of the risks and benefits of alcohol consumption, *Australian Journal of Public Health*: **16**, 38-42.

Halpernfelsher B, Millstein S & Ellen J (1996). Relationship of alcohol use and risky sexual behaviour: A review and analysis of findings, *Journal of Adolescent Health*: **19** (5), 331-336.

Hanson GR, Venturelli PJ & Fleckenstein AE (2005). *Drugs and Society*, 9th ed, Jones and Bartlett Publishers: Sudbury, Massachusetts.

Härstedt K (2004). *Vår Gar Gränsen?* Where do we set the limit, Statesn Offentliga Utredningar: Stockholm.

Hartman L F & Oppenheim A L (1950). On Beer and Brewing Techniques in Ancient Mesopotamia, *Journal of the American Oriental Society*: **10** (suppl.).

Harwood H (2000). *Updating Estimates of Economic Costs of Alcohol Abuse in the United States: Estimates, Update Methods, and Data*. Rockville, MD: National Institute on Alcohol Abuse and Alcoholism: US.

Hastings G, Anderson S, Cooke E & Gordon R (2005). Alcohol marketing and young people's drinking: A review of the research. *Journal of Public Health Policy*: **26**, 296-311. .

Haworth A & Simpson R (Eds.) (2004). *Moonshine Markets: Issues in Unrecorded Alcohol Beverage Production and Consumption*, Brunner-Routledge: New York.

Heath D B (2000). *Drinking Occasions: Comparative Perspectives on Alcohol and Culture*, Brunner/Mazel: Philadelphia.

B

Heath DB (1998). Defining beneficial drinking patterns: a social science perspective, Paper presented at the 2nd International Conference on drinking patterns and their consequences, a thematic meeting of the Kettil Bruun Society, February: Perth.

Heath BD (1995) *International handbook on alcohol and culture*, Greenwood Publishing Group: Westport, Connecticut, USA.

Henderson M, Hutcheson G & Davies J (1996). *Alcohol and the Workplace*, World Health Organisation: Geneva.

Heyman G M (2000). An economic approach to animal models of alcoholism, *Alcohol Research and Health*: **24**, 132-139.

Hibell B, Andersson B, Bjarnason T, Ahlström S, Balakireva O & Kokkevi A (2004). *The ESPAD report 2003: Alcohol and other drug use among students in 35 European countries*, Swedish Council for Information on Alcohol and Other Drugs (CAN) & Pompidou Group at the Council of Europe: Stockholm.

History & Learning (2014). Prohibition and the gangsters, available http://www.historylearningsite.co.uk/prohibition_and_the_gansters.htm accessed 5/2/14.

History of the Alcohol and Tobacco Tax Division (n.d.) Library of the Distilled Spirits Institute: US.

HMSO (2003). Licensing Act 2003, Her Majesty's Stationery Office, available http://www.opsi.gov.uk/acts/acts2003/20030017.htm accessed 17/7/14.

Hobbs D, Hadfield P & Lister S (2002). Door lore: the art and economics of intimidation, *British Journal of Criminology*: **42**, 352-370.

Hobbs D, Hadfield P, Lister, S (2003). *Bouncers: violence and governance in the night time economy*, Oxford University Press: New York.

Holden L (2004). Mixed messages, alcohol confusion, p.11, 29 June, *The Irish Times*: Dublin.

Holder H D & Wagenaar A C (1994). Mandated server training and reduced alcohol-involved traffic crashes: A time series analysis of the Oregon experience, *Accident, Analysis and Prevention*: **26**, 89-97.

Holmyard, E J (1990). *Alchemy*, Courier Dover Publications.

Home Office (2004). Alcohol audits, strategies and initiatives: lessons from Crime and Disorder Reduction Partnerships, Home Office: London.

Home Office (2004b). *Alcohol and Sexual Violence: Key Findings from The Research*: London.

Home Office (2010). *Selling alcohol responsibly: Good Practice Examples from the Alcohol Retail and Hospitality Industries*, Home Office: UK.

Homel R, Tomsen S & Thommeny J (1992). Public drinking and violence: not just an alcohol problem, *Journal of Drug Issues*: **22**, 679-97.

Homel R, Hauritz M, Wortley R, McIlwain G & Carvoth R (1997). Preventing alcohol related crime through community action: The Surfers Paradise Safety Action Project. In R Homel (Ed.), *Policing for prevention: Reducing crime, public intoxication, and injury*, 35-90, Criminal Justice Press: Monsey, NY.

Homel R, Carvolth R, Hauritz M, McIlwain G & Teague R (2004). Making licensed venues safer for patrons: What environmental factors should be the focus of interventions? , *Drug and Alcohol Review*: **23**, 19-29.

Houston, M (2002). Drinking just the one to your health, p. 15, 23 Sept, *Irish Times*: Dublin.

How many drinks (2014). Life isn't easy being a student, available howmanydrinks.org accessed 30/06/16.

How many drinks (2014b). Drunk in bars, from: howmanydrinks.org accessed 30/06/14.

How Stuff Works (2014). How alcohol works, available science.howstuffworks.com/ alcohol6.htm accessed 3/5/14.

HSCIC (2014). Statistics on Alcohol - England, Health and Social Care Information Centre, available /www.hscic.gov.uk/catalogue/PUB14184 accessed 14/9/14.

Hsu C & McDonald D (2002). An examination on multiple celebrity endorsers in advertising, *Journal of Product & Brand Management*: **11**, 19-30.

Hu, T (1950). *The Liquor Tax in the US: 1791-1947*, Columbia University Press: New York.

IBA (2008). *A Guide to Social Responsibility*, International Bartenders Association, Graphic Support: The Netherlands.

IBN Live (2009) In right spirit, Gujarat must end prohibition, 14 July, available at http:// ibnlive.in.com/news/ftn-in-right-spirit-gujarat-must-end-prohibition/97059-3.html accessed 1/2/14.

ICAP(2001b). *Building Blocks Action Checklist*, International Centre for Alcohol Policies: Washington, DC.

ICAP (2002). *ICAP Reports 12: Alcohol and Licensed Premises*, ICAP: Washington DC.

ICAP (2002b). *Industry Views on Beverage Alcohol Advertising and Marketing, with Special Reference to Young People*. Prepared for the World Health Organization, ICAP: Washington, DC.

ICAP (2002c). *Violence and Licensed Premises*, ICAP: Washington, DC.

ICAP (2002d). *Drinking Age Limits*. ICAP Report 4, ICAP: Washington, DC.

ICAP (2003). *International Drinking Guidelines*, International Centre for Alcohol Policies Report 14: Washington, DC.

ICAP (2006). *The Structure of the Beverage Alcohol Industry*, International Centre for Alcohol Policies, March, available www.icaPorg   accessed 9/5/14.

ICAP (2008). *Guide to Building Partnerships*. International Centre for Alcohol Policies: Washington, DC.

ICAP (2014). *Self-Regulation Guides*, available http://www.icaPorg/PolicyTools/Toolkits/ SelfregulationGuides/tabid/245/DefaulTaspx accessed 19/6/14.

ICAP (2014a). *Initiatives Reporting: Industry Actions to Reduce Harmful Driving*, available http://reporting.global-actions.org/uploads/cc759416-ef7f-43cd-a8ba-25aaa5fbf13e/ Drink-resp-7M-X-4m.jpg accessed 7/7/14.

ICC (2014b). *Consolidated Code of Advertising and Marketing Communication Practice*, available http://www.iccwbo.org/uploadedFiles/ICC/policy/marketing/ Statements/330%20Final%20version%200f%20the%20Consolidated%20 Code%20 with%20covers.pdf   accessed 23/6/14.

ICAP (2014c). *Policy Options - Alcohol and the Elderly*, International Centre for Alcohol Policies, available http://www.icap.org/PolicyTools/ICAPBlueBook/BlueBookModules/ 23AlcoholandtheElderly/tabid/181/Default.aspx#5 accessed 3/6/14.

B

ICAP (2014d). *Alcohol and the Workplace*, available http://www.icap.org/PolicyTools/ ICAPBlueBook/BlueBookModules/22AlcoholandtheWorkplace/tabid/542/Default.aspx accessed 7/7/14.

ICAP (2014e). *An Integrated Approach to Alcohol Policies*, International Centre for Alcohol Policies: Washington, DC.

ICAP (2014f) Beverage alcohol labelling requirements by country, available at http:// www.icaPorg/table/alcoholbeveragelabeling accessed 9/10/14.

ICC (2004). ICC framework for responsible food and beverage communications, International Chamber of Commerce, available http://www.iccwbOorg/id990/ indeXhtml accessed 12/6/14.

Internal Revenue Service (1921, 1966, 1970). Alcohol and Tobacco Summary Statistics: US.

International Agency for Research on Cancer (IARC) (2007). *Monograph 96: Alcoholic Beverage Consumption and Ethyl Carbonate (Urethane)*: Lyon, France.

ILO - International Labour Organization (1949). *Convention (no. 95) on the Protection of Wages, Article 4*, available http://www.ilo.org/public/english accessed 13/7/14.

ILO (1996). *Management of Alcohol and Drug-Related Issues in The Workplace, an ILO Code of Practice*: Geneva.

ILO (2002). *Women and Men in the Informal Economy: A Statistical Picture*. International Labour Office/Employment Sector: Geneva.

ILO (2009). *Encyclopaedia of Occupational Health and Safety, 4th ed*. International Labour Office: Geneva.

Irish Independent (2004). Bouncer at gay bar gouged man's eye court told, 21 Oct: Dublin.

Isralowitz, R (2004). *Drug Use: A Reference Handbook*, ABC-CLIO: Santa Barbara, California.

IUPAC, (1997). *Compendium of Chemical Terminology, 2nd Ed, Alcohols*, International Union of Pure and Applied Chemistry: USA.

Jackson KM, Sher KJ & Park A (2005). Drinking among college students: Consumption and consequences. In: Galanter, M, Ed., *Recent Developments in Alcoholism, Vol 17: Alcohol Problems in Adolescents and Young Adults*, 85-117, Springer: New York.

Jacobson J L, Jacobson S W, Sokol R J, Martier S S, Ager J W & Kaplan-Estrin M G (1993). Teratogenic effects of alcohol on infant development, *Alcoholism: Clinical and Experimental Research*: **17**, 174-183.

Jennison K M (2004). The short-term effects and unintended long-term consequences of binge drinking in college: A 10-year follow-up study, *American Journal of Drug and Alcohol Abuse*: **30**, 659-684.

Jensen J R (1971). *The Winning of the Midwest: Social and Political Conflict, 1888-1896, Vol 2*, University of Chicago Press, Chicago: USA.

Jernigan D (2000). Applying commodity chain analysis to changing modes of alcohol supply in a developing country, *Addiction*: **95**, 465-475.

Jin Z, Xiang C, Cai Q, Wei X & He J (2013). Alcohol consumption as a preventive factor for developing rheumatoid arthritis: a dose-response meta-analysis of prospective studies, *Annals of the Rheumatic Diseases*: **73**(11), 1962-67.

Johnsson K O & Berglund M (2003). Education of key personnel in student pubs leads to a decrease in alcohol consumption among the patrons: A randomized controlled trial, *Addiction*: **98**, 627-633.

Jones A W (1990). Physiological aspects of breath-alcohol measurement, *Alcohol, Drugs and Driving*: **6**, 1-25.

Jones L, James M, Jefferson T, Lushey C, Morleo M, Stokes E, Sumnall HR, Witty K & Bellis M A (2007). *A Review of Effectiveness and Cost Effectiveness of Interventions Delivered in Primary and Secondary Schools to Prevent and/or Reduce Alcohol Use by Young People Under 18 Years Old*. NICE: London.

Jones S & Gordon R (2013). *Regulation of alcohol advertising: Policy options for Australia*, Evidence Base, issue 2: Australia.

Jung, C G (1916). *Collected Papers on Analytical Psychology*. Bailliere, Tindall and Cox:London.

Kao W H, Puddey I B, Boland L L, Watson R L & Brancati F L (2001). Alcohol consumption and the risk of Type II diabetes mellitus: Atherosclerosis risk in communities study, *American Journal of Epidemiology*: **154**, 748-757.

Kaplan S & Prato C G (2007). Impact of BAC limit reduction on different population segments: A Poisson fixed effect analysis, *Accident Analysis and Prevention*: **39**(6), 1146-54.

Kaufman Kantor G & Asdigian N L (1997). Gender differences in alcohol-related spousal aggression. In R W Wilsnack & S C Wilsnack (Eds.), *Gender and alcohol: Individual and social perspectives*, pp 312–334, Rutgers Centre of Alcohol Studies: New Brunswick, NJ.

Kim S, De La Rosa M, Rice C P & Delva J (2007). Prevalence of smoking and drinking among older adults in seven urban cities in Latin America and the Caribbean, *Substance Use and Misuse*: **42**, 1455-1475.

Kirchner J E, Zubritsky C, Cody M, Coakley E, Chen H T & Ware J H (2007). Alcohol consumption among older adults in primary care, *Journal of General Internal Medicine*: **22**, 92-97.

Kjaerheim K, Mykletun R, Aasland OG, Haldorsen T & Andersen A (1995). Heavy drinking in the restaurant business: the role of social modelling structural factors of the work-place, *Addiction*: **90**, 1487-1495.

Kondili L A, Taliani G, Cerga G, Tosti M E, Babameto A & Resuli B (2005). Correlation of alcohol consumption with liver histological features in non-cirrhotic patients, *European Journal of Gastroenterology & Hepatology*: **17**, 155-159.

Koppes L L, Twisk J W, Snel J, Van Mechelen W & Kemper H C (2000). Blood cholesterol levels of 32-year-old alcohol consumers are better than of non-consumers, *Pharmacology, Biochemistry, and Behaviour*: **66**, 163-167.

Koppes LLJ, Dekker JM, Hendriks HFJ, Bouter LM & Heine RJ (2004). Moderate alcohol consumption lowers the risk of type 2 diabetes, A meta-analysis of prospective observational studies, available http://care.diabetesjournals.org/content/28/3/719.full#aff-2 accessed 8/6/14.

Krout J A (1967). *The Origins of Prohibition*, Russell & Russell: New York.

Kuntsche E, Knibbe R, Gmel G & Engels R (2005). Why do young people drink? A review of drinking motives, *Clinical Psychology Review*: **25**(7), 841-861.

Kuntsche E, Stewart S H & Cooper M L (2008). How stable is the motive-alcohol use link? A cross-national validation of the Drinking Motives Questionnaire Revised among adolescents from Switzerland, Canada, and the United States, *Journal of Studies on Alcohol and Drugs*: **69**(3), 388-396.

B

Kuo M, Wechsler H, Greenberg P & Lee H (2003). The marketing of alcohol to college students, *American Journal of Preventive Medicine*: **25** (3), 204-211.

KyiPost (2010). Tobacco, alcohol advertising bans take effect in printed media, available www.kyivpost.com/content/ukraine/tobacco-alcohol-advertising-bans-take-effect-in-pr-56294.html   accessed 12/6/14.

la Hausse P (1988). *Brewers, Beerhalls and Boycott. A History of Liquor in South Africa*, Ravan Press: Johannesburg.

Langdana, F (2009). *Macroeconomic Policy: Demystifying Monetary and Fiscal Policy* (2nd Ed), 29th March. Springer Science & Business Media, Business & Economics.

Latendresse SJ, Rose RJ, Viken RJ, Pulkkinen L, Kaprio J & Dick DM (2008). Parenting mechanisms in links between parents' and adolescents' alcohol use behaviours, *Alcoholism: Clinical and Experimental Research*: **32**(2), 322-330.

Ledermann S & Tabah F (1951). Nouvelles données sur la mortalite d'origine alcoolique, *Population*: **6**(1), 41-58.

Lee H (1963). *How dry we were: prohibition revisited*, Englewood Cliffs, Prentice Hall: US.

Lee J E, Hunter D J, Spiegelman D, Adami H O, Albanes D & Berstein, L (2007). Alcohol intake and renal cell cancer in a pooled analysis of 12 prospective studies, *Journal of National Cancer Institute*: **99**, 801-810.

Leigh JP & Jiang WY (1993). Liver cirrhosis deaths within occupations and industries in the California occupational mortality study, *Addiction*: **88**, 767-780.

Lewis S J, Zuccolo L, Davey Smith G, Macleod J, Rodriguez S & Draper E S (2012). Foetal Alcohol Exposure and IQ at Age 8: Evidence from a Population-Based Birth-Cohort Study, PLoS ONE: **7**(11).

Leyton J (2003). How cinco de mayo works, available at www.howstuffworks.com accessed 2/2/14.

Liberto J G, Oslin D W & Ruskin P E (1992). Alcoholism in older persons: A review of the literature, *Hospital and Community Psychiatry*: **43**, 975-984.

Lieber C S (1997). Gender differences in alcohol metabolism and susceptibility In R W Wilsnack & S C Wilsnack (Eds.), *Gender and Alcohol: Individual and Social Perspectives*, Rutgers Centre of Alcohol Studies: New Brunswick, NJ.

Lipsey M W, Wilson D B, Cohen M A & Derzon J H (1997). Is there a causal relationship between alcohol use and violence? A synthesis of evidence. In M Galanter (Ed.), *Recent Developments in Alcoholism:Vol 13, Alcohol and Violence*, 245-282 Plenum Press: New York.

Lister S, Hobbs D & Hall S (2000). Violence in the night time economy. Bouncers: the reporting, recording and prosecution of assaults, *Policing and Society*: **10**, 383-402.

Lodgsdon JE (1994). Ethanol, In Kroschwitz JI *Encyclopaedia of Chemical Technology* 9, 4thed, John Wiley & Sons: New York.

Loh E W & Ball D (2000). Role of the GABA (A) beta2, GABA (A) alpha6, GABA (A) alpha1 and GABA (A) gamma2 receptor subunit genes cluster in drug responses and the development of alcohol dependence, *Neurochemistry International*: **37**, 413-423.

Los Angeles Times (2002). FTC Says Alcohol Type Not Aimed at Minors, 5 June: US.

Lowe G (1994). Pleasures of social relaxants and stimulants: the ordinary person's attitudes and involvement. In Warburton DM, Ed. *Pleasure: The Politics and the Reality*, 95-108, Wiley: Chichester, UK.

Lowe G & Taylor S B (1997). Effects of alcohol on responsive laughter and amusement, *Psychological Reports*: **80**, 1149-1150.

Luca A, García-Pagán J C, Bosch J, Feu F, Caballería J & Groszmann R J (1997). Effects of ethanol consumption on hepatic hemodynamics in patients with alcoholic cirrhosis, *Gastroenterology*: **112**, 1284-1289.

Lucia, S P (1963). *A History of Wine as Therapy*, Lippincott: Philadelphia, PA.

Lyall, S (2003). Something cheap in the state of Denmark, 13 Oct, p. 4A, *Liquor: The New York Times*: USA.

Lyons RA, Lo SV, Monaghan S & Littlepage BN, C (1995). Moderate drinking also improves health, *British Medical Journal*: **310**, 326.

MacAvoy, M (2002). Alcohol ethics & society – where to from here, *Drinks Industry Ireland*, November, Louisville Publishing Ltd: Co. Wicklow.

MacRae, D (1870). *The Americans at Home: Pen-and-Ink Sketches of American Men, Manners, and Institutions, Vol II*: Edmonston and Douglas: Edinburgh.

Maezawa, Y, Yamauchi, M, Toda, G, Suzuki, H & Sakurai, S (1995). Alcohol-metabolizing enzyme polymorphisms and alcoholism in Japan, *Alcoholism: Clinical and Experimental Research*: **19**, 951-954.

Maguire M, Nettleton H (2003). *Reducing Alcohol-Related Violence and Disorder: an Evaluation of the 'TASC' Project*. Home Office Research Study, Home Office: London.

Mail Foreign Service, (2009). Holidaymaker latest to die in poison scandal, *Irish Daily Mail*, 3 June: Dublin.

Mäkelä K & Mustonen H (1988) Positive and negative consequences related to drinking as a function of annual alcohol intake, *British Journal of Addiction*: **83**, 403-408.

Mäkelä K & Mustonen H (2000). Relationships of drinking behaviour, gender and age with reported negative and positive experiences related to drinks, *Addiction*: **95**, 727-736.

Mäkelä K & Simpura J (1985). Experiences related to drinking as a function of annual alcohol intake and by age and sex, *Drug and Alcohol Dependence*: **15**, 389-404.

Mäkelä P, Rossow I & Tryggvesson K (2002). Who drinks more or less when policies change? The evidence from 50 years of Nordic studies. In R Room (Ed.), *The Effects of Nordic Alcohol Policies: What Happens to Drinking and Harm When Control Systems Change?* Publication No 42, Nordic Council for Alcohol and Drug Research: Helsinki.

Malzburg B (1949). A study of first admissions with alcohol psychoses in New York State 1943-44, *Quarterly Journal of Studies on Alcohol*: **10** (294), 430-431.

Mangione T W, Howland J, Amick B, Cote J, Lee M & Bell N (1999). Employee drinking practices and work performance, *Journal of Studies on Alcohol*: **60**(2), 261-270.

Mann R E, Smart R G & Govoni, R (2003). The epidemiology of alcoholic liver disease, *Alcohol Research and Health*: **27**, 209-219.

Manning W G, Blumberg L & Moulton L H (1995). The demand for alcohol: The differential response to price, *Journal of Health Economics*: **14**, 123-148.

B

Marciniak ML (1992) Filters, Strainers and Siphons in Wine and Beer Production and Drinking Customs in Ancient Egypt, *Annual Alcohol Epidemiology Symposium of the Kettil Bruun Society for Social and Epidemiological Research on Alcohol,* May 30th – June 5th: Toronto, Ontario.

Mares S H, van der Vorst H, Lichtwarck-Aschoff A, Schulten I, Verdurmen J E & Otten, R (2011). Effectiveness of the home-based alcohol prevention program "In control: no alcohol!" Study protocol of a randomized controlled trial. *BMC Public Health,* **11,** Article 622.

Marlowe L (2004). Landmark drink-driving decision provokes debate, p. 10, 7 Jan, *Irish Times*: Dublin.

Marshall M (Ed.) (1979). *Beliefs, Behaviours and Alcoholic Beverages: A Cross-Cultural Survey,* University of Michigan Press: Ann Arbor, MI.

Martin S E (Ed.) (1993). *Alcohol and Interpersonal Violence: Fostering Multidisciplinary Perspectives,* National Institute of Health: Rockville, MD.

Martino S C, Ellickson P L & McCaffrey D F (2009). Multiple trajectories of peer and parental influence and their association with the development of adolescent heavy drinking, *Addictive Behaviours*: **34**(8), 693-700.

Mass-Observation (1943). *The Pub and The People, a Work Town Study by Mass-Observation,* Gollancz Ltd: London.

May P A, Gossage J P, Marais A S, Hendricks L S, Snell C L & Tabachnick B G (2008). Maternal risk factors for foetal alcohol syndrome and partial foetal alcohol syndrome in South Africa: a third study, *Alcoholism: Clinical and Experimental Research*: **32**(5), 738-753.

McCafferty E (2008). So, what would your drink diary say about you? *Irish Independent,* 22 April: Dublin.

McCracken G (1987). Advertising: meaning or information, in M Wallendorf and P F Anderson (Eds) *Advances in Consumer Research,* 121-124, Association for Consumer Research: Provo, UT.

McCrickerd K, Chambers L & Yeomans MR (2014). Fluid or fuel? The context of consuming a beverage is important for satiety, PLoS ONE 9(6): e100406.

McDonagh P (2008). Almost half of us have been harmed by booze, *Irish Independent,* 22 April: Dublin.

McGovern P E (2003). *Ancient Wine: The Search for the Origins of Viniculture,* Princeton University Press: Princeton.

McGovern P E, Zhang J, Tang J, Zhang Z, Hall G R, Moreau R A, Nunez A, Butrym E D, Richards M P, Wang C S, Cheng G, Zhao Z & Wang, C (2004). Fermented beverages of pre- and proto-historic China. *Proceedings of the National Academy of Sciences* **101** (51): 17593–17598.

McGrew L J (n.d.). History of alcohol prohibition, Schaffer library of drug policy, available http://www.druglibrary.org/schaffer/library/studies/nc/nc2a.htm accessed 4/1/14.

McKnight A, J (1988). *Development and field test of a responsible alcohol service programme, final report,* National Highway Traffic Safety Administration, US Department of Transportation: Washington.

McKnight A J & Streff F M (1994). The effect of enforcement upon service of alcohol to intoxicated patrons of bars and restaurants, *Accident, Analysis and Prevention*: **26**, 79-88.

MCM (1990). *Conflict and Violence in Pubs*, MCM Research Ltd: Oxford.

McMurran M (eds) (2013). *Alcohol Related Violence – Prevention and Treatment*, Wiley & Sons Ltd: USA.

McPherson K, Cavallo F & Rubin E (1999). Alcohol and breast cancer. In I Macdonald (Ed.), *Health Issues Related to Alcohol Consumption*. 2nd Ed, 215–242, Blackwell Science: Oxford.

MEAS (2011). Nightclub's Rag Week Promotion Breached MEAS Code on Responsible Promotion of Alcohol, available http://www.meas.ie/news-and-research/press-releases/2011/nightclub-s-rag-week-promotion-breached-meas-code-on-responsible-promotion-of-alcohol/ accessed 11/7/14.

Meier P & Seitz H K (2008). Age, alcohol metabolism, and liver disease, *Current Opinion in Clinical Nutrition and Metabolic Care*: **11**, 21-26.

Meister K A, Whelan E M & Kava R (2000). The health effects of moderate alcohol intake in humans: An epidemiologic review, *Critical Reviews in Clinical Laboratory Sciences*: **37**, 261-296.

Mendelson JH, Ellingboe J, Mello NK & Kuehnle J (1978). Effects of Alcohol on Plasma Testosterone and Luteinizing Hormone Levels, *Alcoholism: Clinical and Experimental Research*: **2** (3), 255-258.

Mennella J (2001). Alcohol's effect on lactation, *Alcohol Research and Health*: **25**, 230-234.

Midanik L T (1994). Comparing usual quantity/frequency and graduated frequency scales to assess yearly alcohol consumption: Results from the 1990 US National Alcohol Survey, *Addiction*: **89**, 407-412.

Midford R & McBride N (2001). Alcohol education in schools. In N Heather, J E Peters & T Stockwell (Eds.), *International Handbook of Alcohol Dependence and Problems*, 785-804, John Wiley & Sons Ltd: Chichester, UK.

Milgram G G (2001). Alcohol influences: The role of family and peers. In E Houghton & A Roche (Eds.), *Learning about Drinking*, 85-107, Brunner-Routledge: Philadelphia.

Min JA, Lee K & Ki DJ (2010). The application of minerals in managing alcohol hangover: a preliminary review, *Current Drug Abuse Reviews*: **3** (2), 110-115.

Mitchell, J (2003). Wine - to your health, 14 Sept, *Sunday Tribune*: Dublin.

MMC (2014). Mcgarvin Moberly Construction – workplace policy, available at http://mcgarvinmoberly.com/crusher.html accessed 10/6/14.

Modell JG & Mountz JM (1990). Drinking and flying: the problem of alcohol use by pilots, *New England Journal of Medicine*: **323**, 455-461.

Mohler-Kuo M, Dowdall G W, Koss M P & Wechsler H (2004). Correlates of rape while intoxicated in a national sample of college women, *Journal of Studies on Alcohol*: **65**, 37-45.

Monaghan L (2002). Regulating unruly bodies: work tasks, conflict and violence in Britain's night time economy, *The British Journal of Sociology*: **53**, 403-429.

Moncrieff J & Farmer R (1998). Sexual abuse and the subsequent development of alcohol problems, *Alcohol and Alcoholism*: **33**, 592-601.

B

Moore A A, Endo J O & Carter M K (2003). Is there a relationship between excessive drinking and functional impairment in older persons? *Journal of the American Geriatrics Society*: **51**, 44-49.

Moore D (1990). Drinking the construction of ethnic identity and social process in Western Australian youth subculture, *British Journal of Addiction*: **85**, 1265-1278.

Moos R H, Brennan P L, Schutte K K & Moos B S (2005). Older adults' health and changes in late-life drinking patterns, *Aging and Mental Health*: **9**, 49-59.

Moreira M T, Smith L A & Foxcroft D (2009). Social norms interventions to reduce alcohol misuse in university or college students. *Cochrane Database of Systematic Reviews*, B.

Mosher JM (1984). The impact of legal provisions on barroom behaviour: toward an alcohol problems prevention policy, *Alcohol*: **1**, 205-211.

Moskal A, Norat T, Ferrari P & Riboli E (2007). Alcohol intake and colorectal cancer risk: A dose-response meta-analysis of published cohort studies, *International Journal of Cancer*: **120**, 664-671.

Mumenthaler M S, Taylor J L, O'Hara R & Yesavage J A (1999). Gender differences in moderate drinking effects, *Alcohol Research and Health*: **23**, 55-64.

Murphy R (2002). *Developing an Alcohol and Drug Policy for your Workplace*, Western Health Board: Ireland.

Murphy J (2005). Dealing with intoxication, *Licensing World*, November, Jemma Publications Ltd: Dublin.

Murphy J (2006). Hangover remedies – The morning after, time tested antidotes, *Licensing World Trade Directory*, Jemma Publications Ltd: Dublin.

Murphy J (2008). Prevention of conflict and violence in licensed premises, *Licensing World*, June, Jemma Publications Ltd: Dublin.

Murphy J (2011). Maintaining a drug free pub, November, *Licensing World*, Jemma Publications Ltd: Dublin.

Murphy J (2013). *Principles and Practices of Bar and Beverage Management*, Goodfellow Publishers Ltd: Oxford.

Murty B R (2004). The biochemistry of alcohol toxicity, October, *Resonance*: India.

Nakanishi N, Suzuki K & Tatara K (2003). Alcohol consumption and risk for development of impaired fasting glucose or Type II diabetes in middle-aged Japanese men, *Diabetes Care*: **26**, 48-54.

National Commission on Law Observance and Enforcement (1931) *Report on the Enforcement of the Prohibition Laws of the US*, 71st Cong, US.

National Institute of Health (2014). *Understanding Alcohol, Teachers Guide*, available science. education.nih.gov/supplements/nih3/alcohol/guide/lesson2.htm accessed 3/4/14.

NBWA (2014). Beer Servers America, The Beer Institute and National Beer Wholesalers Association, available http://www.beerservesamerica.org/ accessed 11/5/14.

Neafsey E & Collins, M (2011). Moderate alcohol consumption and cognitive risk, *Neuropsychiatric Disease and Treatment*: **7** (1), 465-484.

Nelson J P (1997). *Broadcast advertising and US demand for alcoholic beverages: System-wide estimates with quarterly data*, US Federal Trade Commission: Washington, DC.

Nelson T F & Wechsler H (2003). School spirits: Alcohol and collegiate sports fans, *Addictive Behaviours*: **28**, 1-11.

Nelson J P (2006). Alcohol advertising in magazines: Do beer, wine, and spirits ads target youth? *Contemporary Economic Policy*: **24** (3), 357-369.

Nelson J P (2010). What is learned from Longitudinal Studies of Advertising and Youth Drinking and Smoking? *International Journal of Environmental Research and Public Health*: **7**(3), 870-926.

Neumark YD, Friedlander Y, Durst R, Leitersdorf E, Jaffe D & Ramchandani VA (2004). Alcohol dehydrogenase polymorphisms influence alcohol-elimination rates in a male Jewish population, *Alcoholism: Clinical and Experimental Research*: **28**, 10-14.

Neville S (2008). Low price alcohol is poisonous, court told, *Evening Herald*, 15 Feb: Ireland.

New South Wales Department of Gaming and Racing (2004). *Liquor Accords: Local Solutions for Local Problems*: Sydney, Australia.

New York Times (1988). Beer (Soon) for Icelanders, 11 May, available at www.nytimes.com /1988/05/11/world/beer-soon-for-icelanders.html accessed 3/2/14.

New Zealand Security Association (2006). Education, available www.security.org.nz/ index.php accessed 15/6/14.

Nicolás JM, Fernández-Sola J, Estruch R, Paré JC, Sacanella E & Urbano-Márquez A (2002). The effect of controlled drinking in alcoholic cardiomyopathy, *Annals of Internal Medicine*: **136**, 192-200.

NIH (2014). *Mixing alcohol with medicines*, National Institute on alcohol abuse and alcoholism, available http://pubs.niaaa.nih.gov/publications/Medicine/medicine.htm accessed 11/5/14.

Niroomand F, Hauer O, Tiefenbacher C P, Katus H A & Kuebler W (2004). Influence of alcohol consumption on restenosis rate after percutaneous transluminal coronary angioplasty and stent implantation, *Heart*: **90**, 1189-1193.

Nolen-Hoeksema S (2004). Gender differences in risk factors and consequences for alcohol use and problems, *Clinical Psychology Review*: **24**, 981-1010.

Norström T (2000). Outlet density and criminal violence in Norway, 1960-19951, *Journal of Studies on Alcohol*: **61**, 907-91.

Norström T (2001). Alcohol and mortality: The post-war experience in the EU countries, *Addiction*: **96**(S.1), 1-129.

Norström T & Skög O J (2003). Saturday opening of alcohol retail shops in Sweden: An impact analysis, *Journal of Studies on Alcohol*: **64**, 393-401.

NRA (1996). *Bar Code – Serving Alcohol Responsibly Server Guide*, The Education Foundation of the National Restaurant Association: USA.

Nummer B (2012). Brewing With Lactic Acid Bacteria, available at http://morebeer.com/ articles/brewing_with_lactic_acid_bacteria accessed 3/10/14.

Obisesan T O, Hirsch R, Kosoko O, Carlson L & Parrott M (1998). Moderate wine consumption is associated with decreased odds of developing age-related macular degeneration in NHANES-1, *Journal of the American Geriatrics Society*: **46**, 1-7.

O'Brien K (2014). Alcohol Industry Sponsorship and Hazardous Drinking in UK University Sport, available http://alcoholresearchuk.org/alcohol-insights/alcohol-industry-sponsorship-and-hazardous-drinking-in-uk-university-sport/ accessed 12/7/14.

B

O'Brien K & Kypri K (2008). Alcohol industry sponsorship of sport and hazardous drinking among New Zealand sportspeople, *Addiction*: **103**(12), 1961-1966.

O'Brien KS, Miller PG, Kolt GS, Martens MP & Webber A (2011). Alcohol industry and non-alcohol industry sponsorship of sportspeople and drinking, *Alcohol and Alcoholism*: **46**, 210-13.

Occupational Health and Safety Act 1910 (1970). United States.

O'Connor A (2007). The Claim: A Little Alcohol Can Help You Beat a Cold, 18 Dec, *New York Times*, available http://www.nytimes.com/2007/12/18/health/18real.html?_r=1& accessed 15/8/14.

Odegard P H (1928). *Pressure Politics - the Story of the Anti-saloon League*, Columbia University Press: New York.

O'Guinn T, Allen C & Semenik R (2003). *Advertising and Integrated Brand Promotion, 3rd Ed*, South-Western Publishing: Mason Ohio.

Oldenburg, R (1999). *The Great Good Place: Cafes, Coffee Shops, Bookstores, Bars, Hair Salons, and Other Hangouts at The Heart of a Community*, Marlowe & Company: New York.

O'Halloran G (2009). Man died after acute alcohol consumption, *The Irish Times*, p. 4, 23 June: Dublin.

O'Halloran G (2011). Barman died of alcohol poison, *Evening Herald*, 13 Sept, Ireland.

O'Leary C, Jacoby P, D'Antoine H, Bartu A & Bower C (2012). Heavy prenatal alcohol exposure and increased risk of stillbirth, *British Journal of Obstetrics and Gynaecology*: **119**(8), 945-952.

O'Leary D (2000). Ethanol, available at http://www.ucc.ie/academic/chem/dolchem/html/comp/ethanol.html accessed 12/10/14.

Olsen J, Bolumar F, Boldsen J & Bisanti L (1997). Does moderate alcohol intake reduce fecundability? A European multicentre study on infertility and subfecundity. *Alcoholism: Clinical and Experimental Research*: **21**, 206-212.

O'Malley P M, Bachman J G, Johnston L D & Schulenberg J E (2004). Studying the transition from youth to adulthood: Impacts on substance use and abuse.In J S House, F T Juster, R L Kahn, H Schuman & E Single (Eds.), *A Telescope on Society: Survey Research and Social Science at The University of Michigan and Beyond*, 305-329, University of Michigan Press: Ann Arbor, MI.

Onder G, Landi F, Della Vedova C, Atkinson H, Pedone C & Cesari M (2002). Moderate alcohol consumption and adverse drug reactions among older adults, *Pharmacoepidemiology and Drug Safety*: **11**, 385-392.

OPM (2014). Alcoholism in the Workplace: A Handbook for Supervisors, available http://www.opm.gov/policy-data-oversight/worklife/reference-materials/alcoholism-in-the-workplace-a-handbook-for-supervisors/ accessed 3/6/14.

Osilla K C, dela Cruz E, Miles J N, Zellmer S, Watkin, K & Larimer M E (2010). Exploring productivity outcomes from a brief intervention for at-risk drinking in an employee assistance program, *Addiction Behaviour*: **35**(3), 194-200.

Paganini Hill A, Kawas C H & Corrada M M (2007). Type of alcohol consumed, changes in intake over time and mortality: The Leisure World Cohort Study, *Age and Ageing*: 36, 203-209.

Parks K A & Miller B A (1997). Bar victimization of women, *Psychology of Women Quarterly*: **21**, 509-525.

Pascarella ET, Goodman KM, Seifert TA, Tagliapietra-Nicoli G, Park S & Whitt EJ (2007). College student binge drinking and academic achievement: A longitudinal replication and extension. *Journal of College Student Development*, **48**(6), 715-727.

Paschall M J, Freisthler B & Lipton R I (2005). Moderate alcohol use and depression in young adults: Findings from a national longitudinal study. *American Journal of Public Health*: **95**, 453-457.

Pasteur L (1879). *Studies on fermentation: The diseases of beer, their causes, and the means of preventing them*, Macmillan Publishers.

Patra J, Bakker R, Irving H, Jaddoe V W, Malini S & Rehm J (2011). Dose-response relationship between alcohol consumption before and during pregnancy and the risks of low birth weight, preterm birth and small for gestational age - a systematic review and meta-analyses, *British Journal of Obstetrics and Gynaecology*: **118**(12), 1411-1421.

Patrick C H (1952). *Alcohol, Culture, and Society*, Duke University Press, Durham: NC (reprint edition by AMS Press, New York, 1970).

Pawan GLS (1973). Alcoholic drinks and hangover effects, *Proceeding of the Nutrition Society*: **32** (1), 15A.

Pedersen CS (1979). *Microbiology of Food Fermentations*, AVI Publishers, USA.

Pedlow G (1998). Alcohol in emerging markets: Identifying the most appropriate role for the alcohol beverage industry. In M Grant (Ed.), *Alcohol and Emerging Markets: Patterns, Problems, and Responses*, 333–352, Brunner/Mazel: Philadelphia.

Peele S & Brodsky, A (2000). Exploring psychological benefits associated with moderate alcohol use: a necessary corrective to assessments of drinking outcomes, *Drug and Alcohol Dependence*: **60**, 241-247.

Penning R, van Nuland M, Fliervoet LA, Olivier B & Verster JC (2010). The pathology of alcohol hangover, *Current Drug Abuse Reviews*: **3** (2), 68-75.

Penning R, McKinney A & Verster JC (2012). Alcohol hangover symptoms and their contribution to the overall hangover severity, *Alcohol and Alcoholism*: **47** (3), 248-252.

Penning R, de Haan LG & Verster JC (2011). Caffeinated drinks, alcohol consumption, and hangover severity, *The Open Neuropsychopharmacology Journal*: **4**, 36-39.

Perkins H W (1997). College student misperceptions of alcohol and other drug norms among peers: Exploring causes, consequences, and implication for prevention programs. In *Designing Alcohol and Other Drug Prevention Programs in Higher Education: Bringing Theory into Practice*, 177–206, Higher Education Centre for Alcohol and Other Drug Prevention: Newton, MA.

Perkins H W, Meilman P W, Leichliter J S, Cashin J R & Presley C A (1999). Misperceptions of the norms for the frequency of alcohol and other drug use on college campuses, *Journal of American College Health*: **47**, 253-258.

Perkins, H W (2002). Social norms and the prevention of alcohol misuse in collegiate contexts, *Journal of Studies on Alcohol*: (**S14**), 164-172.

Perkins H W, Linkenbach J, Lewis M & Neighbors C (2010). Effectiveness of social norms media marketing in reducing drinking and driving: A state-wide campaign, *Addictive Behaviours*: **35**, 866-874.

B

Pernanen K (1991). *Alcohol in Human Violence*, The Guilford Press: New York.

Piasecki TM, Robertson BM & Epler AJ (2010). Hangover and risk for alcohol use disorders: existing evidence and potential mechanisms, *Current Drug Abuse Reviews*: **3** (2), 92-102.

Pidd K, Boeckmann R & Morris M (2006). Adolescents in transition: The role of workplace alcohol and other drug policies as a prevention strategy, *Drugs: Education, Prevention, and Policy*: **13**(4), 353-365.

Pittler MH, Verster JC, Ernst E (2005). Interventions for preventing or treating alcohol hangover: systematic review of randomized controlled trials, *British Medical Journal (Clinical research ed.)*: **331** (7531), 1515-1518.

Plant, M L (1997). *Women and Alcohol: Contemporary and Historical Perspectives*, Free Association Books: London.

Plant M & Plant M (1997). Alcohol education and harm minimisation. In M Plant, E Single & T Stockwell (Eds.), *Alcohol: Minimising the Harm. What Works?* Free Association Books: New York.

Plant M L, Abel E L & Guerri C (1999). Alcohol and pregnancy. In I Macdonald (Ed.), *Health Issues Related to Alcohol Consumption. 2nd Ed*, 182–213, Blackwell Science: Oxford.

Plant M L, Miller P & Plant M A (2005). The relationship between alcohol consumption and problem behaviours: Gender differences among British adults, *Journal of Substance Use*: **10**, 22-30.

Pliner P & Cappell H (1974). Modification of affective consequences of alcohol: a comparison of social and solitary drinking, *Journal of Abnormal Psychology*: **83**, 418-425.

Pope C (2009). A drink or two, p.7, April 14, *The Irish Times-Health Plus*: Dublin.

Popham, R E (1978) The social history of the tavern. In Smart RG, Cappell HD, Glaser FB, Israel Y, Kalant H, Popham RE, Schmidt W & Sellers EM (Eds.) *Research Advances in Alcohol and Drug Problems: Volume 8*. New York: Plenum Press.

Porjesz B & Begleiter H (1998). Genetic basis of event-related potentials and their relationship to alcoholism and alcohol use, *Journal of Clinical Neurophysiology*: **15**, 45-57.

Porter SR & Pryor J (2007). The effects of heavy episodic alcohol use on student engagement, academic performance, and time use. *Journal of College Student Development*, **48**(4), 455-467.

Portman Group (2014). Alcohol Labelling, available http://www.portmangroup.org.uk/codes/alcohol-marketing/alcohol-labelling accessed 10/6/14.

Portman Group (2000). Keeping the peace: A guide to the prevention of alcohol-related disorder, available http://www.portman-group.org.uk/uploaded_files/documents/35_49_KeepingthePeace.pdf accessed 18/7/14.

Prat G, Adan A, Sánchez-Turet M (2009). Alcohol hangover: a critical review of explanatory factors. *Human Psychopharmacology: Clinical and Experimental*: **24** (4), 259-267.

Preedy VR & Watson RR, Eds (2005). *Comprehensive Handbook of Alcohol-Related Pathology*. Elsevier Science: London.

Preseley CA, Meilman PW & Lyerla R (1993). *Alcohol and Drugs on American College Campuses: Use, Consequences, and Perceptions of the Campus Environment, Volume I, 1989-91*, Southern Illinois University.

Puddey I B, Beilin L J, Vandongen R, Rouse I L & Rogers P (1985). Evidence for a direct effect of alcohol consumption on blood pressure in normotensive men: A randomized controlled trial, *Hypertension*: **7**, 707-713.

Pulkkinen L & Pitkanen T (1994). A prospective study of the precursors to problem drinking in young adulthood, *Journal of Studies on Alcohol*: **55**, 578-587.

Quigley B M, Leonard K E & Collins R L (2003). Characteristics of violent bars and bar patrons, *Journal of Studies on Alcohol*: **64** (6), 765-772.

Raging Alcoholic (2014). Alcohol health problems, available http://ragingalcoholic.com/alcohol-health-problems/ accessed 13/6/14.

Raistrick D (1999). Tackling alcohol together - towards a national alcohol policy for the UK, *Alcohol and Alcoholism*: **34**, 113-114.

Ramskogler K, Hertling I, Riegler A, Semler B, Zoghlami A & Walter H (2001). Possible interaction between ethanol and drugs and their significance for drug therapy in the elderly, *Wiener Klinische Wochenschrift*: **113**, 363-370.

Ramstedt, M (2001). Alcohol and suicide in 14 European countries, *Addiction*: **96**(S.1), 59-75.

Rau W & Durand A (2000). The Academic ethic and college grades: does hard work help students to "make the grade"? *Sociology of Education*, **73**(1), 19-38.

Read JP, Wood MD & Kahler CW (2003). Examining the role of drinking motives in college student alcohol use and problems, *Psychology of Addictive Behaviours*: **17**, 13-23.

Rehm J & Gmel G (1999). Patterns of alcohol consumption and social consequences. Results from an 8-year follow-up study in Switzerland, *Addiction*: **94**, 899-912.

Rehm J, Sempos C T & Trevisan M (2003). Alcohol and cardiovascular disease: More than one paradox to consider. Average volume of alcohol consumption, patterns of drinking and risk of coronary heart disease. A review, *Journal of Cardiovascular Risk*: **10**, 15-20.

Rehm J, Rehn N, Room R, Monteiro M, Gmel G & Jernigan D (2003). The global distribution of average volume of alcohol consumption and patterns of drinking, *European Addiction Research*: **9**, 147-156.

Rehm J, Kanteres F & Lachenmeier DW (2010). Unrecorded consumption, quality of alcohol and health consequences, *Drug and Alcohol Review*: **29**, 426-436.

Rehm J, Baliunas D, Brochu S, Fischer B, Gnam W & Patra, S (2006). *The costs of substance abuse in Canada 2002*, Canadian Centre on Substance Abuse: Ottawa, Canada.

Reid R J, Hughey J & Peterson N A (2003). Generalizing the alcohol outlet assaultive violence link: Evidence from a US Midwestern city, *Substance Use and Misuse*: **38**, 1971-1982.

Reisch G (2007). How are non-alcoholic beer and wine made? available at www.chow.com/food-news/53912/how-are-nonalcoholic-beer-and-wine-made accessed 13/10/14.

Reynolds R I, Holder H D & Gruenewald P J (1997). Community prevention and alcohol retail access, *Addiction*: **92**, s261-s272.

Rigakos GS (2004). *Nightclub security and surveillance*, The Canadian Review of Policing Research: Ottawa.

Rimm E B & Moats C (2007). Alcohol and coronary heart disease: Drinking patterns and mediators of effect. *Annals of Epidemiology*: **17**(Suppl.), S3-7.

B

Riserus U & Ingelsson E (2007). Alcohol intake, insulin resistance, and abdominal obesity in elderly men, *Obesity*: **15**, 1766-1773.

Road Safety Authority (2014). Drink Drive limits and the corresponding penalties, available at http://www.rsa.ie accessed 19/7/14.

Robinson R (2006) *The Oxford Companion to Wine, 3rd Ed*, P 234. Oxford Univ. Press: Oxford.

Roche AM, Bywood PT, Borlagdan J, Lunnay B, Freeman T, Lawton L, Tovell A & Nicholas R (2007). *Young people and alcohol: The role of cultural influences*. National Centre for Education and Training on Addiction: Adelaide.

Rodgers B, Korten AE, Jorm AF, Jacomb PA, Christensen H & Henderson S (2000). Non-linear relationships in associations of depression and anxiety with alcohol use, *Psychological Medicine*: **30**, 412-432.

Rodgers, P (2006). From that first sip, drinking damages and it's worse for women, p. 16, 24 Oct, *Irish Independent*: Dublin.

Roehrs T, Papineau K, Rosenthal L & Roth T (1999). Ethanol as a hypnotic in insomniacs: Self administration and effects of sleep and mood, *Neuropsychopharmacology*: **20**, 279-286.

Rohsenow DJ & Howland J (2010). The role of beverage congeners in hangover and other residual effects of alcohol intoxication: a review, *Current Drug Abuse Reviews*:3(2), 76-79.

Roncek D W & Maier P A (1991). Bars, blocks, and crimes revisited: Linking the theory of routine activities to the empiricism of hot spots, *Criminology*: **29**, 725-753.

Rong G X (2014). *Grandiose survey of Chinese alcoholic drinks and beverages*, Chinese Administration of Alcoholic Beverages, from: www.sytu.edu.cn/zhgjiu/umain.htm accessed 11/2/14.

Romeri E, Baker A & Griffiths C (2007). Alcohol-related deaths by occupation, England and Wales, 2001-05, *Health Statistics Quarterly*: **35**, 6-12.

Room R & Rossow I (2001). Share of violence attributable to drinking, *Journal of Substance Use*: **6**, 218-228.

Room R, Jernigan D, Carlini-Marlatt B, Gureje O, Mäkelä K & Marshall M (2002). *Alcohol and developing societies: a public health approach*. Helsinki: Finnish Foundation for Alcohol Studies and Geneva: World Health Organization.

Room R, Graham K, Rehm J, Jernigan D & Monteiro M (2003). Drinking and its burden in a global perspective: Policy considerations and option, *European Addiction Research*: **9s**, 165-175.

Roseingrave L (2010). Youth died after vodka drinking game, 5 Nov, *Irish Times*: Dublin.

Rossow I & Hauge R (2004). Who pays for the drinking? Characteristics of the extent and distribution of social harms from others' drinking, *Addiction*: **99**, 1094-1102.

Rotondo S, Di Castelnuovo A & de Gaetano G (2001). The relationship between wine consumption and cardiovascular risk: From epidemiological evidence to biological plausibility, *Italian Heart Journal*: **2**, 1-8.

RRAI (2010). Responsible Retailing of Alcohol in Ireland, available http://www.rrai.ie/Member_Resources/Default.110.html   accessed 13/7/14.

Rumbold G, Malpass A, Lang E, Cvetkovski S & Kelly W (1998). *An evaluation of the Geelong Local Industry Accord: final report*, Turning Point Alcohol and Drug Centre: Melbourne.

Ryan S M, Jorm A F & Lubman D I (2010). Parenting factors associated with reduced adolescent alcohol use: a systematic review of longitudinal studie, *Australian and New Zealand Journal of Psychiatry*: **44s**, 774-783.

Rydon P & Stockwell T R (1997). Local regulation and enforcement strategies for licensed premises. In Plant M, Single E, Eds. *Alcohol: minimising the harm*, Free Association Books: London.

Saar I (2009). The social costs of alcohol misuse in Estonia, *European Addiction Research*: **15**(1), 56-62.

Saitz R F (1987). The roles of bars and restaurants in preventing alcohol-impaired driving: An evaluation of server intervention, *Evaluation and the Health Professions*: **10**, 5-27.

Salonsalmi A, Laaksonen M, Lahelma E & Rahkonen O (2009). Drinking habits and sickness absence: the contribution of working conditions, *Scandinavian Journal Public Health*: **37**(8), 846-854.

Sargent JD, Wills TA, Stoolmiller M, Gibson J & Gibbons, F (2006). Alcohol use in motion pictures and its relation with early-onset teen drinking. *Journal of Studies in Alcohol*: **67**, 54-65.

Sariola, S (1954). Prohibition in Finland, 1919-1932, its background and consequences, *Quarterly Journal of Studies in Alcohol*: **15**(3), 477-490.

Sarkola T, & Eriksson CJP (2003). Testosterone increases in men after a low dose of alcohol, *Alcoholism, Clinical and Experimental Research*: **27** (4), 682-5.

Sarkola T, Fukunaga T, Mäkisalo H, Eriksson CJP (2000). Acute effect of alcohol on androgens in premenopausal women, *Alcohol and Alcoholism*: **35** (1), 84-90.

Saunders JB, (1998). Defining beneficial patterns of drinking: a clinical perspective, Paper presented at the 2nd International Conference on drinking patterns and their consequences, a thematic meeting of the Kettil Bruun Society, February: Perth.

Saunders J B & DeBurgh S (1999). The distribution of alcohol consumption. In M Grant & J Litvak (Eds.), *Drinking Patterns and their Consequences*, 129–152, Taylor & Francis: Washington, DC.

Savitz D A, Schwingl P J & Keels M A (1991). Influence of paternal age, smoking, and alcohol consumption on congenital anomalies, *Teratology*: **44**(4), 429-440.

Schep LJ, Slaughter RJ, Vale JA & Beasley DM (2009). A seaman with blindness and confusion, 30 September, *British Medical Journal*: **339**.

Schmidt LA, Mäkelä P, Rehm J, Room R (2010). Alcohol: equity and social determinants. In Blass E, Kurup, AS, eds *Equity, social determinants and public health programmes*. World Health Organization: Geneva.

Schubiner, H (2005). Substance abuse in patients with attention-deficit hyperactivity disorder: Therapeutic implications, *CNS Drugs*: **19**, 643-655.

Schulenberg JE, Maggs JL & O'Malley PM (2003). How and why the understanding of developmental continuity and discontinuity is important: The sample case of long-term consequences of adolescent substance use. In: Mortimer JT, and Shanahan MJ, eds. *Handbook of the Life Course*, 413-436, Kluwer Academic/Plenum: New York.

Schulenberg JE & Maggs JL (2002). A developmental perspective on alcohol use and heavy drinking during adolescence and the transition to young adulthood. *Journal of Studies on Alcohol*: (**S14**), 54-70.

B

Scott DM, Taylor RE (2007). Health-related effects of genetic variations of alcohol-metabolizing enzymes in African Americans, *Alcohol Research & Health*: **30**(1), 18-21.

Scribner R A, Theall K P, Mason,K, Simonsen N, Schneider S K & Towvim L G (2011). Alcohol prevention on college campuses: The moderating effect of the alcohol environment on the effectiveness of social norms marketing campaigns, *Journal of Studies on Alcohol and Drugs*: **72**, 232-239.

SCU Wellness Centre (2014). Mixing alcohol with other drugs, available http://www.scu.edu/wellness/topics/alcohol/mixingalcohol.cfm accessed 15/7/14.

Scully P (1992). Liquor and Labor in the Western Cape. In J Crush and C Ambler (Eds.), *Liquor and Labor in Southern Africa*, 56-77, University of Ohio Press: Athens, OH.

Seitz H K & Meier P (2007). The role of acetaldehyde in upper digestive tract cancer in alcoholics, *Translational Research*: **149**, 293-297.

Shay F (1934). Ten Best Cocktails of 1934, p. 40, *Esquire* vol. 2, December: USA.

Sherwood T F (1945). The evolution of the still, *Annals of Science*: **5** (3), 186.

Shi L, Stevens GD (2005). Vulnerability and unmet health care needs – the influence of multiple risk factors, *Journal of General Internal Medicine*: **20**, 148-154.

Shioya T (2007). Does cooking alcohol really burn it all off? available at www.chow.com/food-news/54140/does-cooking-alcohol-really-burn-it-all-off/ accessed 3/11/13.

Shults R A, Elder R W, Sleet D A, Nichols J L, Alao M O & Carande-Kulis V G (2001). Reviews of evidence regarding interventions to reduce alcohol-impaired driving, *American Journal of Prevention and Medicine*: **21**(Suppl.4, 66-88).

Sieck C J & Heirich M (2010). Focusing attention on substance abuse in the workplace: a comparison of three workplace interventions, *Journal of Workplace Behavioural Health*: **25**, 72-87.

Sillanaukee P, Koivula T, Jokela H, Pitkajarvi T & Seppa K (2000). Alcohol consumption and its relation to lipid-based cardiovascular risk factors among middle-aged women: The role of HDL (3) cholesterol, *Atherosclerosis*: **152**, 503-510.

Sinclair A (1962). *The Era of Excess*, Little Brown: Boston.

Singh H, Masih B, Satpath, S K, Duseja A & Chawla Y (2001). Financial burden of alcohol abuse in patients with alcoholic liver disease, *Tropical Gastroenterology*: **22**, 172.

Single E (1990). *Paths Ahead for Server Interventions in Canada*. Rockville, MD: Office for Substance Abuse Prevention, US Department of Health and Human Services.

Single E (1997). Public drinking, problems and prevention measures in twelve countries: Results of the WHO project on public drinking, *Contemporary Drug Problems*: **24**, 425-48.

Single E & Leino VE (1998). The levels, patterns, and consequences of drinking. In: Grant M and Litvak J, eds *Drinking Patterns and their Consequences*, 7-24, Taylor and Francis: Washington, DC.

Single E & Easton B (2001). Estimating the economic costs of alcohol misuse: Why we should do it even though we shouldn't pay too much attention to the bottom-line results, Paper presented at the Annual Meeting of the Kettil Bruun Society for Social and Epidemiological Research on Alcohol: Toronto, Canada.

Single E, Collins D, Easton B, Harwood H, Lapsley H, Kopp P & Wilson E (2003). *International Guidelines for Estimating the Costs of Substance Abuse, 2nd Ed*, WHO: Geneva.

Simons L A, Simons J, McCallum J & Friedlander Y (2006). Lifestyle factors and risk of dementia: Dubbo study of the elderly, *Medical Journal of Australia*: **184**, 68-70.

Sloan F A, Stout E M, Whetten-Goldstein K & Liand L (2000). *Drinkers, Drivers, and Bartenders. Balancing Private Choices and Public Accountability*, University of Chicago Press: Chicago, IL.

Smart R G (Ed.) *Research Advances in Alcohol and Drug Problems, Vol 4*, Plenum: New York.

Smart R G & Mann R E (1995). Treatment, health promotion and alcohol controls and the decrease of alcohol consumption and problems in Ontario: 1975-1993, *Alcohol and Alcoholism*: **30**, 337-343.

Smith K L, Wiggers J H, Considine R J, Daly J B & Collins T (2001). Police knowledge and attitudes regarding crime, the responsible service of alcohol and a proactive alcohol policing strategy, *Drug and Alcohol Review*: **20**, 181-191.

Smith LA and Foxcroft D, R (2009). The effect of alcohol advertising, marketing and portrayal on drinking behaviour in young people: systematic review of prospective cohort studies. *BMC Public Health*, **9**:51.

Smith-Squire A (2008). Binge drinking as a student gave me breast cancer at 25, *Irish Daily Mail*: Ireland.

Snyder LB, Milici F F, Slater M, Sun H, Strizhakova, Y (2006). Effects of alcohol advertising exposure on drinking among youth. *Archives of Paediatrics & Adolescent Medicine*: **160**(1), 18-24.

Soloff P H, Lynch K G & Moss H B (2000). Serotonin, impulsivity, and alcohol use disorders in the older adolescent: A psych biological study, *Alcoholism: Clinical and Experimental Research*: **24**, 1609-1619.

Solomon R & Prout L (1996). *Alcohol Liability in Canada and Australia: Sell, Serve and Be Sued*, National Centre for Research into the Prevention of Drug Abuse, Curtin University of Technology: Perth.

Song H J, Kim H J, Choi N K, Hahn S, Cho Y J & Park B J (2008). Gender differences in gastric cancer incidence in elderly former drinkers, *Alcohol*: **42**, 363-368.

Spicer R S & Miller T R (2005). Impact of a workplace peer-focused substance abuse prevention and early intervention program, *Alcoholism, Clinical and Experimental Research*: **29**(4), 609-611.

Stack, S (2011). Dead man drank 10 shots in one glass, *Metro - Evening Herald*, 5 May: Dublin.

Stacy AW, Zogg J B, Unger J B & Dent C W (2004). Exposure to televised alcohol ads and subsequent adolescent alcohol use. *American Journal of Health Behaviour*: 28(6), 498-509.

Standerwick K, Davies C, Tucker L & Sheron N (2007). Binge drinking, sexual behaviour and sexually transmitted infection in the UK, *International Journal of STDs & AIDS*: **18**(12), 810-813.

Stephens D & Dudley R (2004). The drunken monkey hypothesis: the study of fruit eating animals could lead to an evolutionary understanding of human alcohol abuse, *Natural History Magazine*, December.

Stephens R, Ling J, Heffernan T M, Heather N & Jones K (2008). A review of the literature on the cognitive effects of alcohol hangover, *Alcohol and Alcoholism*: **43**(2), 163-170.

B

Stevens T, Conwell D L & Zuccaro G (2004). Pathogenesis of chronic pancreatitis: An evidence-based review of past theories and recent developments, *American Journal of Gastroenterology*: **99**, 2256–2570.

Stimson G, Grant M, Choquet M & Garrison P (2007). *Drinking in Context: Patterns, Interventions, and Partnerships*, Routledge: New York.

Stockwell T (2001). Responsible alcohol service: lessons from evaluations of server training and policing initiatives, *Drug and Alcohol Review*: **20**(3), 257-265.

Stockwell T, Hawks D, Lang E & Rydon P (1996). Unraveling the preventive paradox for acute alcohol problems, *Drug and Alcohol Review*: **15**, 7-15.

Stockwell T, Lang E & Rydon P (1993). High risk drinking settings: The association of serving and promotional practices with harmful drinking, *Addiction*: **88**, 1519-1526.

Stockley C & Saunders J B (2010). The biology of intoxication, In A Fox & M MacAvoy (Eds.), *Expressions of Drunkenness (Four Hundred Rabbits)*, 13-52, Routledge: New York.

Stone BM (1980). Sleep and low doses of alcohol, *Electroencephalography and Clinical Neurophysiology*: **48** (6), 706-709.

Stryer L (1975). *Biochemistry*, W H Freeman and Company: US.

Student Wellness (2014). Types of Depressants, available http://www.treatment4addiction.com/drugs/depressants/ accessed 12/7/14.

Sweeny C (2007). Remains of speakeasy found in cyber cafe parking lot, April 17, *Pipe Dream*: Binghamton University, New York.

Sweeney T (2012). The drink diaries, *Evening Herald*, 7 May: Dublin.

Szabo G (2007). Moderate drinking, inflammation and liver disease, *Annals of Epidemiology*: **17**(Suppl.), S49-54.

The Age (2003). Lone brewer small beer in Pakistan, March 11, www.theage.com.au accessed 3/2/14.

The Guardian (n.d.). How does alcohol affect your athletic performance?, available http://www.theguardian.com/lifeandstyle/the-running-blog/2014/apr/23/how-does-alcohol-affect-athletic-performance accessed 10/4/14.

The Guardian (2004). Irish bartenders on trial over alcohol death, available www.guardian.co.uk/world/2011/may/04/irish-barmen-trial-alcohol-death accessed 10/3/13.

Thomas V S & Rockwood K J (2001). Alcohol abuse, cognitive impairment, and mortality among older people, *Journal of the American Geriatrics Society*: **49**, 415-420.

Thombs DL (2006). *Introduction to Addictive Behaviour, 3rd Ed*, Guildford Press: New York.

Till BD & Shimp TA (1998). Endorsers in advertising: The Case of Negative Celebrity Information, *Journal of Advertising*: **27**, 67-83.

Tillitt M H (1932). *The Price of Prohibition*, Harcourt, Brace & Co: New York City.

Timberlake J H (1963). *Prohibition and the Progressive Movement*, Harvard University Press: Cambridge.

Tomsen S (1997). A top night: Social protest, masculinity and the culture of drinking violence, *British Journal of Criminology*: **37**, 90-102.

Toomey T L, Kilian G R, Gehan J P, Perry C L, Jones-Webb R & Wagenaar A C (1998). Qualitative assessment of training programs for alcohol servers and establishment managers, *Public Health Reports*: **113**, 162-169.

Trevisan M, Dorn J, Falkner K, Russell M, Ram M & Muti P (2004). Drinking pattern and risk of non-fatal myocardial infarction: A population-based case-control study, *Addiction*: **99**, 313-322.

Turner C (1990). How much alcohol is in a standard drink? An analysis of 125 studies, *British Journal of Addiction*: **85**, 1171-1175.

Turner J, Perkins H W & Bauerle J (2008). Declining negative consequences related to alcohol misuse among students exposed to a social norms marketing intervention on a college campus, *Journal of American College Health*: **57**, 85-94.

Turner T B, Bennett V L & Hernandez H (1981). The beneficial side of moderate alcohol use, *John Hopkins Medical Journal*: **148**, 53-63.

Turris, R & Ray A E (2010). Sustained parenting and college drinking in first-year students, *Developmental Psychobiology*: 52, 286-294.

Tyrrell F (2004). Launch of drink-testing kit aims to prevent drug rape, p.1, *Irish Times – Health Supplement*, 13 April: Dublin.

University of East Anglia (2009). Moderate alcohol intake reduces gallstone risk, 31 May, available http://www.uea.ac.uk/mac/comm/media/press/2009/may/gallstonerisk accessed 11/7/14.

UNWTO (2014). *World Tourism Barometer, Vol. 12*, January, World Tourism Organization, available www.unwto.org accessed 10/6/14.

US Passports & International Travel (2014). Saudi Arabia - learn about your destination, available at http://www.Travel.state.gov   accessed 5/2/14.

USDA (2004) *National Nutrient Database for Standard Reference*, USDA Nutrient Data Laboratory Release 16-1, available www.nal.usda.gov accessed 10/11/14.

USDA (2007). USDA Table of Nutrient Retention Factors, Release 6(Report), US Dept of Agriculture.

US Legal (2014). Alcoholic Beverage Labelling Act law and legal definition, available http://definitions.uslegal.com/a/alcohol-beverage-labeling-act/ accessed 29/7/14.

Vermeulen-Smit E, Koning IM, Verdurmen JEE, van der Vorst H, Engels R & Vollegbergh WAM (2012). The influence of parental and maternal drinks patterns with two partner families at the initiation and development of adolescent drinking, *Addictive Behaviour*: 37, 1248-1256.

Verster J C (2006). Congeners and alcohol hangover: differences in severity among Dutch college students after consuming beer, wine or liquor, *Alcoholism: Clinical and Experimental Research*: **30** (Suppl. 6), 53A.

Verster JC (2009). The hair of the dog: a useful hangover remedy or a predictor of future problem drinking?, *Current Drug Abuse Reviews*: **2** (1), 1-4.

Verster JC & Penning R (2010). Treatment and prevention of alcohol hangover, *Current Drug Abuse Reviews*: **3** (2), 103-109.

Verster JC, Stephens R, Penning R, Rohsenow D, McGeary J, Levy D, McKinney A, Finnigan F, Piasecki TM, Adan A, Batty GD, Fliervoet LA, Heffernan T, Howland J, Kim DJ, Kruisselbrink LD, Ling J, McGregor N, Murphy RJ, van Nuland M, Oudelaar M, Parkes A, Prat G, Reed N, Slutske WS, Smith G and Young M (2010). The Alcohol Hangover Research Group consensus statement on best practice in alcohol hangover research, *Current Drug Abuse Reviews*: **3** (2), 116-126.

B

Vickers K S, Patten C A, Bronars C, Lane K, Stevens S R & Croghan I T (2004). Binge drinking in female college students: The association of physical activity, weight concern, and depressive symptoms, *Journal of American College Health*: 53, 133-140.

Voet D & Voet J G (1995). *Biochemistry*, 2ⁿᵈ Ed, John Wiley & Sons: New York, NY.

Vouillamoz J F, McGovern P E, Ergul A, Söylemezoğlu G K, Tevzadze G, Meredith C P & Grando M S (2006). Genetic characterization and relationships of traditional grape cultivars from Transcaucasia and Anatolia. *Plant Genetic Resources: characterization and utilization*: **4** (2), 144.

Vvedensky I N (1915). *An Experience in Enforced Abstinence*, Moskva: Izdanie moskovskogo stolichnogo popechitel'stva o narodnoĭ trezvostI.

Wagenaar A C & Holder H D (1991). Effects of alcoholic beverage server liability on traffic crash injuries, *Alcoholism: Clinical and Experimental Research*: 15, 942-947.

Wakim-Fleming J & Mullen K D (2005). Long-term management of alcoholic liver disease, *Clinics in Liver Disease*: **9**, 135-149.

Wallin E, Norstrom T & Andreasson S (2003). Alcohol prevention targeting licensed premises: A study of effects on violence, *Journal of Studies on Alcohol*: **64**, 270-277.

Waters, J (2003). Drinking masks our dark side, *Irish Times*, 12 May: Dublin.

Weathermon R & Crabb D W (1999). Alcohol and medication interactions, *Alcohol Research and Health*: **23**, 40-54.

Wechsler H, Dowdall G, Maenner G, Gledhill-Hoyt J & Hang L (1998). Changes in binge drinking and related problems among american college students between 1993 and 1997: Results of the Harvard School of Public Health College Alcohol Survey. *Journal of American College Health*, **47**(2), 57-68.

Wechsler H, Lee J E, Kuo M, Seibring M, Nelson T F & Lee H (2002). Trends in college binge drinking during a period of increased prevention efforts. Findings from 4 Harvard School of Public Health College Alcohol Study surveys: 1993–2001, *Journal of American College Health*: **50**, 203-217.

Wechsler H, Lee J E, Hall J, Wagenaar A C & Lee H (2002). Second hand effects of student alcohol use reported by neighbours of colleges: The role of alcohol outlets, *Social Science and Medicine*: **55**, 425-435.

Wechsler H, Nelson T E, Lee J E, Seibring M, Lewis C & Keeling R P (2003). Perception and reality: A national evaluation of social norms marketing interventions to reduce college students' heavy alcohol use, *Journal of Studies on Alcohol*: **64**, 484-494.

Wegscheider S (1976). *The Family Trap*, Johnson Institute: Minnesota, USA.

Weintraub T A, Saitz R & Samet J H (2003). Education of preventive medicine residents: Alcohol, tobacco, and other drug abuse, *American Journal of Preventive Medicine*: **24**, 101-105.

Wells S, Graham K, West, P (1998). The good, the bad and the ugly: responses by security staff to aggressive incidents in public drinking settings, *Journal of Drug Issues*: **28**, 817-836.

Wen X J, Balluz L & Town M (2012). Prevalence of HIV risk behaviours between binge drinkers and non-binge drinkers aged 18- to 64-years in US, *Journal of Community Health*: **37**(1), 72-79.

Whelan G (2003). Alcohol: A much neglected risk factor in elderly mental disorders, *Current Opinion in Psychiatry*: **16**, 609-614.

White H R & Gorman D M (2000). Dynamics of the drug-crime relationship. In G LaFree (Ed.), *Criminal justice 2000, Vol 1: The nature of crime: Continuity and change*, 151-218, US Department of Justice: Washington, DC.

White H, R & Jackson K (nd). Social and psychological influences on emerging adult drinking behaviour, available pubs.niaaa.nih.gov/publications/arh284/182-190.htm accessed 3/10/14.

White HR, Johnson V & Buyske S (2000). Parental modelling and parenting behaviour effects on offspring alcohol and cigarette use: A growth curve analysis. *Journal of Substance Abuse*: **12**, 287-310.

WHO (2004). *Global status report: Alcohol policy*, World Health Organization: Geneva.

WHO (2005). *Alcohol Use and Sexual Risk Behaviour*, Mental Health Evidence and Research Team, World Health Organization: Geneva.

WHO (2006). *Framework for Alcohol Policy in the WHO European Region*, WHO: Gevena.

WHO (2007). *WHO Expert Committee on Problems Related to Alcohol Consumption. 2nd report*, WHO: Geneva.

WHO (2009). *Global Status Report on Road Safety*, World Health Organization: Geneva.

WHO (2011a). *The Global Status Report on Alcohol and Health 2011*. available www.who.int/ substance_abuse/publications/global_alcohol_report/en/ accessed 10/01/14.

WHO (2014). *The Global Status Report on Alcohol and Health 2014*. available www.who.int/ substance_abuse/publications/global_alcohol_report/en/ accessed 11/0614.

WHM (2003). *Developing an Alcohol and Drug Policy*, Western Health Board: Galway.

Wichstrom T & Wichstrom L (2009). Does sports participation during adolescence prevent later alcohol, tobacco and cannabis use? *Addiction*: **104**(1), 138-149.

Wiese JG, Shlipak MG, Browner WS (2000). The alcohol hangover, *Annals of Internal Medicine*: **132** (11), 897-902.

Wiggers J, Jauncey M, Considine R, Daly,J, Kingsland M, Purss K (2004). Strategies and outcomes in translating alcohol harm reduction research into practice: the Alcohol Linking Program, *Drug and Alcohol Review*: **23**, 355-364.

Williams F M, Cherkas L F, Spector T D & MacGregor A J (2005). The effect of moderate alcohol consumption on bone mineral density: A study of female twins, *Annals of the Rheumatic Diseases*: **64**, 309-310.

Willis J (2006). Drinking crisis: Change and continuity in cultures of drinking in sub-Saharan Africa, *African Journal of Drug and Alcohol Studies*: **5**, 1-15.

Wilsnack R W & Wilsnack S C (Eds.). (1997). *Gender and alcohol: Individual and social perspectives*, Rutgers Centre of Alcohol Studies: New Brunswick, NJ.

Windle, M (2003). Alcohol use among adolescents and young adults, *Alcohol Research and Health*: **27**, 79-85.

Wissler, C (1932) Stone Age had booze and prohibition, *Popular Science Monthly*, May, **120** (5), 44-45, Popular Science Publishing Co, Inc: New York.

Wolaver, A (2002). Effect of heavy drinking in college on student effort, grade point average, and major choice. *Contemporary Economic Policy*, **20**(4), 415-428.

B

World Health Organization (WHO) (2002). *The World Health Report 2002: Reducing risks, promoting healthy life.* Geneva, available www.who.int/whr/2002/en/ accessed 11/7/14.

Wosie KS & Kalkwarf HJ (2007). Bone density in relation to alcohol intake among men and women in the United States. *Osteoporosis International*: **18**(3), 391-400.

WTTC, (2014). Economic impact research, World Travel & Tourism Council, available at http://www.wttCorg/research/economic-impact-research/ accessed 11/6/14.

Wuorinen H J (1932). Finland's prohibition experiment, *Annals of the American Academy of Political and Social Science*: **163**, 216-226.

Xiao J (1995). China. In: Heath DB, ed. *International Handbook on Alcohol and Culture.* Greenwood Press: Westport, Connecticut.

Xu G L, Liu X F, Yin Q, Zhu W S, Zhang R L & Fan X B (2009). Alcohol consumption and transition of mild cognitive impairment to dementia, *Psychiatry and Clinical Neurosciences*: **63**, 43-49.

Yeomans MR, Caton S & Hetherington MM (2003). Alcohol and Food Intake, *Current opinion in Clinical Nutrition and Metabolic Care*: **6** (6), 639-644.

Yuan Z, Dawson N, Cooper G S, Einstadter D, Cebul R & Rimm A A (2001). Effects of alcohol-related disease on hip fracture and mortality: A retrospective cohort study of hospitalized Medicare beneficiaries, *American Journal of Public Health*: **91**, 1089-1093.

Zacharatos A, Barling J & Iverson R D (2005). High-performance work systems and occupational safety, *Journal of Applied Psychology*: **90**(1), 77-93.

Zuccala G, Onder G, Pedone C, Cesari M, Landi F & Bernabei R (2001). Dose-related impact of alcohol consumption on cognitive function in advanced age: Results of a multicentre survey, *Alcoholism: Clinical and Experimental Research*: **25**, 1743-1748.

Index